AF594857

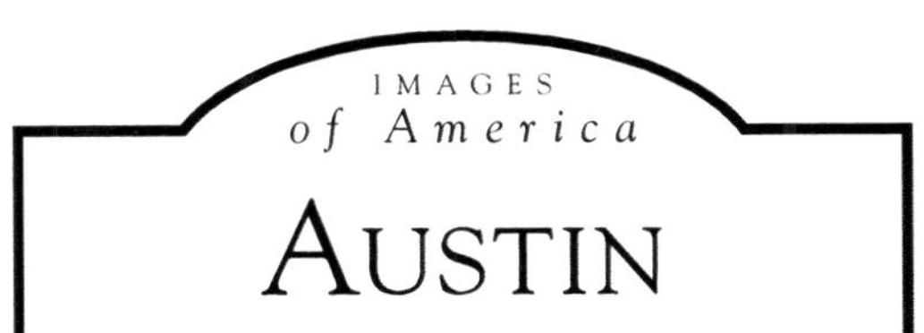
IMAGES
of America
AUSTIN

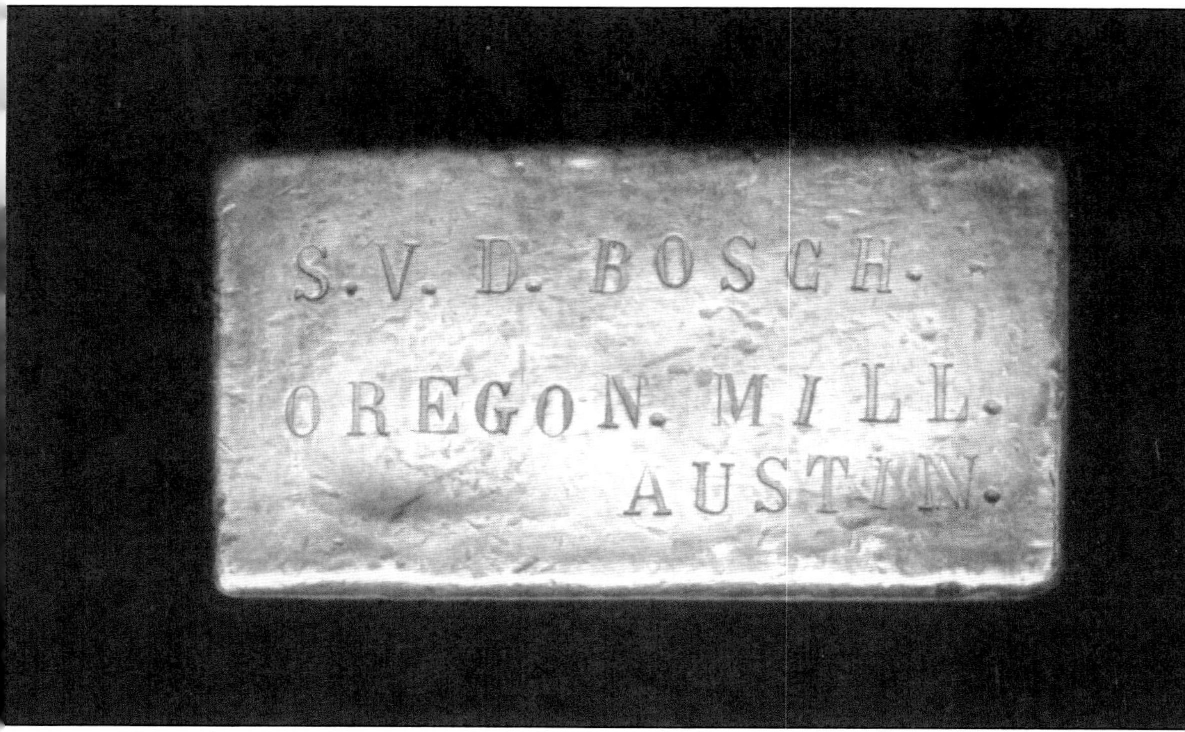

This is what all the fuss was about. Pictured is a bar of Austin silver from the Oregon Mill, located in upper Austin. Its 10 stamps commenced their work in December 1863 and were silenced two years later. This bar of silver was an early pour owned by John Frost, Felix O'Neil, George Buffet, and S. Van Der Bosch. (Courtesy NVHS.)

On the Cover: This image was taken on July 4, 1890. A traveling photographer's studio is seen set up next to the courthouse on Main Street. In celebration of Independence Day, a parade, which included a brass band, was scheduled to march up Main Street (see page 22.) (Courtesy of JBC.)

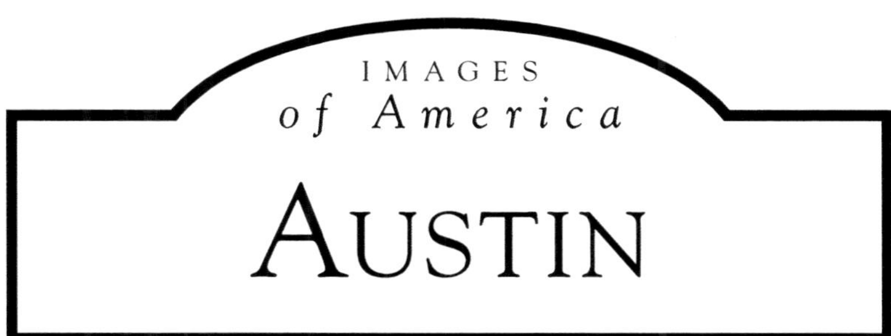

Austin Historical Society

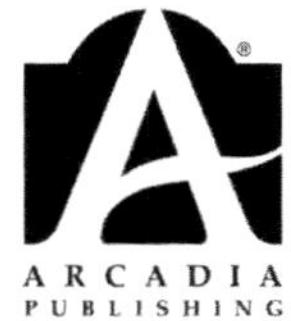

ISBN 978-0-7385-7447-9

Published by Arcadia Publishing
Charleston, South Carolina

Printed in the United States of America

Library of Congress Control Number: 2010937901

For all general information, please contact Arcadia Publishing:
Telephone 843-853-2070
Fax 843-853-0044
E-mail sales@arcadiapublishing.com
For customer service and orders:
Toll-Free 1-888-313-2665

Visit us on the Internet at www.arcadiapublishing.com

Contents

Acknowledgments

The Austin Historical Society wants to thank the town of Austin for its support of this project. Members of the community have helped in two very significant ways: by passing on oral histories and collective memories that we have woven into this pictorial and, most importantly, by having the tenacity to survive so that we would even have a story to tell. We want to thank the Scoggin, Brandt, and Cantrell families for opening up their old photo albums. This book would not have been possible without their generous donations of time and energy. And, in particular, we would like to give recognition to Norm Scoggin, Joy Brandt, Darla Cantrell, Jay Winrod, Wally Trapnell, and Poncho Williams. We also want to thank Lee Brumbaugh and the gang at the Nevada Historical Society for opening up their collections for us; it has been an adventure! Lastly, we are extremely thankful for Irene—may she rest in peace.

Unless otherwise noted, the following abbreviations are used for photograph credits: Scoggin Collection (SC), Joy Brandt Collection (JBC), Cantrell Collection (CC), Austin Historical Society (AHS), and Nevada Historical Society (NVHS).

INTRODUCTION

Austin didn't quite happen all at once. Originally, in 1859, there was the establishment of Jacob's Spring, a Pony Express station about seven miles west of the future town. The express riders often took shortcuts through a canyon that was eventually given the name Pony Canyon. When the Pony Express folded one and a half years later, Jacob's Spring became Jacobsville, and an office or relay station for the Overland Telegraph, which, shortly thereafter, became the Overland Mail and Stage. William Talcot, a wrangler at the station, was cutting wood in Pony Canyon on May 2, 1862, when he found a rich vein of silver in quartz ore. Talcot and his friends organized the Reese River Mining District on May 10, and the ore was sent to Virginia City for assay, where some of the original ore was determined to be twice as rich as that from the Comstock Lode. By Christmas, a small camp, named Clifton, was established at the foot of the canyon.

It did not take long for word to leak out. Braving winter snows, a slow, but steady group of miners, speculators, and merchants began arriving. With the melting snow in the spring of 1863, the trickle became a flood. Clifton became the county seat, and although a mile from the diggings, it offered a relatively flat building area. The population may have reached 500. When David Buel arrived with friends from Virginia City, they inspected the upper canyon, located their mining claims, and plated out the town of Austin. Free townsites were offered to anyone who would help grade a mile-long wagon road up the canyon from Clifton, and Austin was born. The naming seems lost in obscurity, but Austin was either named for Buel's hometown of Austin, Texas, or for his good friend Alvah C. Austin. By September 1863, it was official—Austin became the county seat for Lander, and Clifton slowly disappeared.

Although the silver was still there, along with much speculation, too many mills and not enough ore led to a period of stagnation. In 1864, only $100,000 in silver was produced. The rich silver chloride surface deposits became silver sulfide deposits at depth. A new metallurgical process was invented. The ore was mixed with salt and was then roasted in ovens; this method became known as the Stetefeldt process. From Six Mile Flat, about 80 miles to the west, the salt was packed in on camels, which were originally imported for military purposes. With the sulfur burned off, the silver combined with the salt and became silver chloride, and production boomed. By 1867, the mines were producing over $1 million a year. During the 1860s, much consolidation occurred between the mines, and by 1870 the Manhattan Silver Mining Company controlled or milled most of the ores produced. But by 1872, the decline had set in and production had slowed to $250,000. Mining continued for years but at a much reduced scale. Over the span of 100 years, the total worth of production for the area is estimated around $50 million.

Though mining declined, Austin survived. A census in 1863 counted 6,000 souls, but by 1870 the population dropped to about 1,200 and stayed about there for the next two decades. Prospectors based in Austin went out and founded other camps, such as Hamilton, Eureka, Cortez, Tuscarora, Belmont, Tonopah, and Ione. In 1880, the Nevada Central Railroad was completed with a narrow-gauge connecting Clifton with the Central Pacific Railroad, located 93 miles to the north at Battle Mountain. The short line of Austin City Railway, known as the "Mules Relief," ran from the terminus at Clifton, 2.8 miles up the canyon, to Austin proper. As the county seat for Lander County and commercial center of central Nevada, Austin's banks, mercantile, and freighting companies prospered along with its saloons and churches. But in 1900, a new silver strike in Tonopah, 110 miles to the south, caused the town to lurch, yet again, toward obscurity. The population dipped to 400 and remained so, more or less, for another eight decades. With the Lincoln Highway (today's US Highway 50) passing through town, and with the advent of motor traffic in general, the railroad went bust during the Great Depression in 1938.

Today, the spires of three churches still rise high from the canyon. St. Augustine, built in 1867, is the oldest original Catholic church in Nevada and is being restored as a cultural center for the town. The Methodist church, dating from 1866, was built with mining stock subscriptions. With each share of mining stock, a certain amount of money went to building the church. Of course, the mines failed, but the church still stands. Presently, the church building has been restored as a town hall. St. George, the Episcopal church, was built in 1878 and is an outstanding example of Gothic Revival, and the congregation still meets each Sunday. It is said that 400 ounces of Austin silver was poured into the bell to give it a purer tone.

Austin's most famous saloon, the International, is still in continuous use. Originally located in Virginia City, it was dismantled and freighted to Austin in 1863. The "back bar," having been shipped around the horn and pulled over the sierras, is magnificent. Today, the American Legion Post 45 uses the building that originally housed the courthouse and jail in 1866. The iron bars of Austin's first jail can still be seen on the lower floor. A more modern and larger courthouse was built in 1878, and today this structure houses various town offices, with the second floor still used as a courtroom by the local justice of the peace. In 1897, mining magnate Anson Stokes built his three-story summerhouse out of locally cut granite. Located a short ways out of town and abandoned now, it is known as the "Castle," since it resembles an old Roman hill fortress; Stokes used it for only two summers.

Austin has had its share of famous people. Emma Wixiom, daughter of Dr. Wixiom, became Emma Nevada; her operatic voice was compared to a nightingale. She eventually moved to Europe, where she sang for many years. Al Dolten, editor in chief of Austin's principal newspaper, the *Reese River Reveille*, was originally from Virginia City, where he taught cub reporter Samuel Clemens the newspaper game. He wrote several books depicting early life on the Comstock. Ruel Gridley, Sam's friend from Missouri, was owner and proprietor of the Gridley Store. In 1864, he bet on an election and, having lost, had to carry a sack of floor up Main Street. An auction broke out for the sack of flour, and the proceeds were giving to the Sanitary Fund, the early precursor to the Red Cross. Ruel traveled the West auctioning off the sack again and again, with each camp trying to outbid the next, and, eventually, raised more than $200,000 for the Sanitary Fund. His store still stands and, until recently, was the home of the Austin Museum. Austin was also known for having a woman sheriff, Clara Crowell. Her husband had originally been sheriff, but when he passed away she was elected and served the town from 1919 to 1921.

Harder times befell Austin in 1980 when, after a long fight, the county seat was moved north to the more populous Battle Mountain. Today, Austin has about 300 residents. A school for the first through twelfth grades serves the town and the surrounding ranches. The forest service has an office and oversees part of the Toiyabe National Forest, the largest national forest on the continental United States. A little turquoise is still mined in the area, and a few rock shops display their wares. Two gas stations, two cafés, three motels, and five bars cater to the travelers along US 50, the "Loneliest Highway in America." But Austin continues on.

One

MAIN STREET

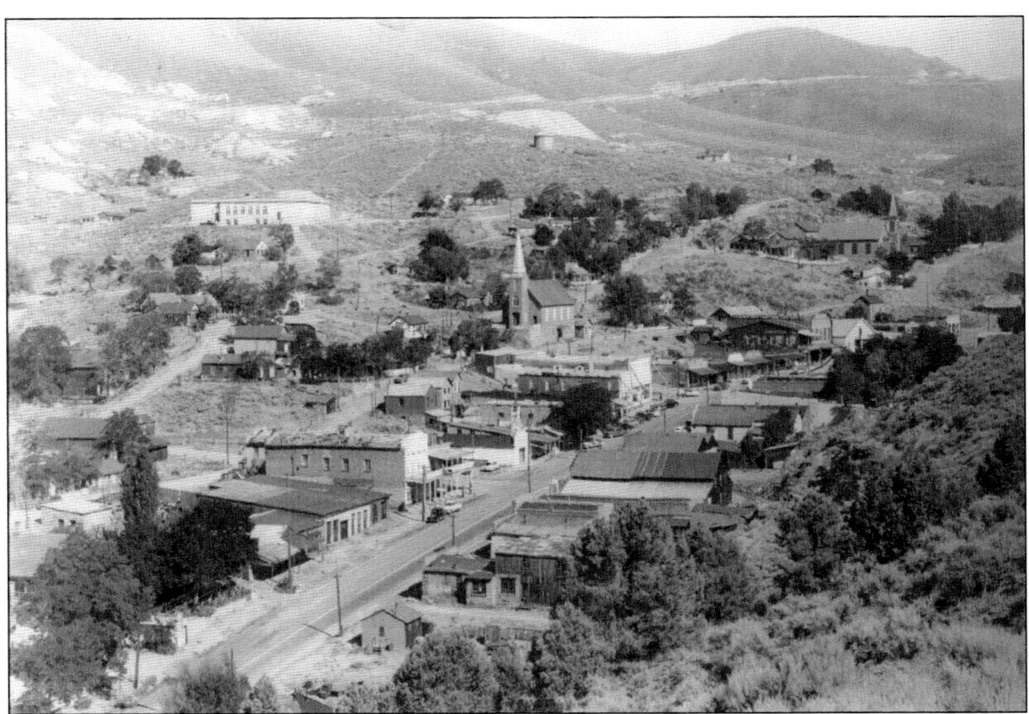

This is Austin's Main Street, pictured around 1950. Highway 50 can be seen snaking down from Austin Summit (7,478 feet) in the upper right-hand corner. Just about everything happened on Main Street. Hotels, liveries, saloons, and mercantile stores lined the street, while cattle drives, parades, and floods ran down it. For a few years, Austin even had a municipal railway to carry miners and supplies into the canyon and the silver out. Austin was the location for the Lander County Courthouse, a bank, the Overland Telegraph Office, and a stage station. In 1913, the Lincoln highway, the nation's first transcontinental highway, ran right down Main Street. Eventually, the horse gave way to the automobile, the livery to the garage, and the hotel to the motor court. Today, Highway 50, the Loneliest Highway in America, is Main Street. (Courtesy of JBC.)

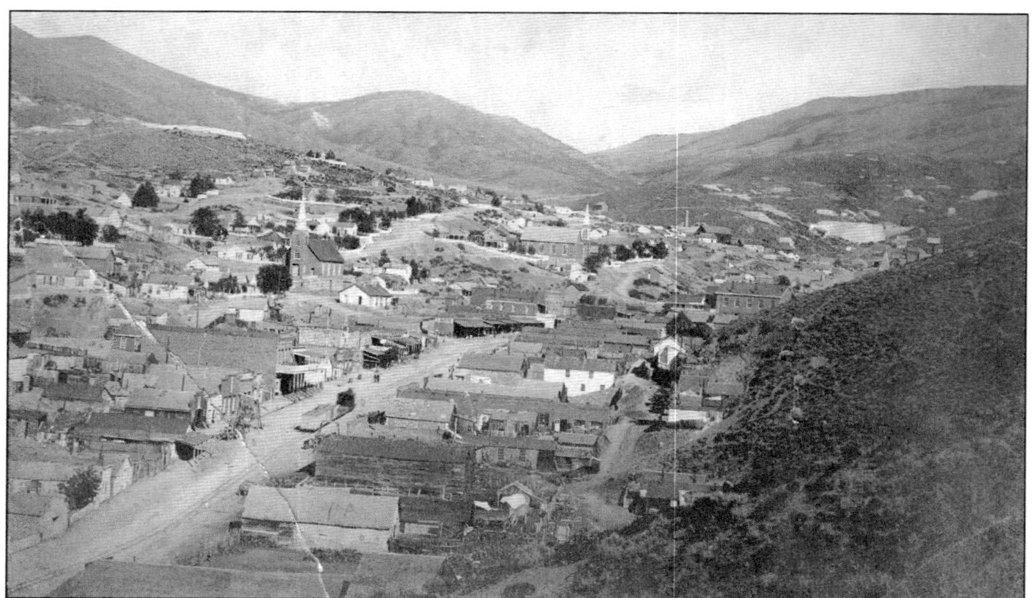

This panorama of Austin dates from about 1880. Main Street runs up the center of the right-hand picture and then out of sight. The Mules Relief (Austin City Railway) can be seen pulling a load of firewood for the mills further up the canyon. And mine tailings pepper the areas above the town. The steeples belonging to Catholic and Methodist churches are quite prominent, and the Episcopal church steeple can barley be seen to the far right. The hills are exposed; the original pinion pines have been cut for building lumber or firewood. (Courtesy of SC.)

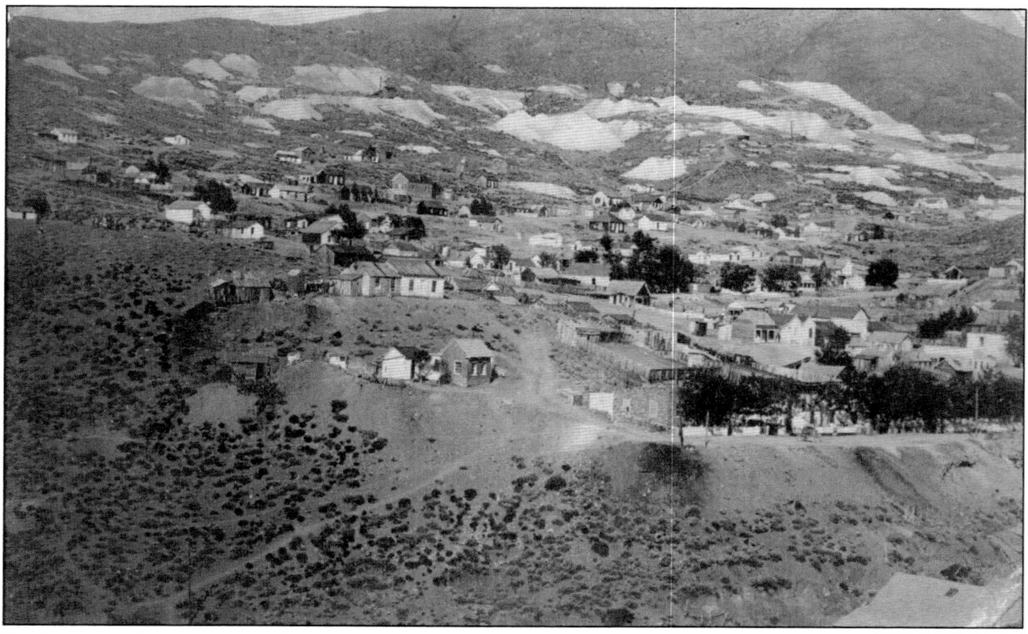

By the time this photograph was taken, cottonwood and black locust shade trees had been planted; many remain today. Austin was constructed with wood that was cut and sawed locally, which was referred to as Reese River lumber, or freighted in from the Sierra Nevada Mountains, about 200 miles to the west. Austin also had its own brickworks, located on Austin Summit. Fired and adobe bricks were used, as well as the local granite. (Courtesy of SC.)

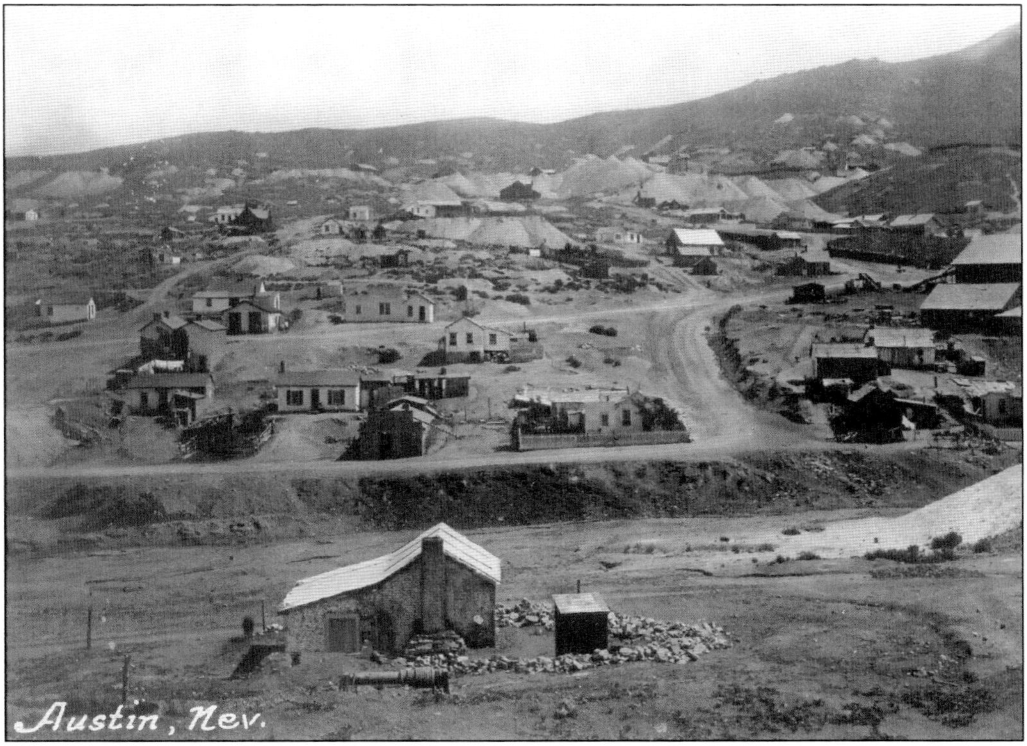

This is another early photograph of upper Austin from around 1870. The Oregon Mill is the industrial building to the right. Main Street runs along the berm in the foreground, and the town's icehouse was the dugout rock building, second from the left on Main Street. (Courtesy of SC.)

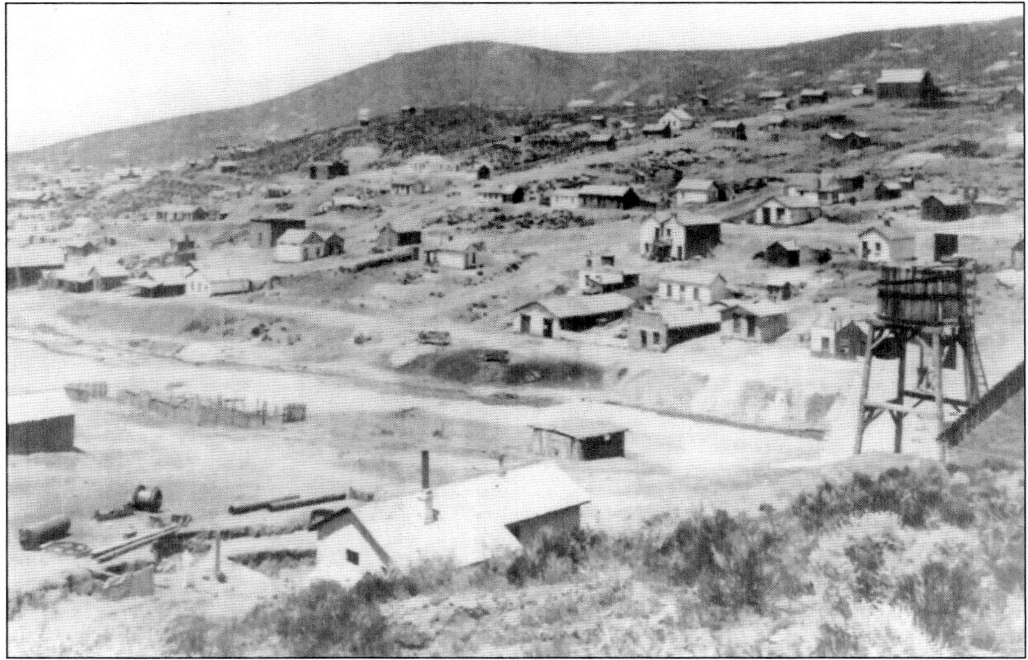

Upper Austin is seen here around 1880, with the Methodist church to the far left. The town's icehouse is the third building from the wooden tower. (Courtesy of AHS.)

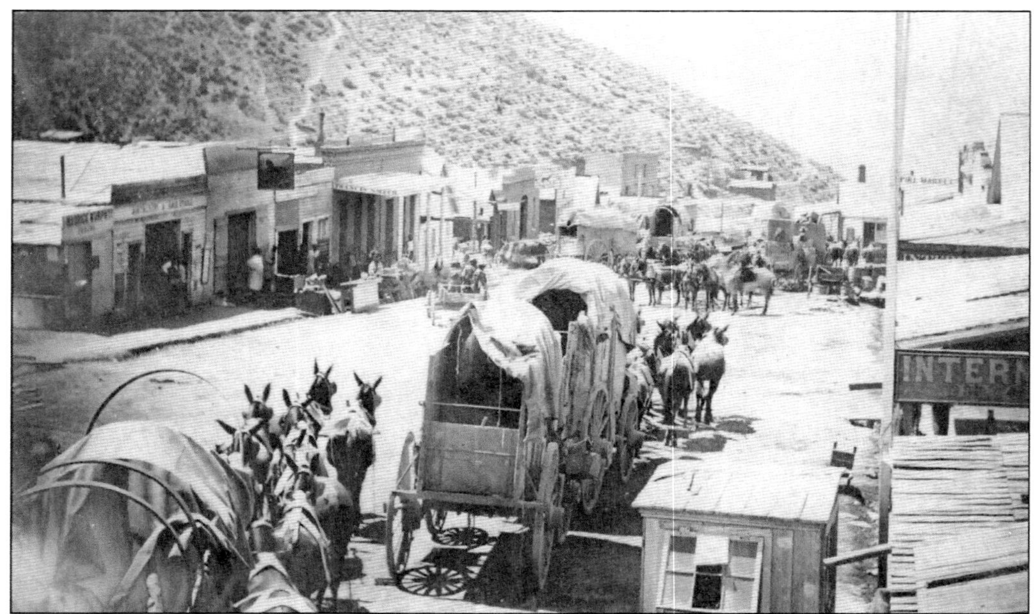

This early Austin view looks down Main Street. A sign for the International Hotel is visible in the right-hand corner. The International was dismantled in Virginia City and freighted piece by piece across 180 miles of desert to Austin in 1863. The International still serves beer and whiskey today. (Courtesy of SC.)

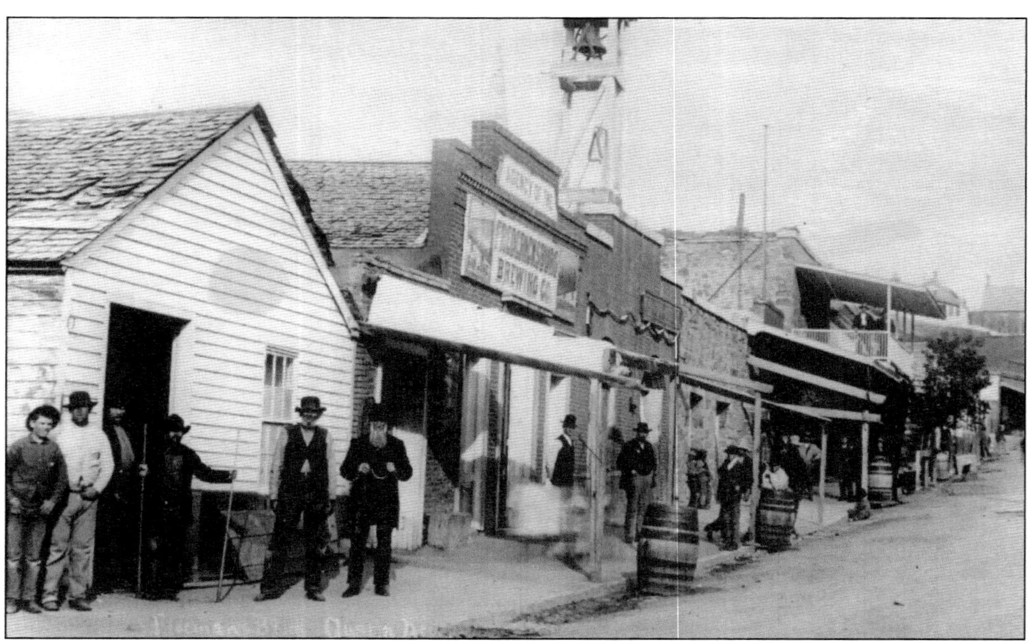

This early view of Austin looks up the north side of Main Street at the intersection of Cedar Street. The businesses are, from left to right, unidentified, Fredericksburg Brewery, Austin Fire Station, Murphy's Store, Silver State saloon, an ice cream parlor, the Commercial Grocery Store, and the Hogan Hotel. The Silver State, remodeled in 1996, is still a saloon today. (Courtesy of JBC.)

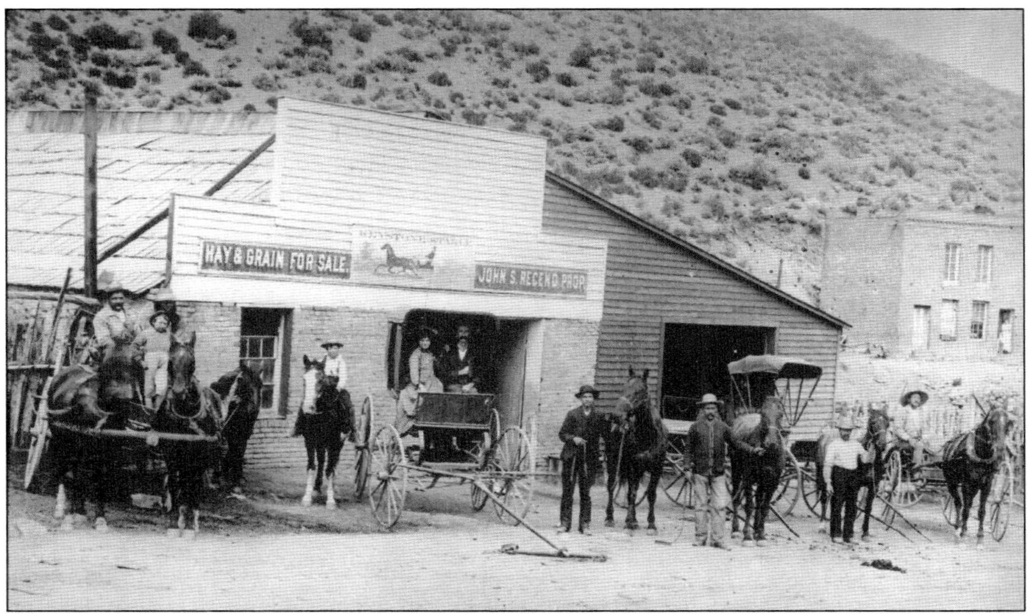

John Recend's livery was located on the south side of Main Street in the middle of the downtown commercial district. Note the man and woman in the buggy who appear dressed up and ready for an outing. (Courtesy of JBC.)

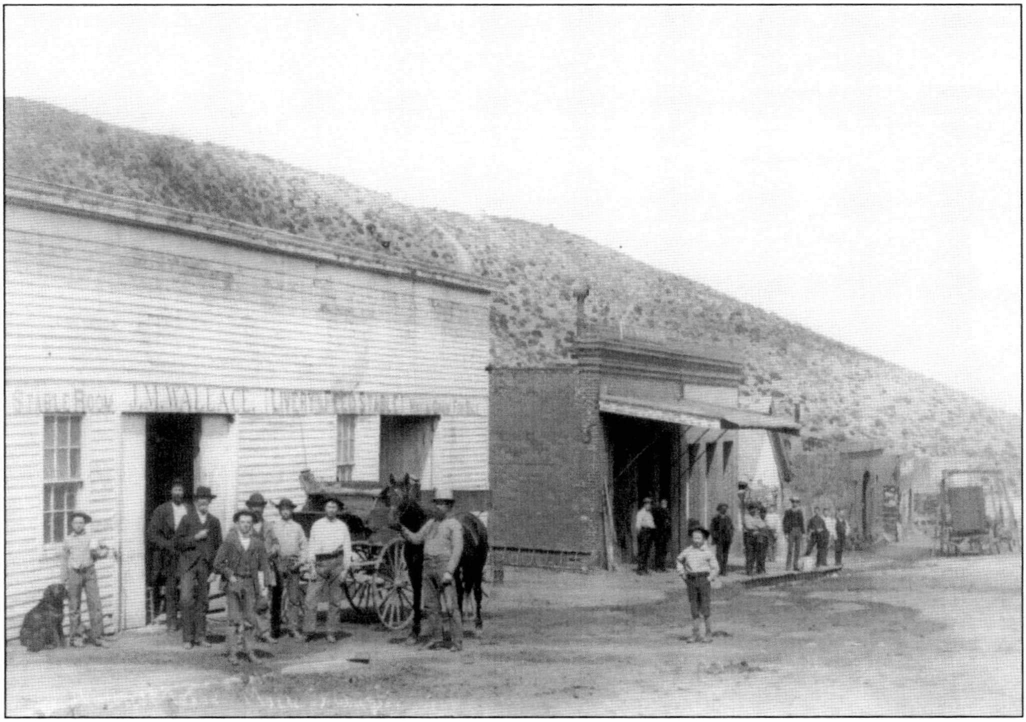

J.M. Wallace's livery was also located on the south side of Main Street, a little to the west and down the canyon from John Recend's livery. (Courtesy of JBC.)

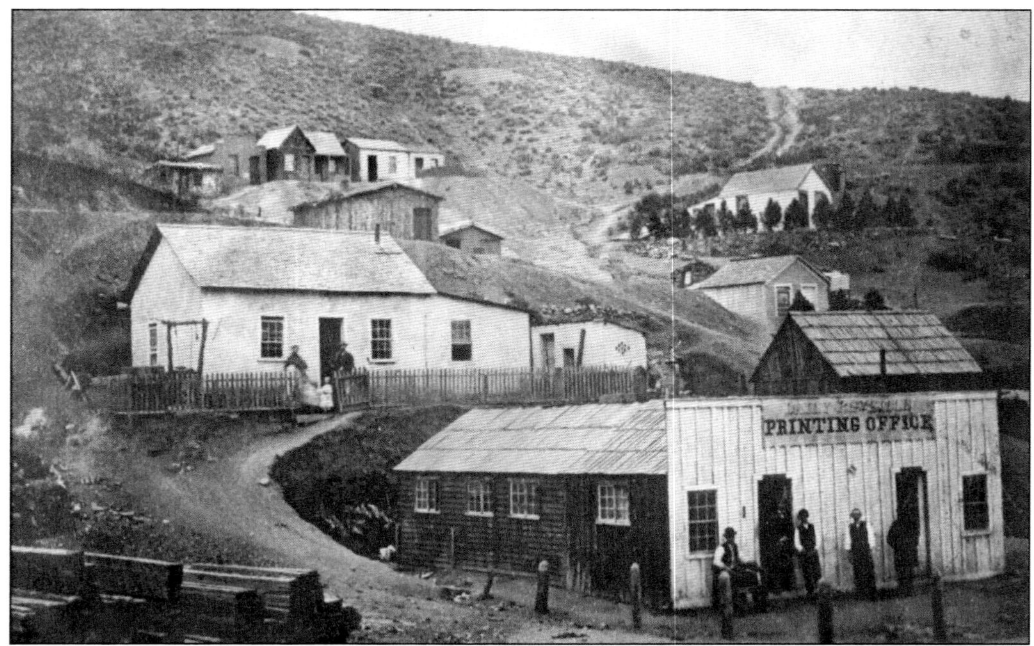

The newspaper *Reese River Reveille* was printed in the building in the foreground, which was located on the south side of Main Street and a short ways up from the courthouse. The *Reveille* published from 1863 until 1993 and was reestablished as a history and tourism periodical in 2004. The area behind the Printing Office Building was originally called Mormon Ravine. (Courtesy of NVHS.)

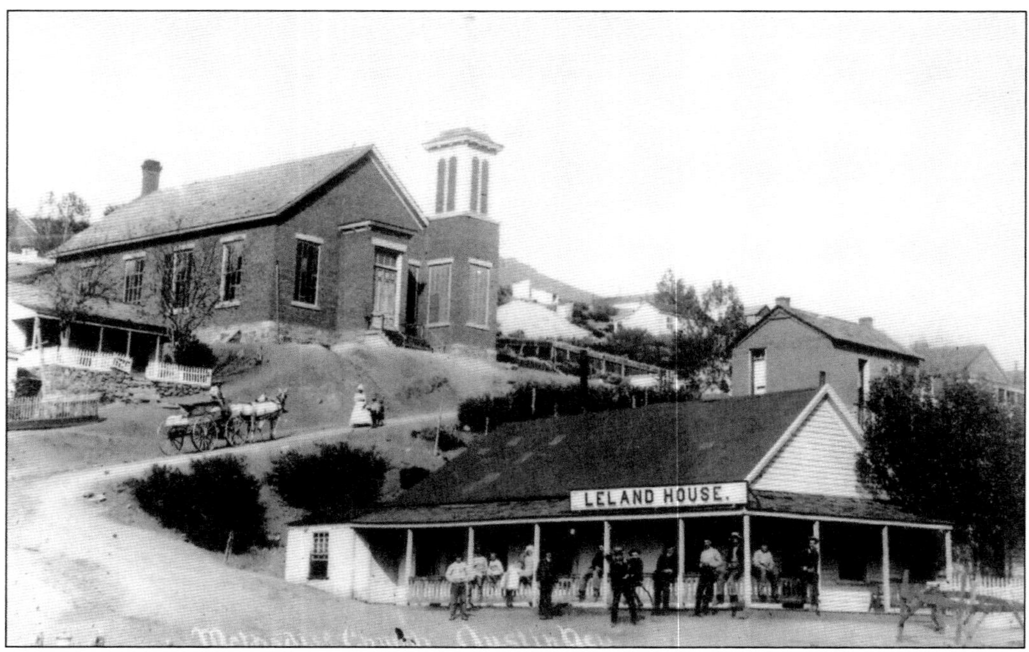

The Leland House was located on the north side of Main Street and faced the Austin City Railroad terminal. It readily received passengers with hot meals and rooms for rent. The house is a private residence today. Behind it, and up the hill, stands the Methodist church. (Courtesy of SC.)

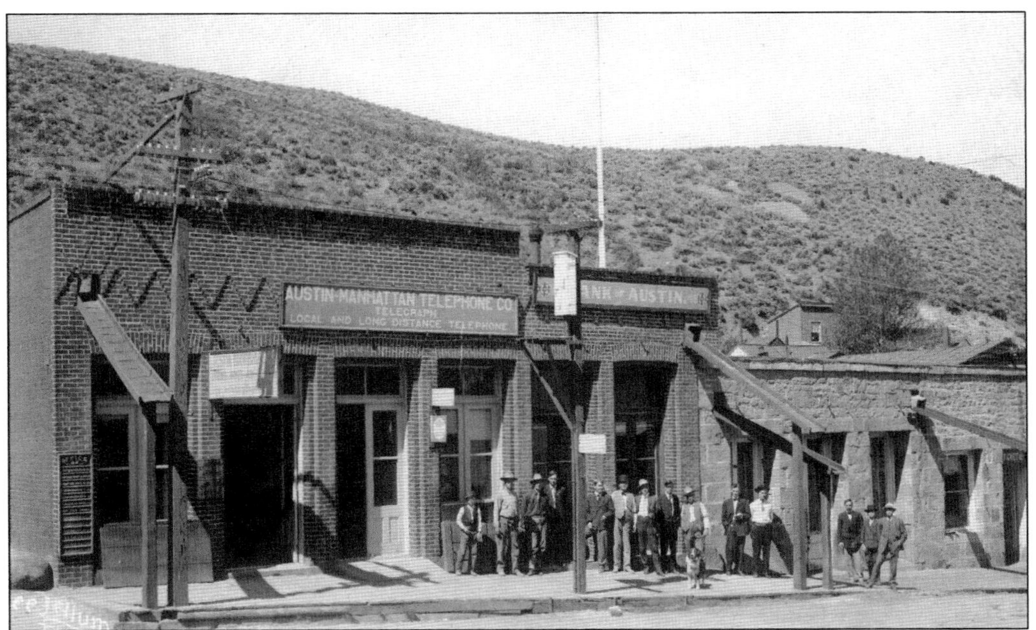

Located on Main Street, the Bank of Austin is seen at the center of this photograph. To the right of the bank was the Wells Fargo office, followed by the Curtis and Gage Assay office, and to the left were the Austin–Manhattan Telephone Company and the Austin Brokerage. The Wells Fargo Building is gone now, but the old bank building houses Austin's library today and the telephone exchange is a bar. (Courtesy of NVHS.)

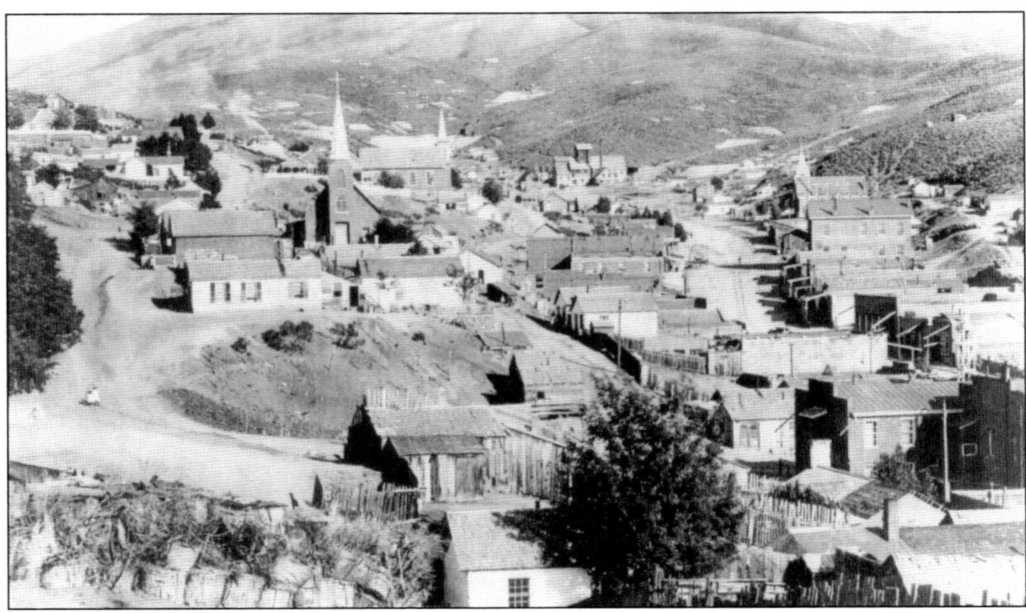

The Mules Relief (Austin City Railway) tracks are shown clearly running up Main Street. The front-facing church is St. Augustine Catholic Church, a little behind it is the Methodist church, and the following large building, toward the center, is the Manhattan Mill Concentrator. Continuing to the right is St. George Episcopal Church, and, right below, the large brick building is the Lander County Courthouse. (Courtesy of JBC.)

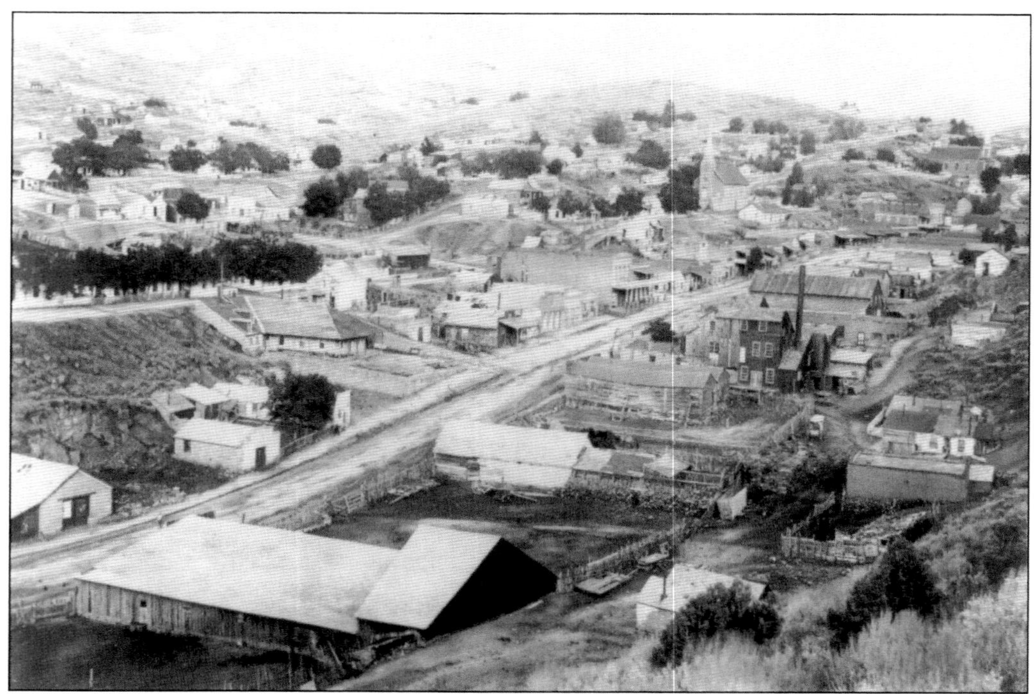

Located in lower Austin, the International Hotel is the large brick building in the center. The liveries on the left of Main Street eventually became motor courts, and now motels. (Courtesy of AHS.)

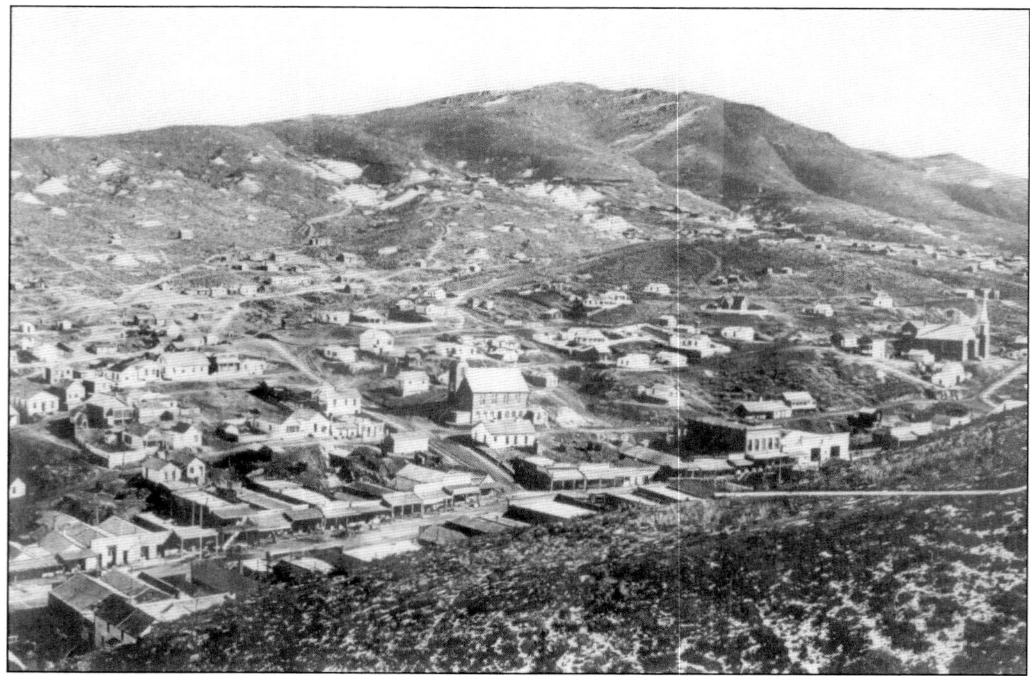

With St. Augustine Catholic Church at center, Main Street is in the foreground, and mine tailings dot the hill. Silver being where you find it, prospectors combed the entire area. (Courtesy of AHS.)

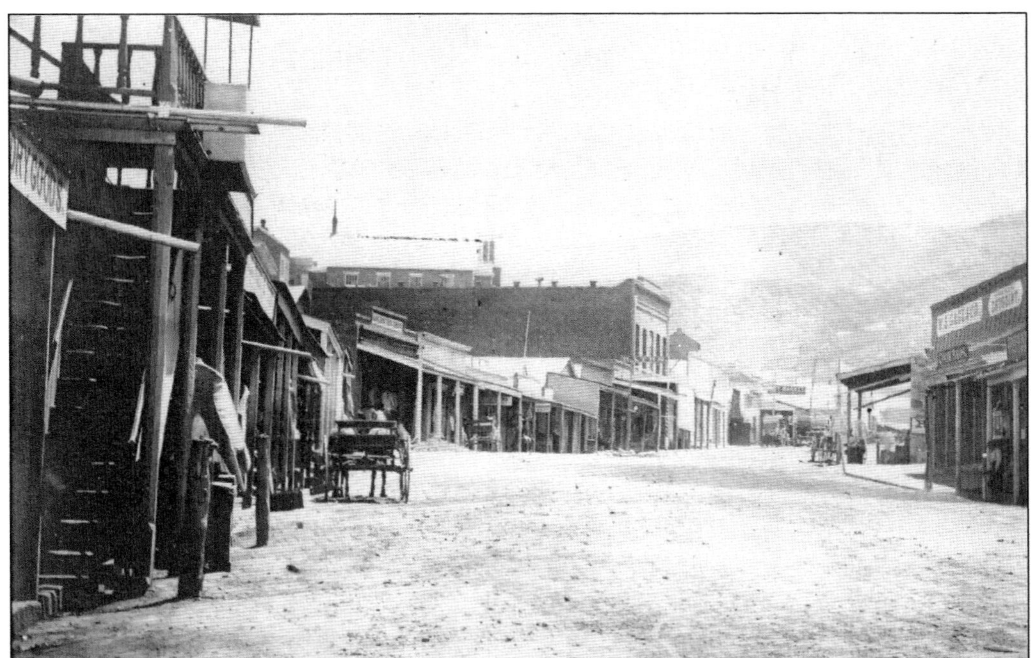

Looking uphill toward the mines, this scene is of Main Street. The prominent brick building in the center is the Masonic hall. The building is still standing, and the lodge has been active since 1864. With many a dance held there, the second story was constructed with a floating floor to relieve strain on the solid beams. The Methodist church rises up behind it. (Courtesy of SC.)

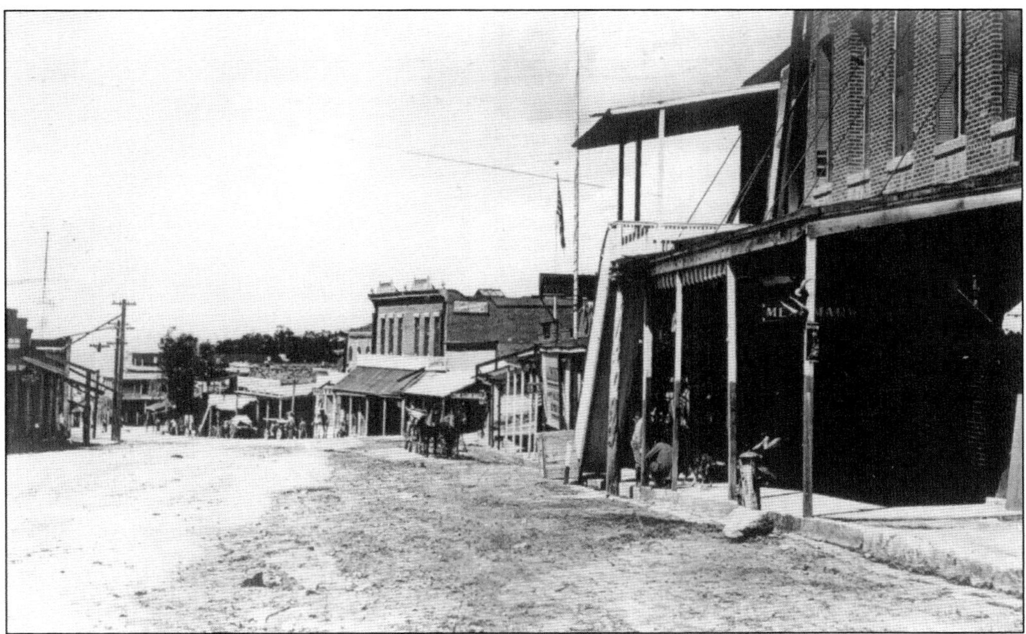

The Masonic hall is located closest to the photographer, and the Hogan Hotel is the two-story building in the center of the image. The International Hotel is on the same side of Main Street as these buildings, but further down past trees. The steps leading to the second-story balcony were hinged. Several floods ravaged Austin, and this feature allowed debris washing down Main Street to pass harmlessly along. (Courtesy of NVHS.)

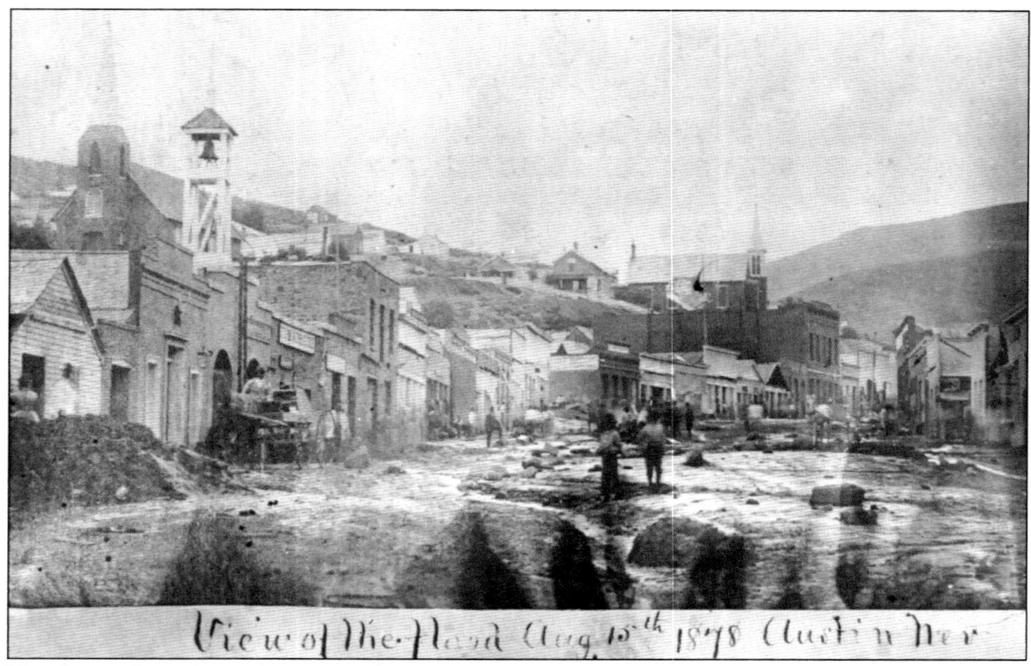

Floods ran down Pony Canyon and onto Main Street in 1868, 1869, 1874, 1878, 1884, 1891, and 1901. Today, a massive culvert runs underneath and diverts the water further down the canyon. Looking up Main Street, one can see the bell tower for the Austin Volunteer Fire Department to the left and the Methodist church rising in the center. (Courtesy of NVHS.)

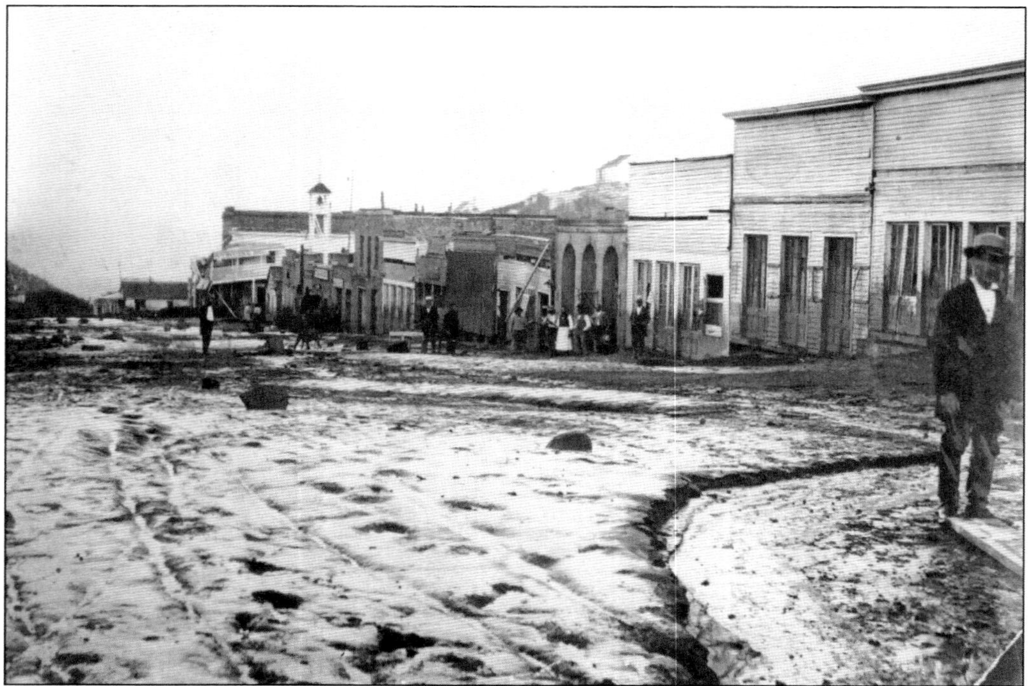

These two photographs show the aftermath of the August 15, 1878, flood. This picture is looking down Main Street. The Austin Volunteer Fire Department bell tower is now further down the street. The International Hotel can be seen behind it. (Courtesy of NVHS.)

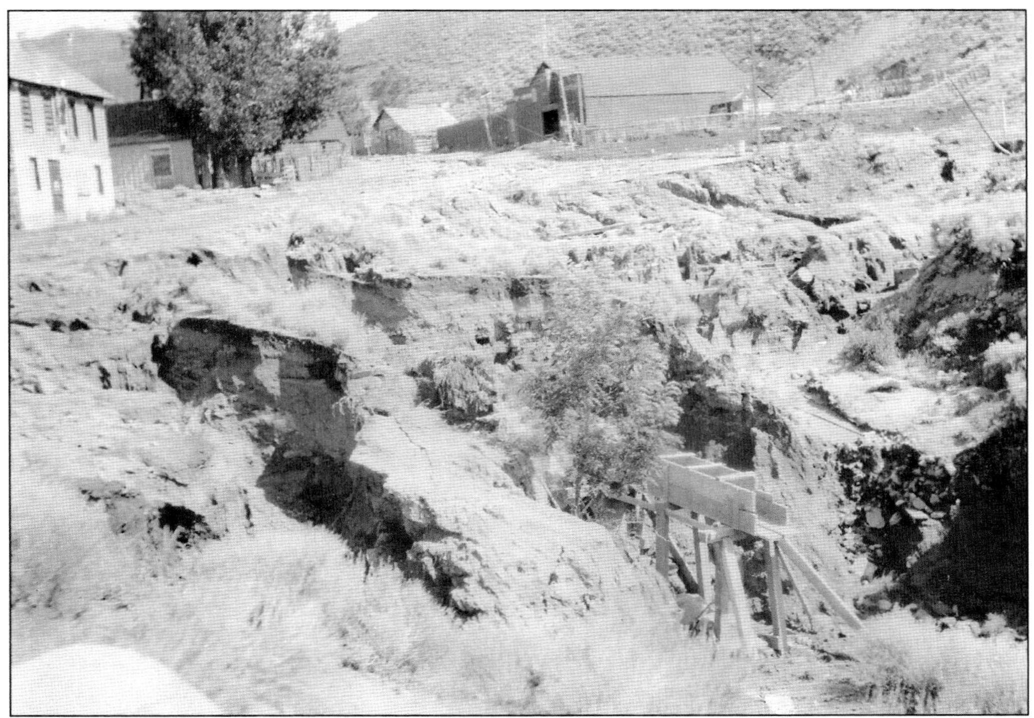

This is Main Street after the flood of 1901. A summer thunderstorm has unleashed a torrent of rain. On the right-hand side of what is left are two old liveries. (Courtesy of SC.)

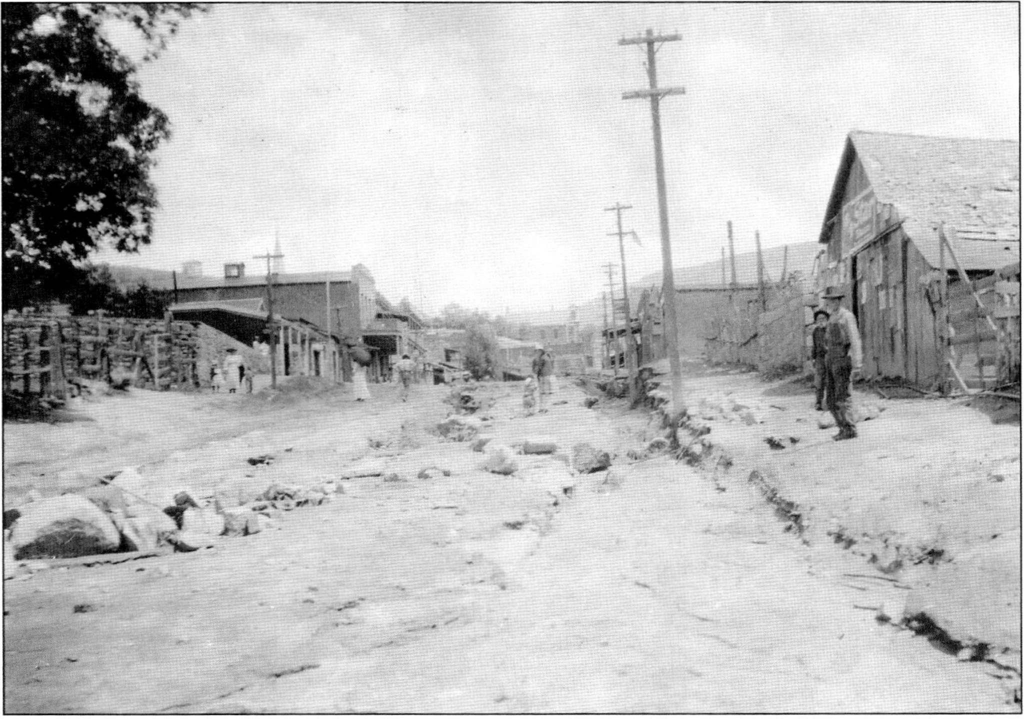

Continuing up Main Street after the 1901 flood, the International Hotel is the large building on the left. On the right is the second livery visible in the picture above. (Courtesy of SC.)

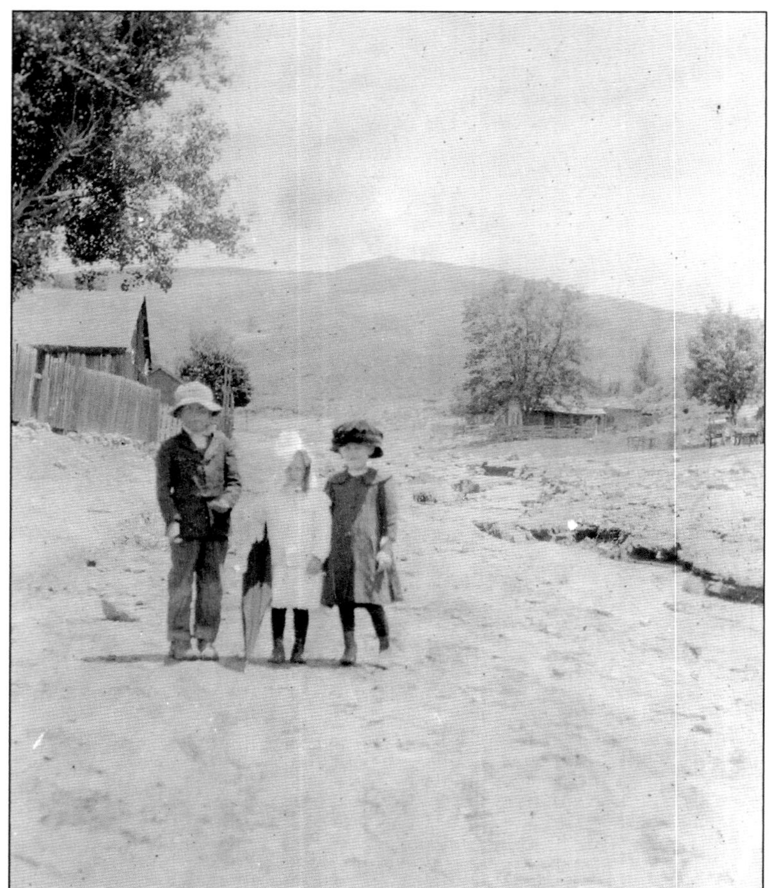

Three children survey the damage of the 1901 flood. This photograph was again taken on Main Street in upper Austin above the Leland House. No rail tracks are seen in these three pictures, as the Mules Relief ceased operation in 1893. (Courtesy of SC.)

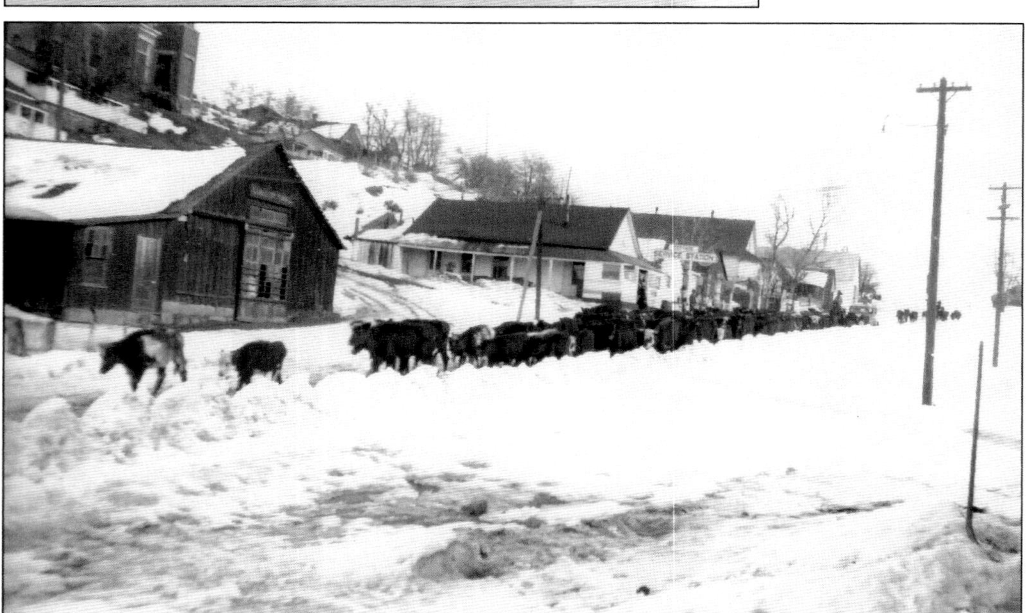

During a Nevada winter, a cattle drive from Austin Summit traveled through Main Street. The Leland House is the house in the center with the wrap around porch. (Courtesy of JBC.)

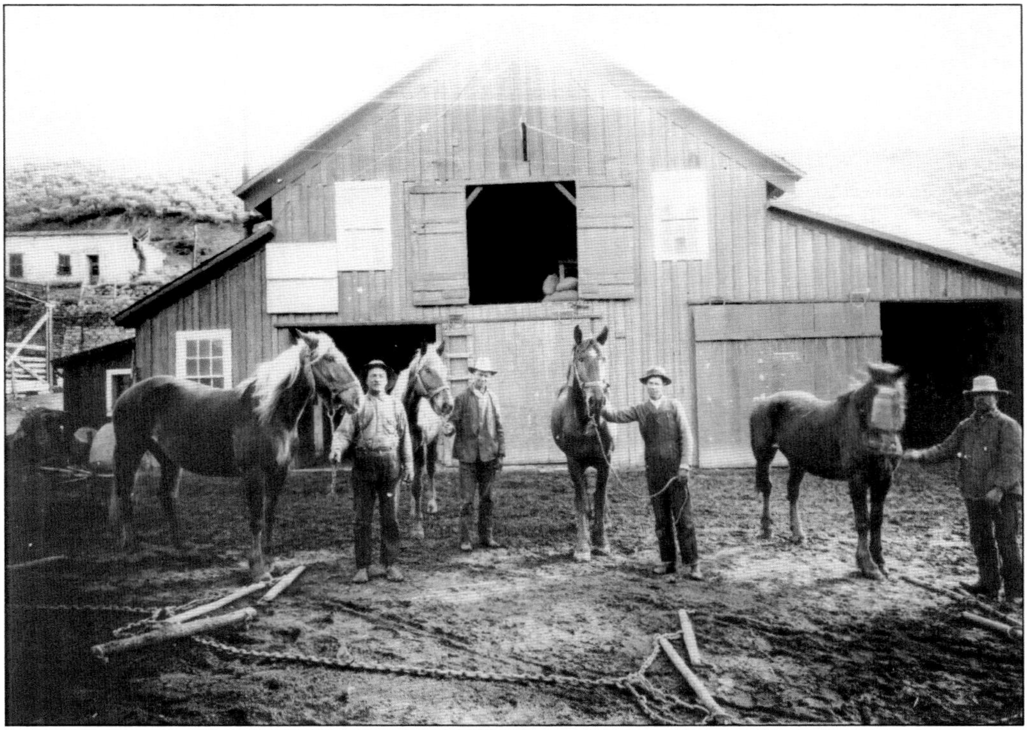

The Stiener Livery was located on Main Street, across from the International Hotel. Those pictured are, from left to right, William Dyer, Walter Frankless, J.M. King, and Jack Phelps. They are retiring a wagon team after a day of work. (Courtesy of NVHS.)

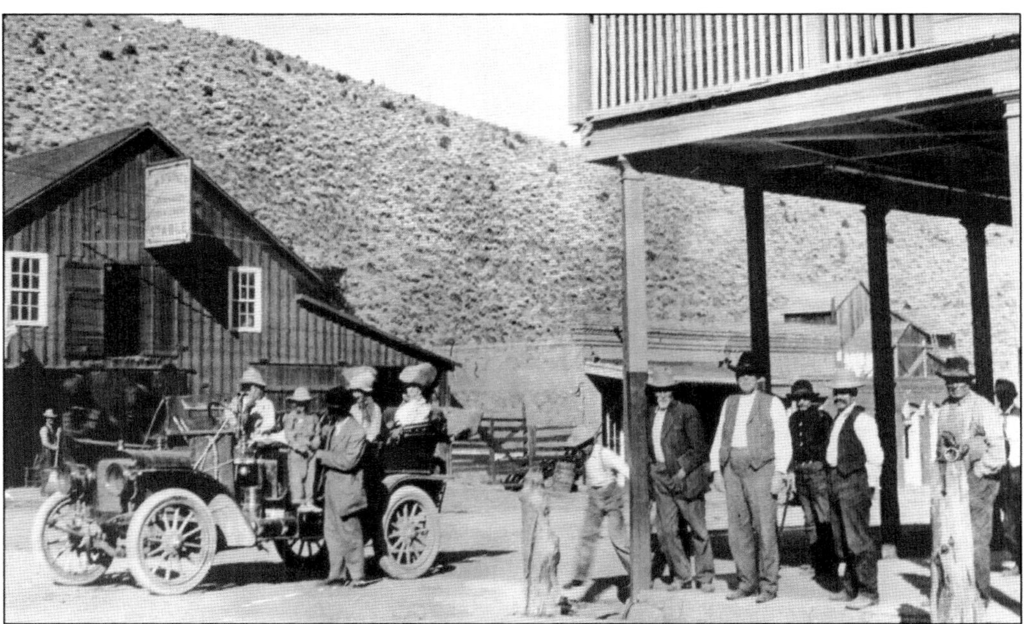

With the Stiener Livery is in the background, Elsie Easton (the passenger in front) and William Easton (the driver) are about to take the wheel of a 1912 Overland touring car. The corner of the International Hotel is to the right. (Courtesy of NVHS.)

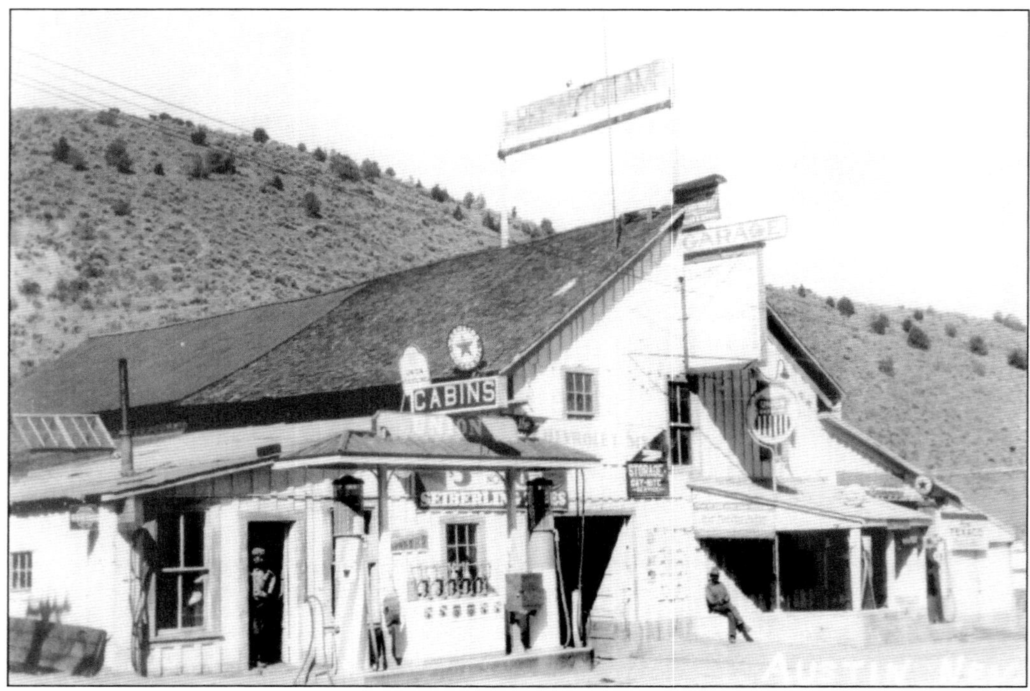

In this image, the Stiener Livery Building has been converted to the Lincoln Garage. Union gasoline, Seiberling tires, Texaco gasoline, and Chevrolet repairs and service are advertised, with cabins available in the back! The Lincoln Highway now runs down Main Street. (Courtesy of JBC.)

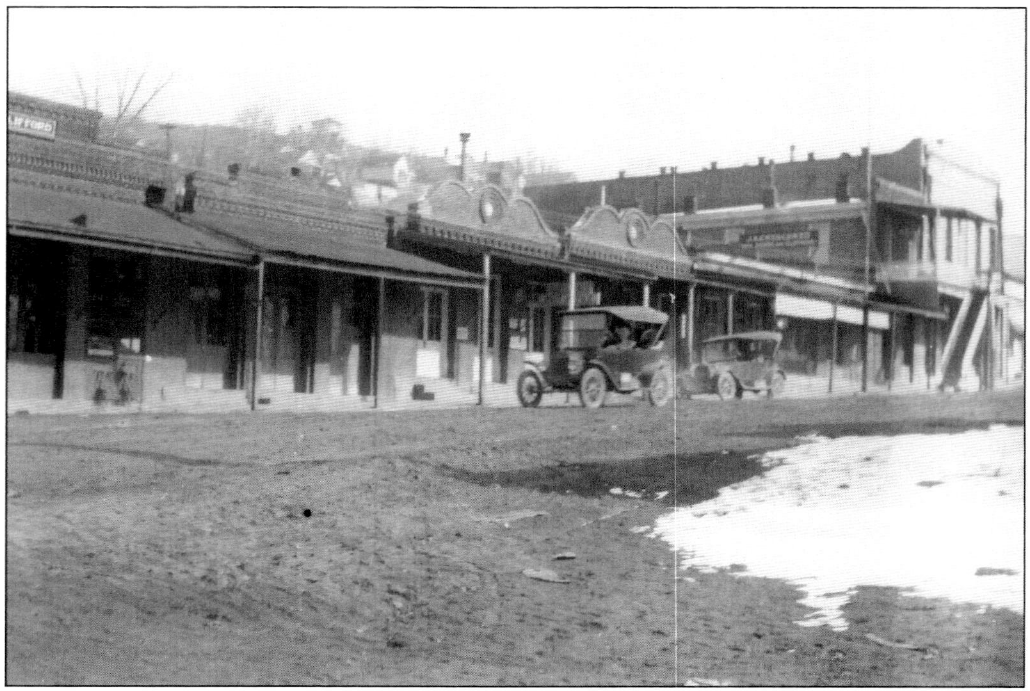

Here, an old Ford is parked on Main Street. The buildings to the left of Lander Lumber are gone, but Lander Lumber (left of the car), and Austin's hardware store can be found in this location today. Up the block is the Masonic hall. (Courtesy of JBC.)

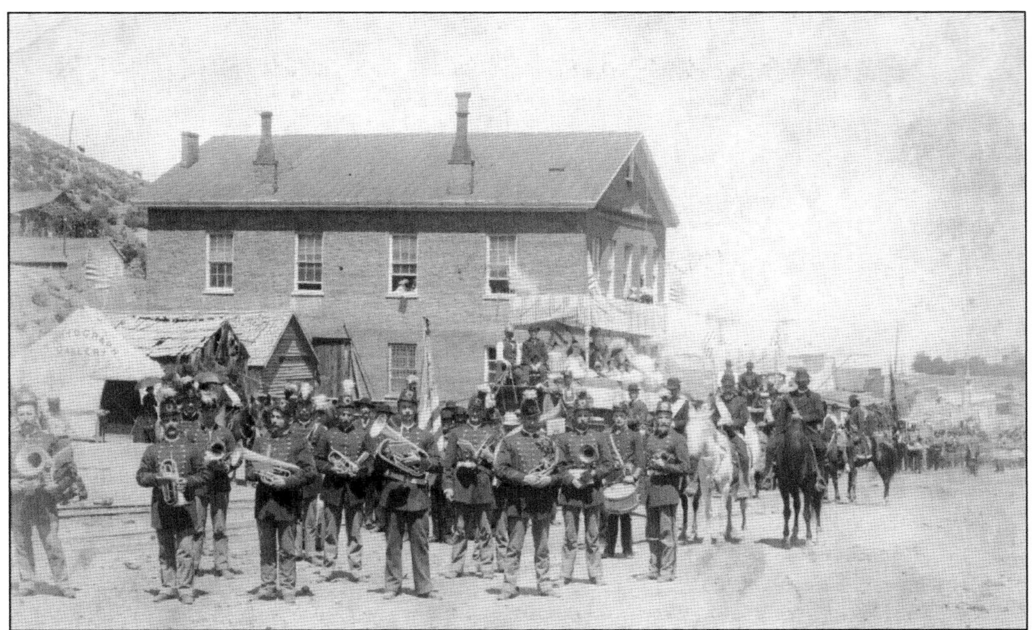

A Fourth of July parade heads up Main Street in 1890. The Lander County Courthouse is in the background. Built in 1878, it was the county's second courthouse in Austin and housed many of the county's offices until 1980. After a bitter election, the county seat was moved 90 miles to the north to Battle Mountain. This picture was taken at the same time as the photograph on the cover of this book. The photographer's studio is visible on the left. (Courtesy of NVHS.)

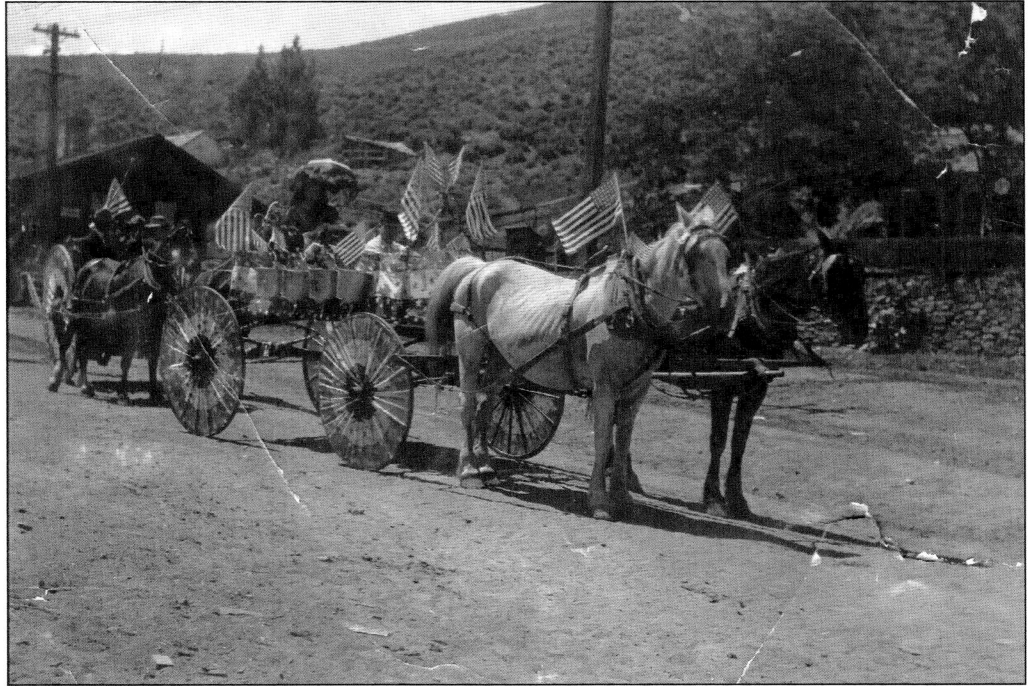

Because of the lack of the Austin City Railway tracks, this Fourth of July float is from the 1890s. The large building in the upper left is the Austin Terminal, which was located directly across from the Leland House. The poor horse has seen better days. (Courtesy of CC.)

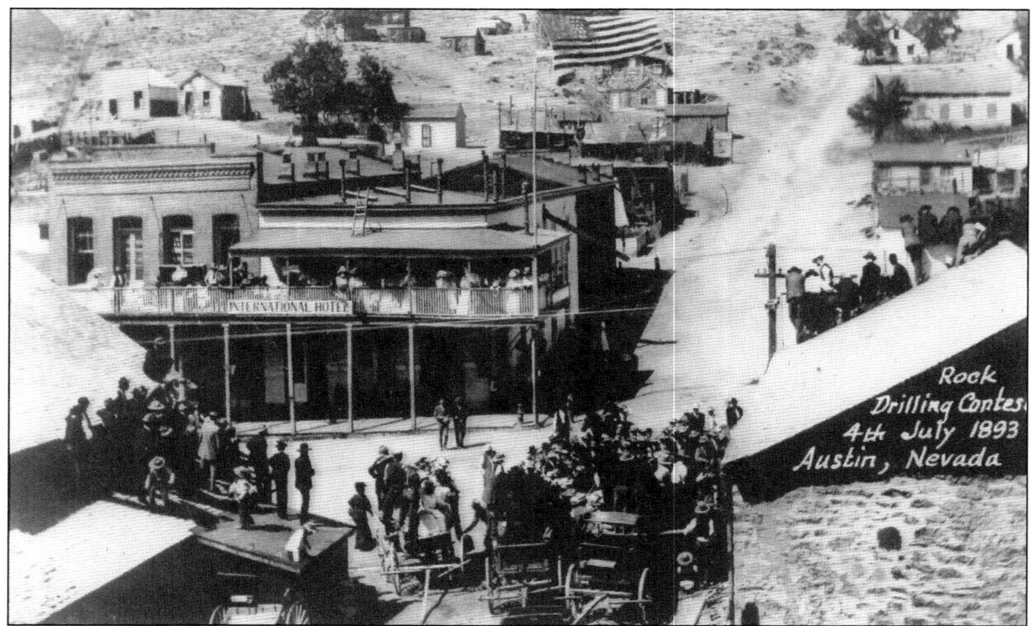

This was taken on July 4, 1893, on Main Street, across from the International Hotel. The crowd watches, as miners try to best each other in a rock-drilling contest. Drilling was done by hand, and Dan Palm won the contest that day. The crowd in the left corner is standing on the roof the old Stiener Livery. And way in the background, up the hill, is China Ridge, Austin's Chinatown. (Courtesy of JBC.)

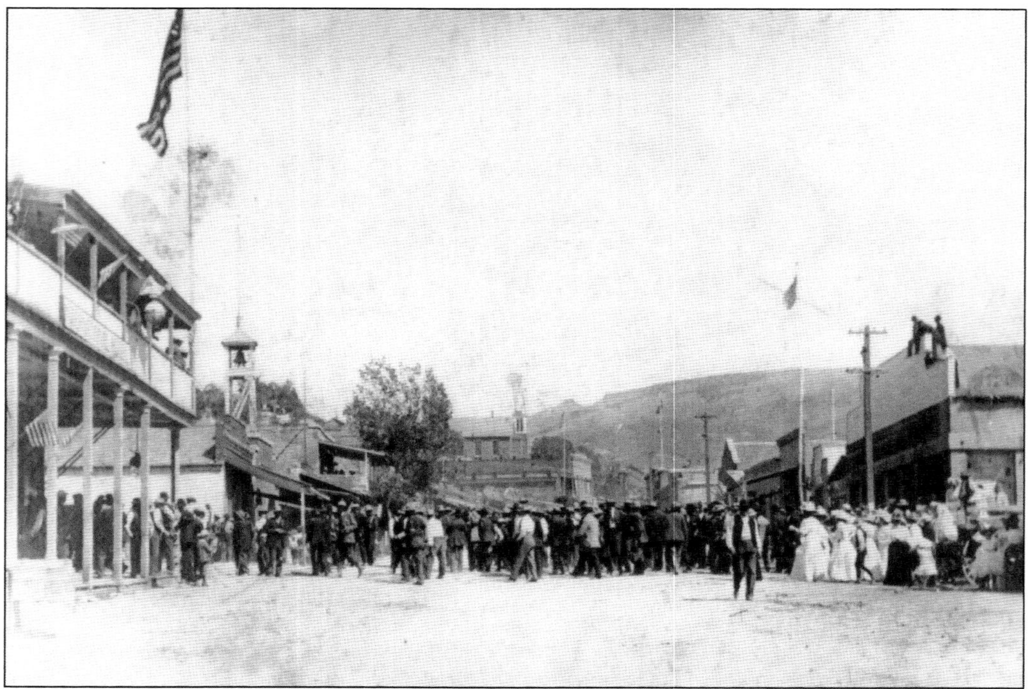

Looking up Main Street, the crowd looks to be dispersing, perhaps time for a beer on this July 4, 1893. Looking further up Main Street, the Masonic hall and Methodist church can be seen. (Courtesy of JBC.)

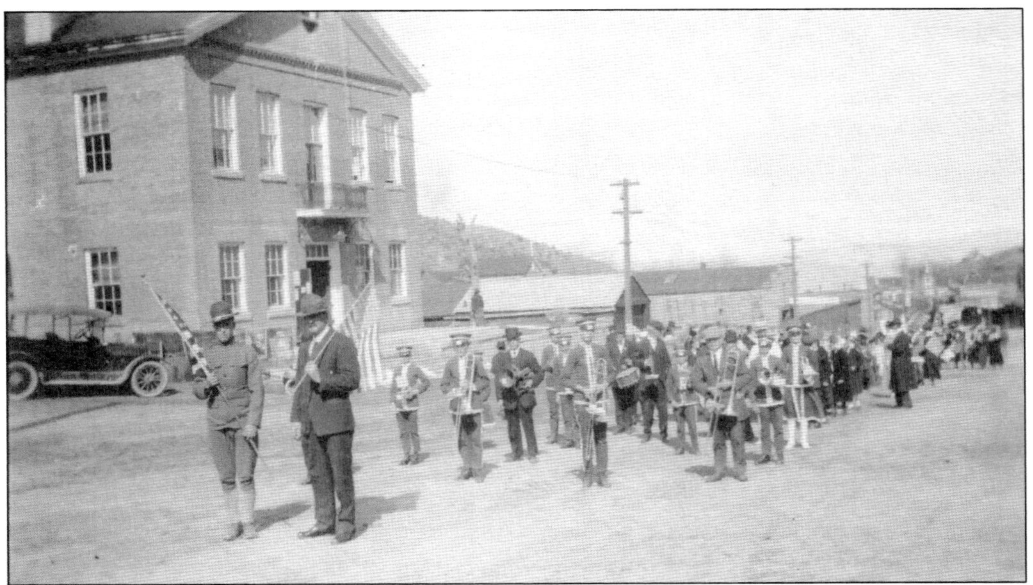

On June 14, 1916, Pres. Woodrow Wilson declared, by presidential decree, Flag Day in the United States, and Austin responded with a parade. The courthouse looms large to the left, and a band makes its way up Main Street. (Courtesy of SC.)

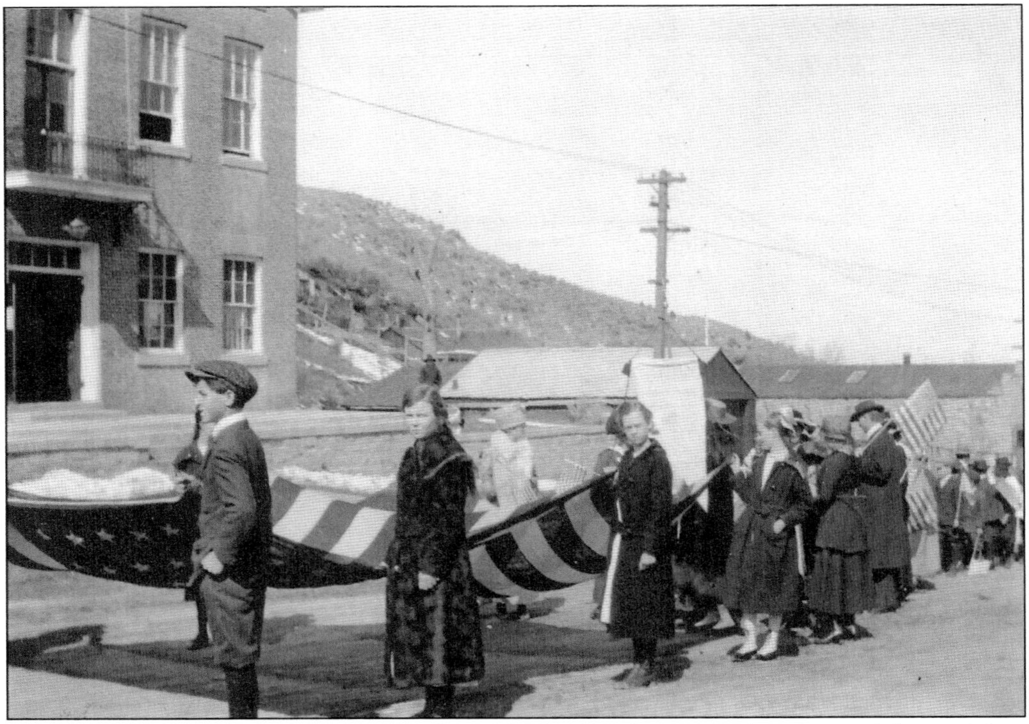

On Flag Day 1916, eight young citizens have the honor of carrying the 48 stared flag up Main Street. Not until 1959 would the flag change with the admission of Alaska. (Courtesy of SC.)

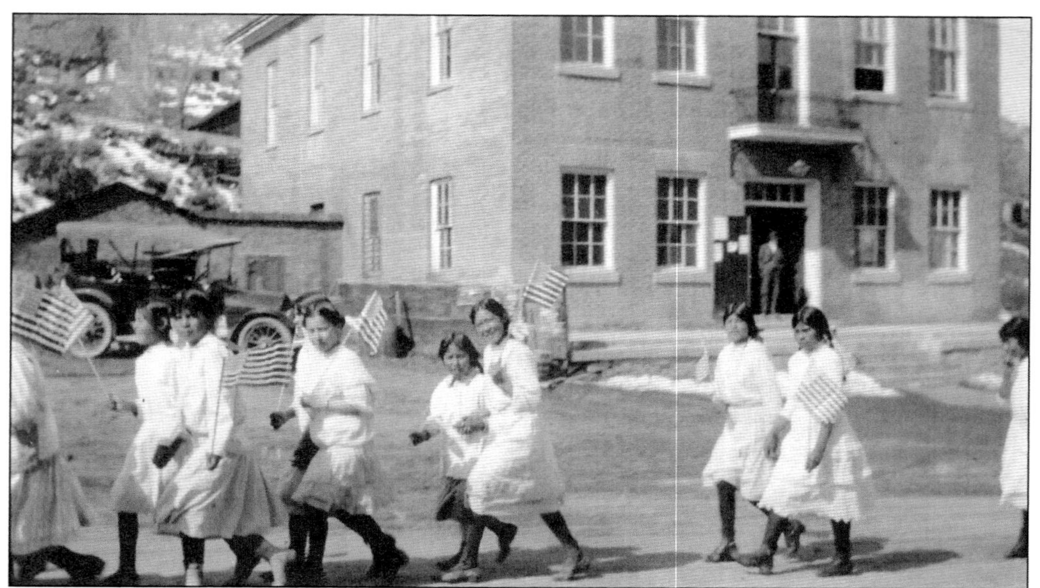

On Flag Day 1916, a contingent of young ladies, dressed in white, is seen bringing up the rear of the parade. Several of people shown are of Native American descent. A little bit of snow remains scattered in the background. Winter can come in September and stay until June in Austin. (Courtesy of SC.)

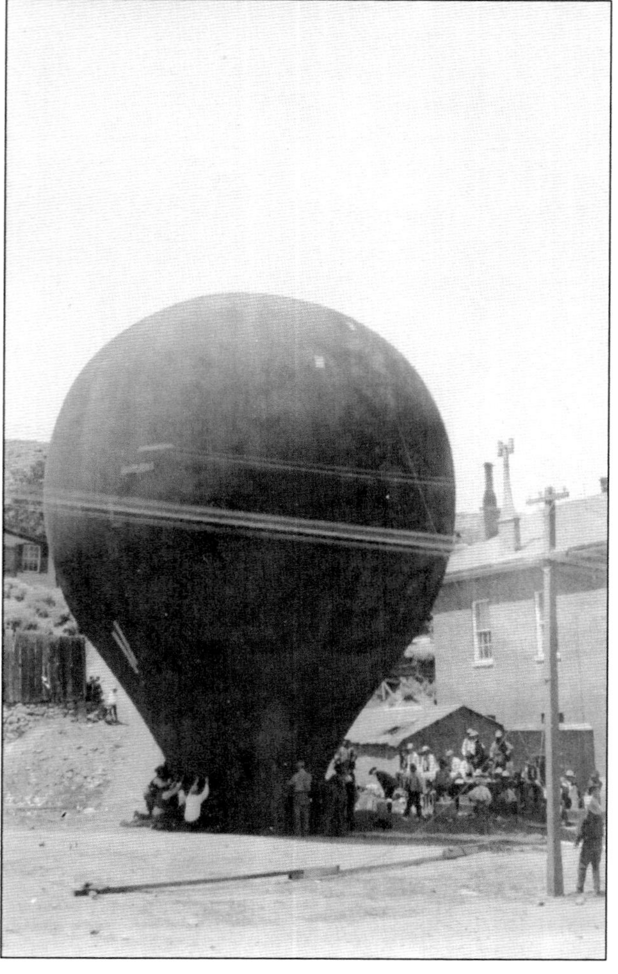

In the summer of 1908, the town gathered to watch a balloon launch next to the courthouse. The traveling aeronaut was known as the "Professor." His flight was cut short after having tangled with the Methodist church's steeple, where he had to be cut down. (Courtesy of NVHS.)

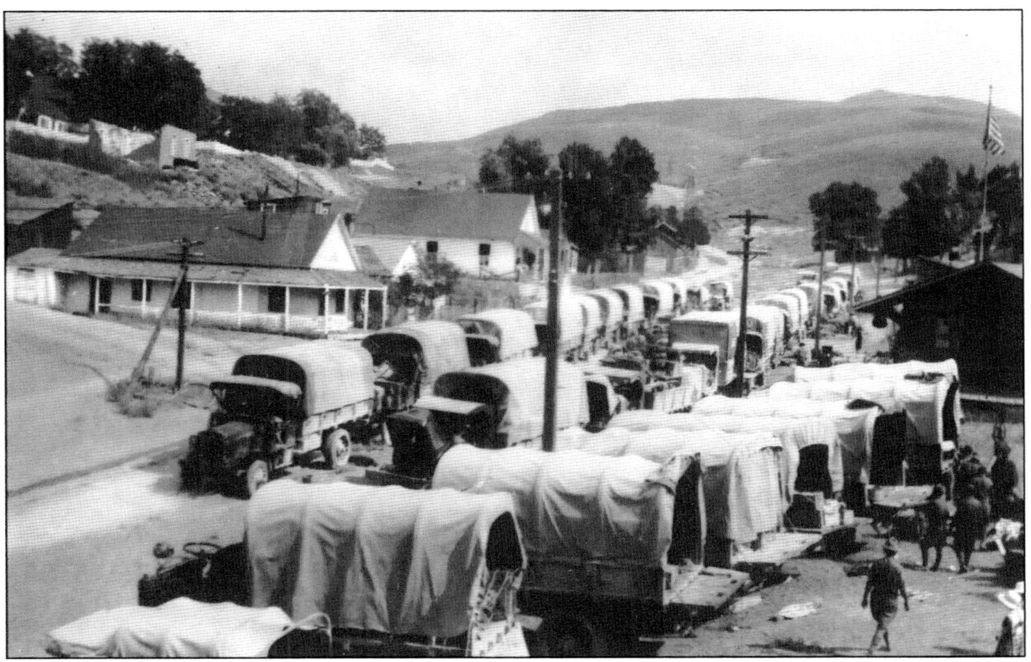

In early July 1919, a convoy of US Army vehicles departed the White House and drove to Gettysburg, Pennsylvania. There they joined the Lincoln Highway and drove on across the nation passing through Austin in late August and arriving in San Francisco early September. The Leland house is the first one on the left. (Courtesy of JBC.)

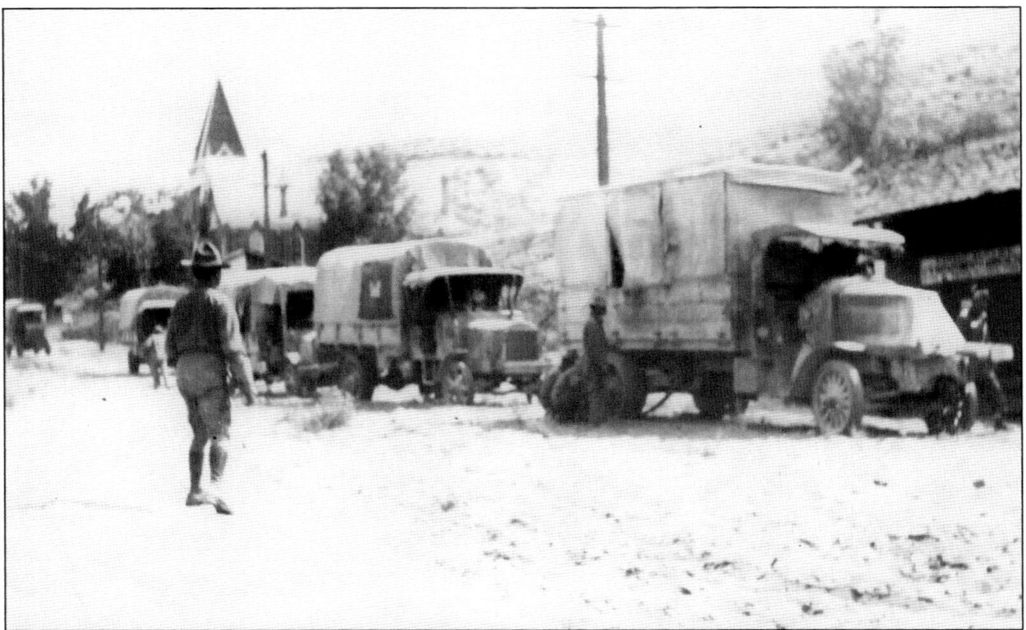

The entire trip was over 3,000 miles, and the convoy came right down Austin's Main Street. A future president, Lt. Col. Eisenhower, was part of the expedition. Between this experience and what he saw of the German highway system during World War II, he was inspired to lead the creation of the interstate highway system in 1956. St. George Episcopal Church's steeple is in the background. (Courtesy of JBC.)

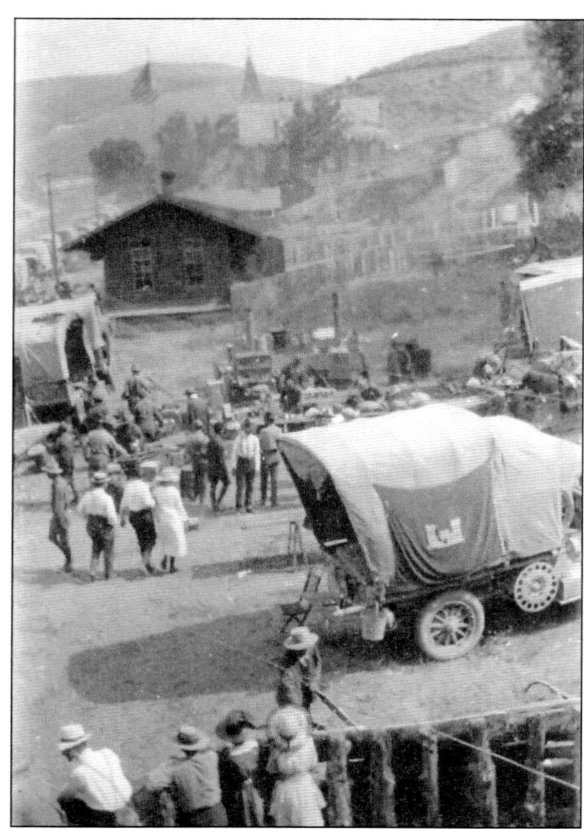

The Army Corp of Engineers' flag is draped on the truck in the foreground. Trucks made by the Four-Wheel Drive Company and Mack Company "Bull Dogs" were part of this expedition. Both companies are still in business today. The dark building to the left is the old Austin City Railway terminal. (Courtesy of JBC.)

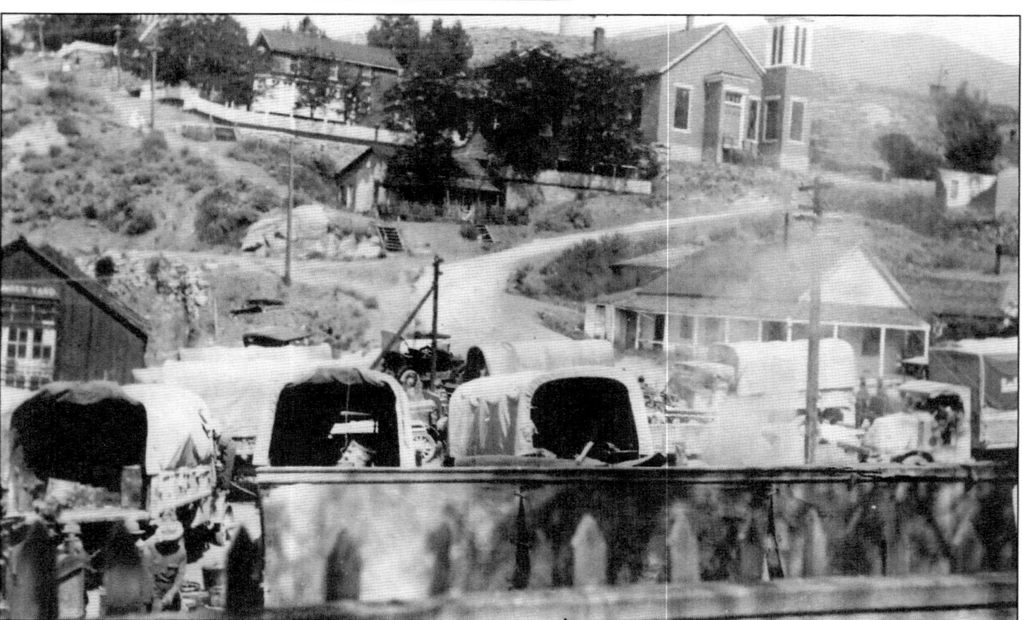

This photograph was taken looking across Main Street. The Leland House and the Methodist church are seen in the background. The convoy stopped in Austin to prepare their noon meal and resumed their drive later that day. It is unknown if there were any desertions. (Courtesy of CC.)

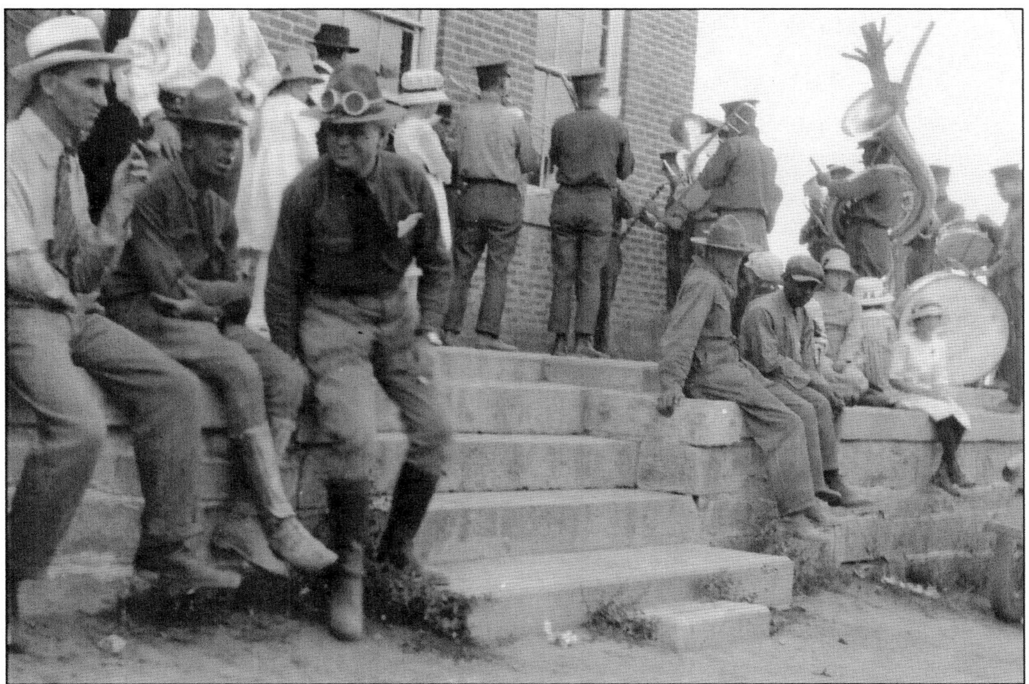

As part of the 1919 convoy, a brass band tunes it up. Soldiers and locals mingle on the courthouse steps. The same granite steps are still there. (Courtesy of JBC.)

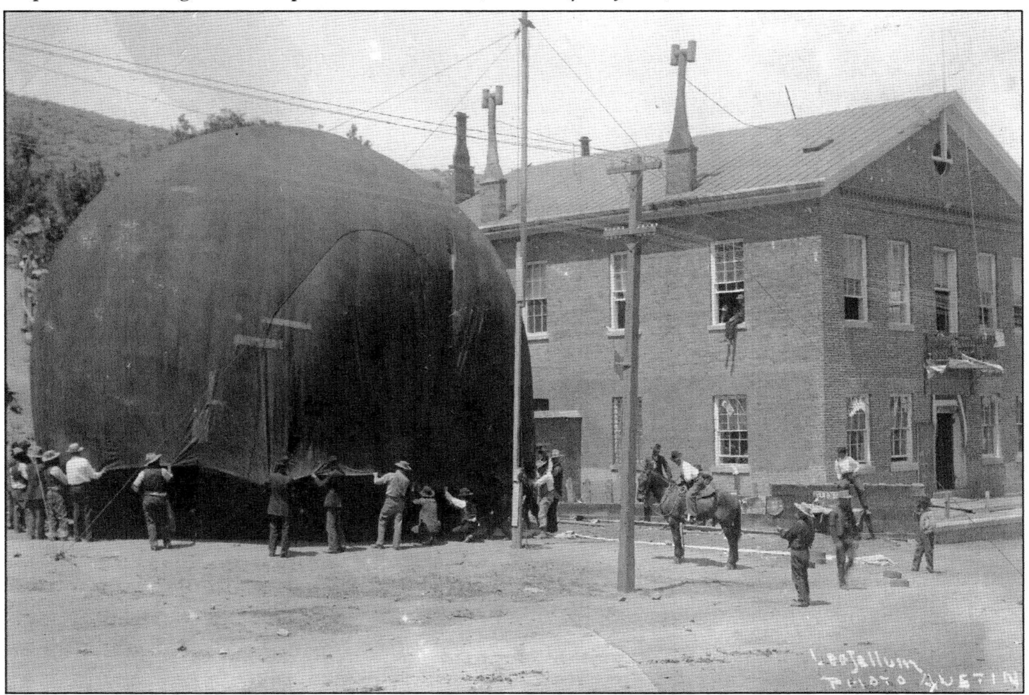

In the summer of 1908, the Professor, a traveling aeronaut, convinced the town into assisting in his one and only balloon launch. The men are holding down the balloon as it fills with hot air. Everyone else is just gawking. Notice the elaborate block and tackle set up for quick removal of the tarp. (Courtesy of AHS.)

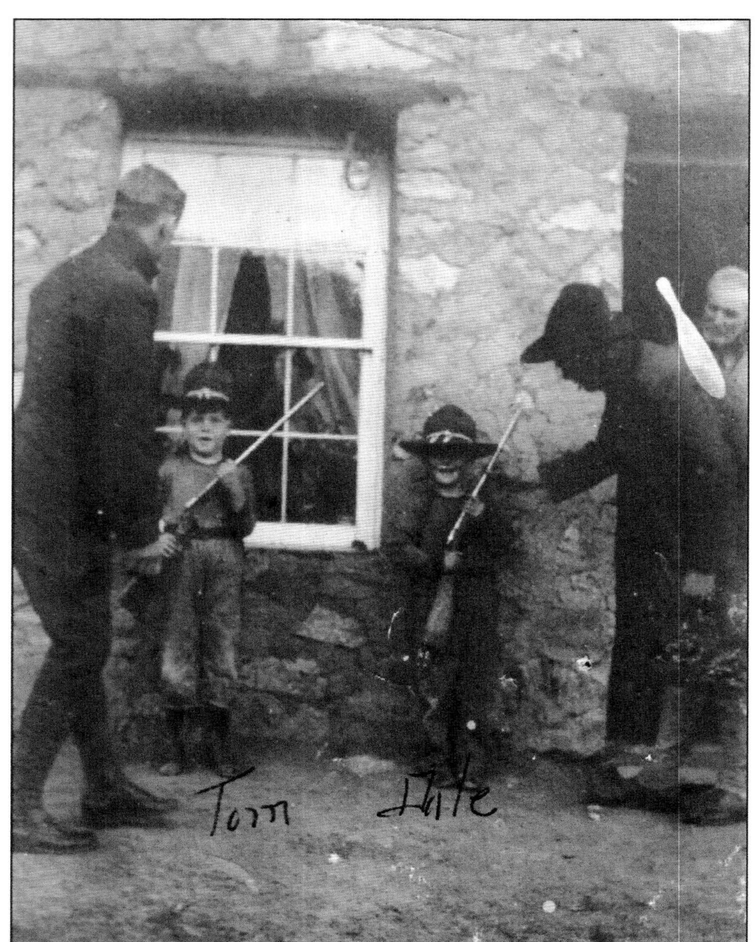

Two recruits, Tom and Dale Acree are being given arms instruction from the soldiers from the 1919 US Army convoy. Their father, Bert Acree, was the Lander County recorder for many years. (Courtesy of CC.)

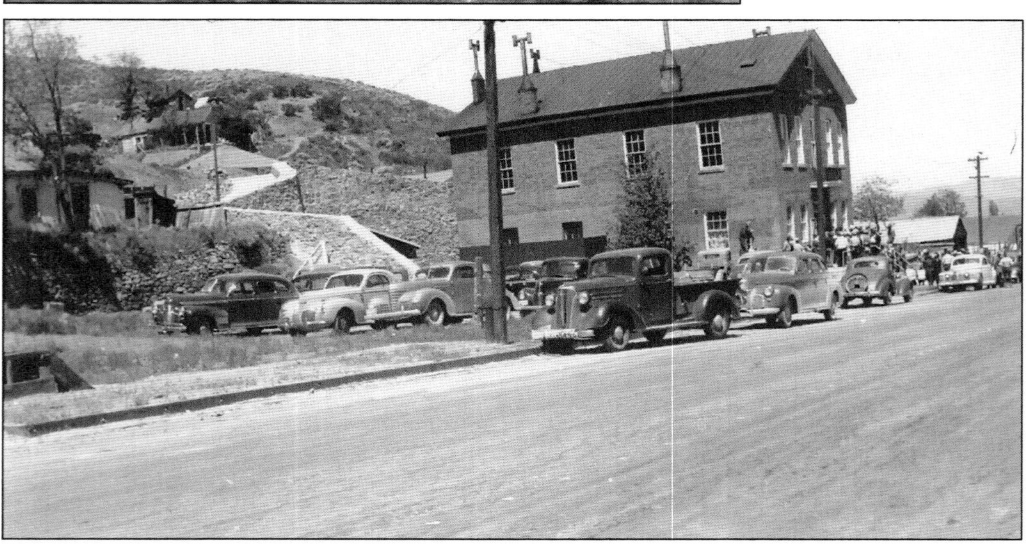

This is the Lander County Courthouse as seen from across Main Street about 25 years after the 1919 Army convoy. Mormon Gulch is visible behind the courthouse (see page 41). (Courtesy of JBC.)

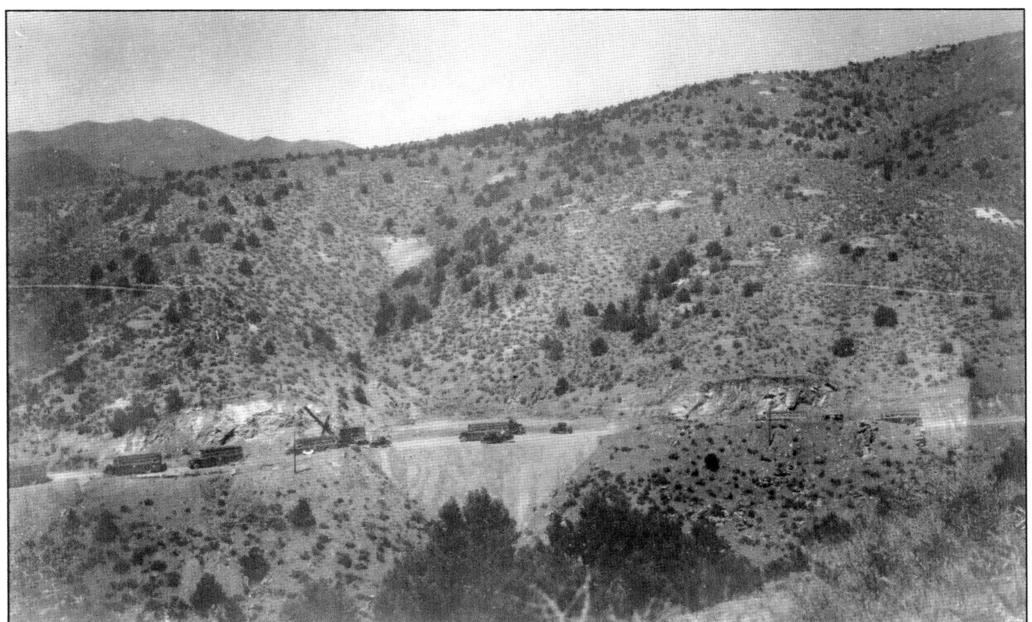

The 1919 Army convoy snakes its way down Pony Canyon and out onto the Reese River Valley. Miners, who were offered a free house lot in Austin for helping, made this original grade. These homesites were closer to the mines than those in the original settlement of Clifton. The Overland Stage, and later Austin City Railway, widened and improved the road over the years. (Courtesy of CC.)

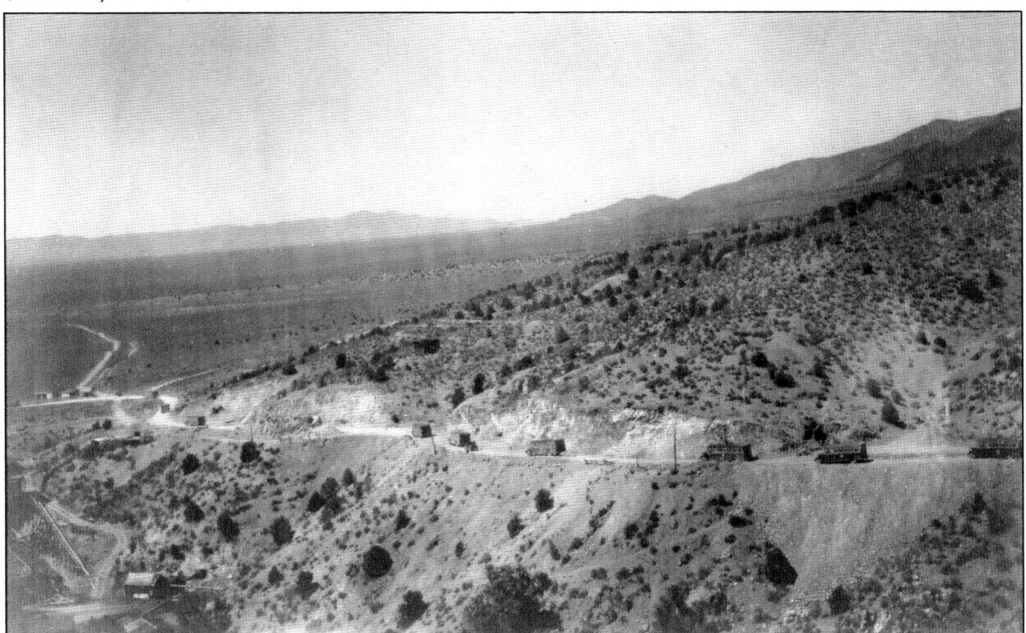

In 1913, the Lincoln Highway was commissioned. It was the first transcontinental highway in America; although, in those days, that may not have meant much more than a dirt track. One can see roadwork going on, as the Army convoy passes by. Eventually, the road was paved, straightened, and graded some more. Today, it is known as US 50, "the Loneliest Highway in America," due to the scarcity of traffic. (Courtesy of CC.)

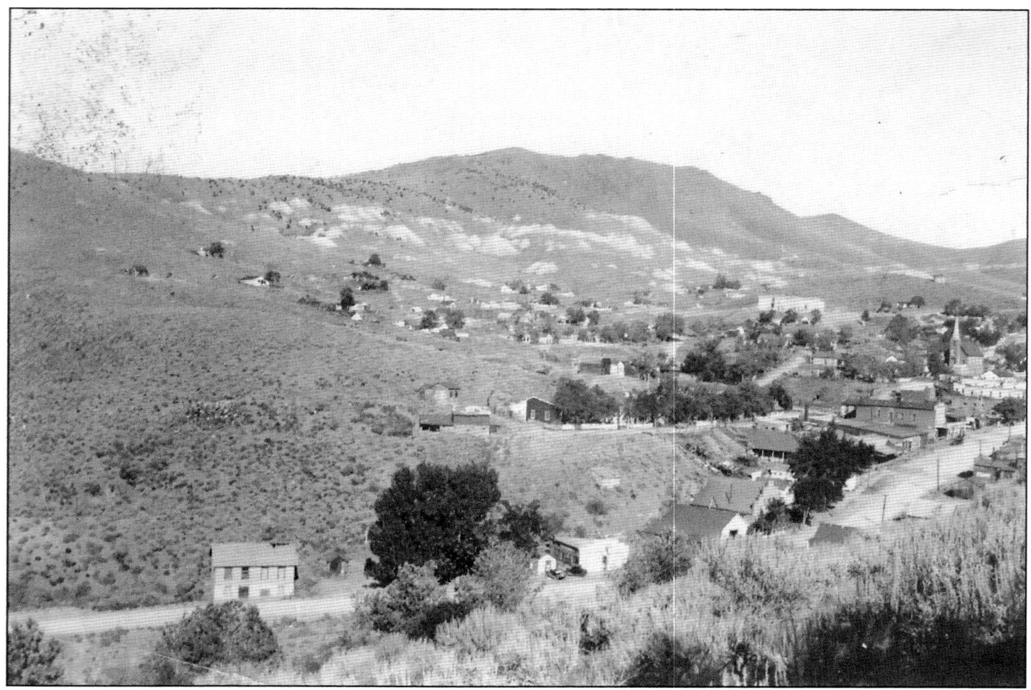

This image is of lower Austin in the 1920s. To the right, the large brick building is the International Hotel, and St. Augustine's steeple is seen above it. China Ridge, Austin's Chinatown, was scattered around the loose bunch of trees in the center of the photograph. (Courtesy of JBC.)

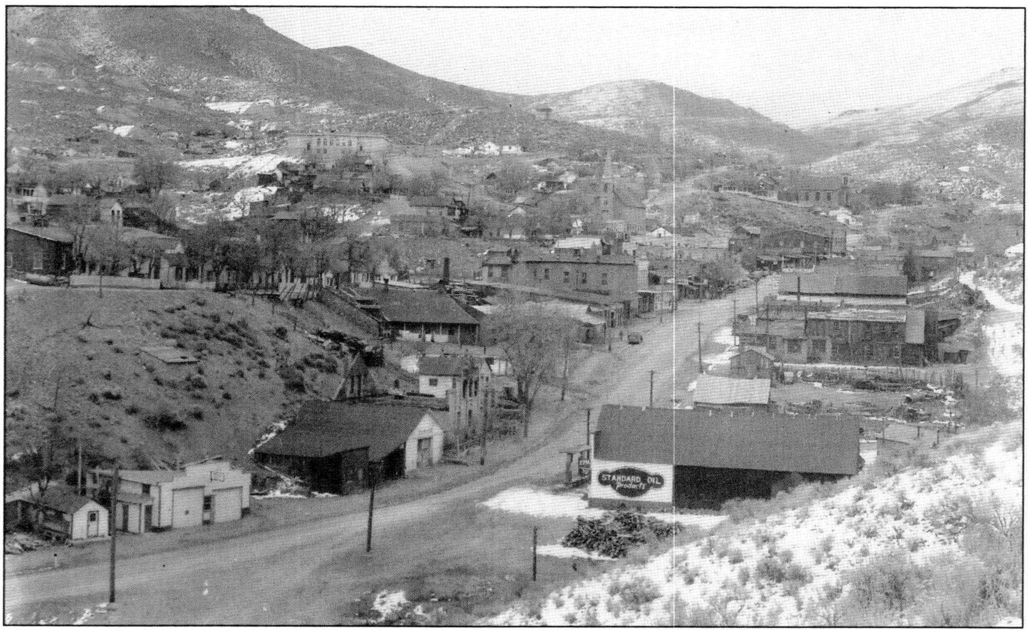

This photograph from around 1930 could be compared to the one on page 11 to see some of the changes to the old town. The liveries on the right of Main Street have started to become motor courts and gas stations. The Standard Oil station is a Chevron station today. The imposing light-colored building on the left, located about two-thirds of the way up the hill, is the new school that was built in 1926. (Courtesy of CC.)

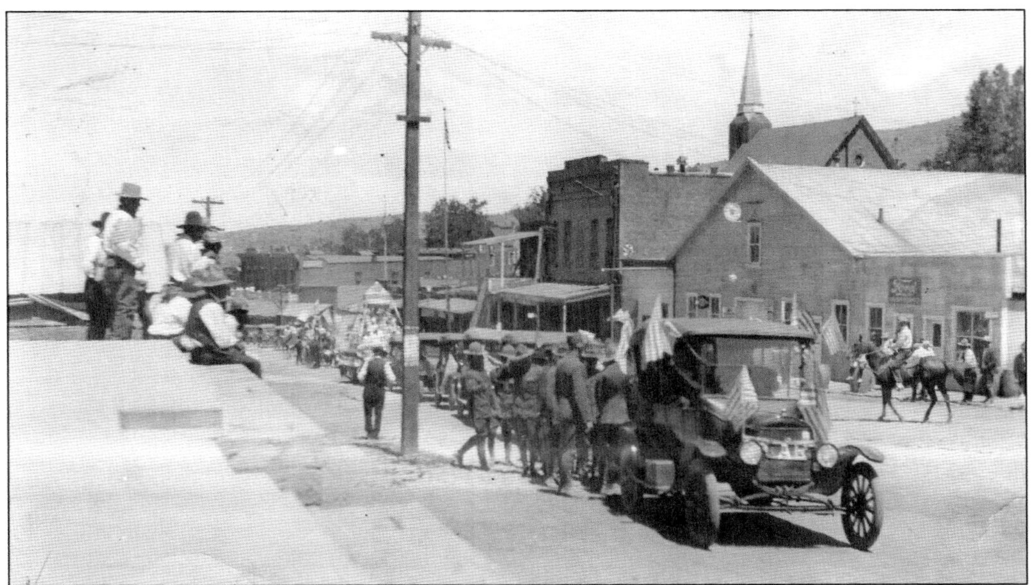

Here is Main Street on July 4, 1908. Today, this area looks much like it did in this photograph taken from the courthouse steps. The review committee still gathers here to judge the many contingents of Austin's Fourth of July parade. The Masonic hall is in the background. (Courtesy of JBC.)

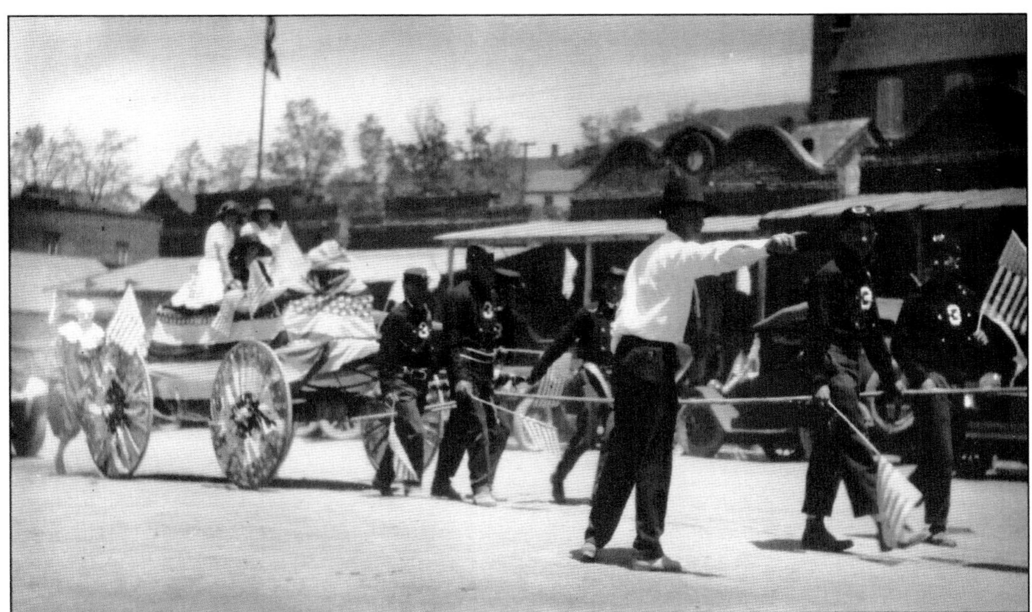

This is Main Street on the Fourth of July. Austin's volunteer firemen are pulling a float of Austin belles up Main Street. It is quite a pull uphill, with a six-percent grade. Today, the town runs its parades down the hill. (Courtesy of JBC.)

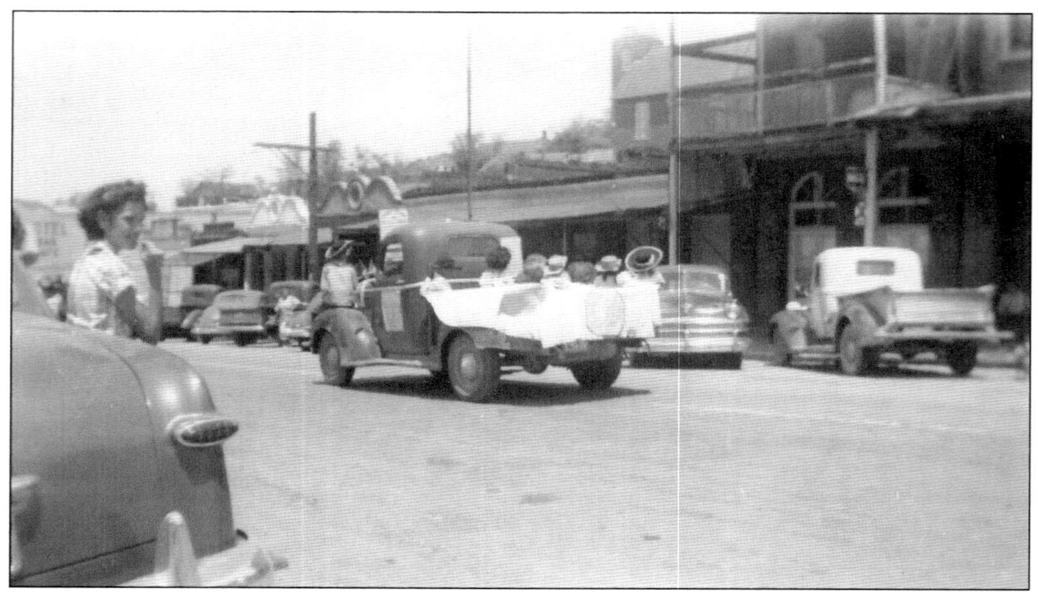

This image is from July 4, 1950. The mode of transportation has changed, but Main Street and the background have not. The Masonic Hall is to the right. (Courtesy of CC.)

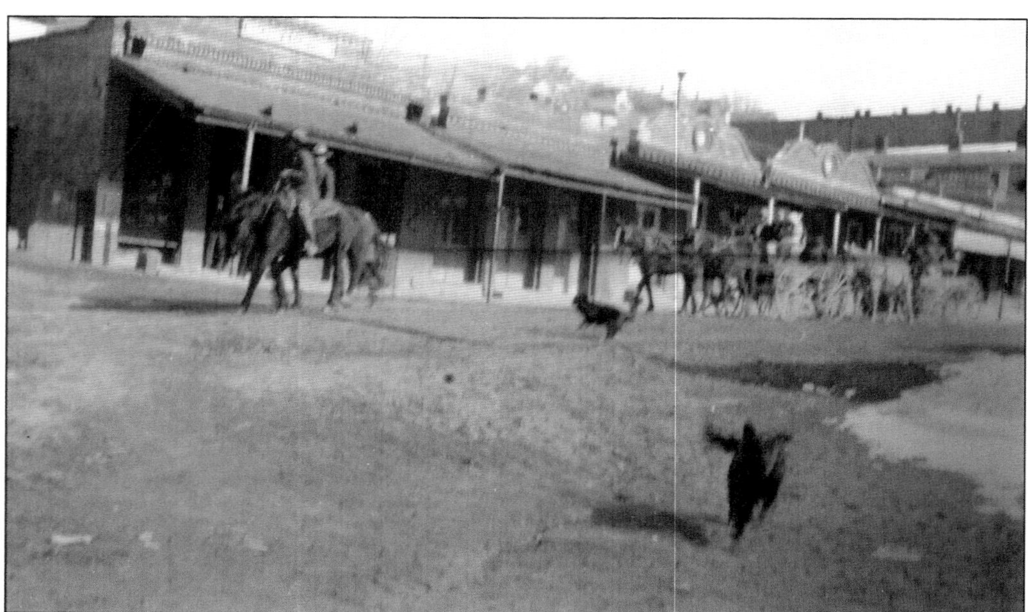

This c. 1910 photograph shows Main Street and the same buildings seen in the above photograph, just taken from another angle. There were no cars present at this time. The two buildings on the left are gone, but the rest of the block is intact. (Courtesy of JBC.)

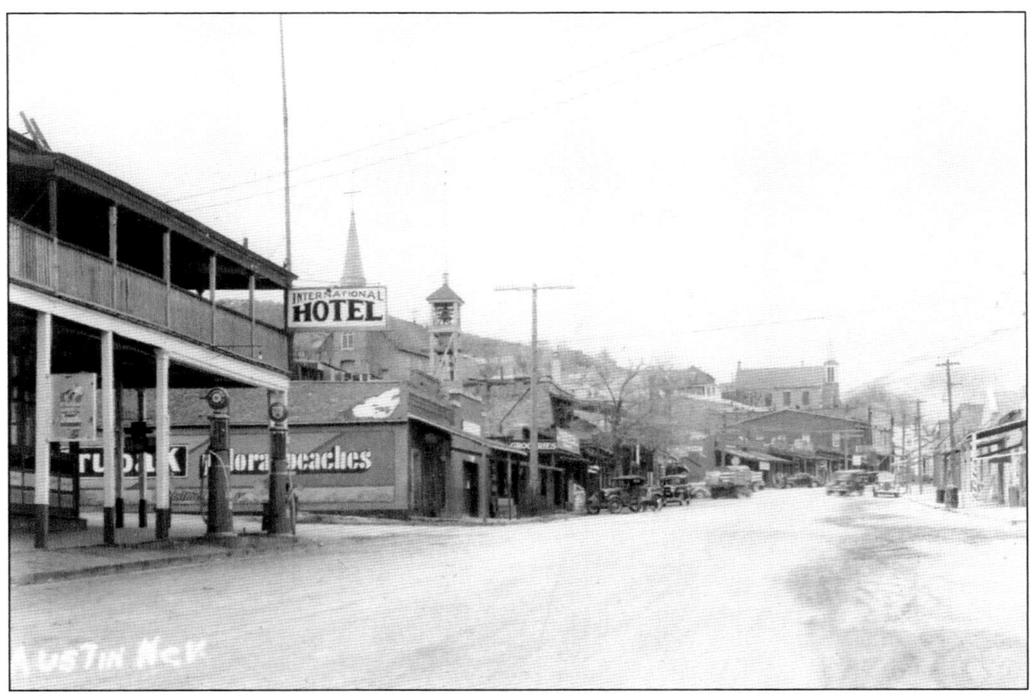

Main Street in the 1930s. The International Hotel, the corner building on the left, is now selling gasoline. The bell tower is atop the Austin Volunteer Firehouse. The bell still rings, and today the building is the town's youth center. (Courtesy of CC.)

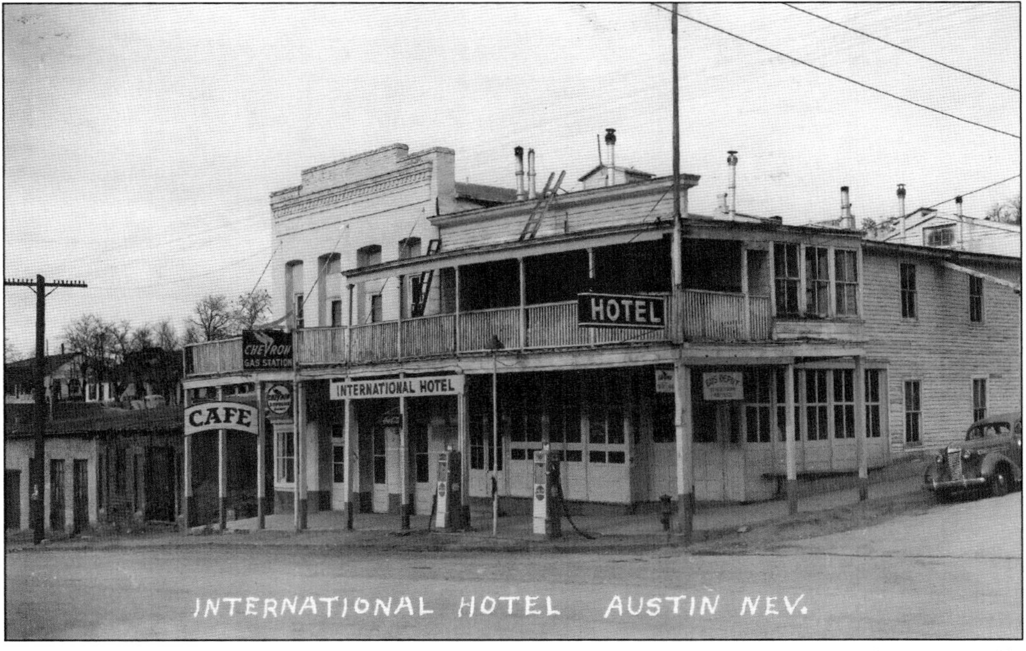

The International Hotel was located at the corner of Cedar and Main Streets. A fire eventually took the wood-framed structure, but the brick building still serves food and whiskey. The whiskey is served in front of the original 1860s back bar. Although the upstairs rooms are no longer rented, a ghost is said to reside there. (Courtesy of JBC.)

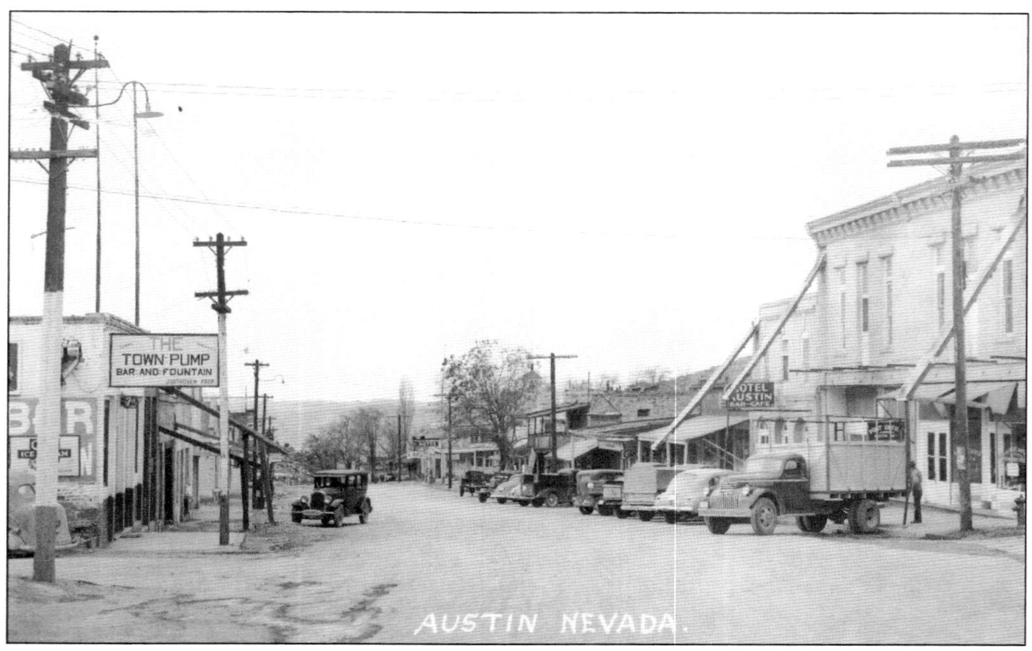

This 1940s view of Main Street is looking down the hill. The Hogan and Austin Hotels are on the right, and the Town Pump is on the left. This building has had many lives, such as a telephone exchange (see page 15), saloon, soda fountain, and a movie theater. (Courtesy of NVHS.)

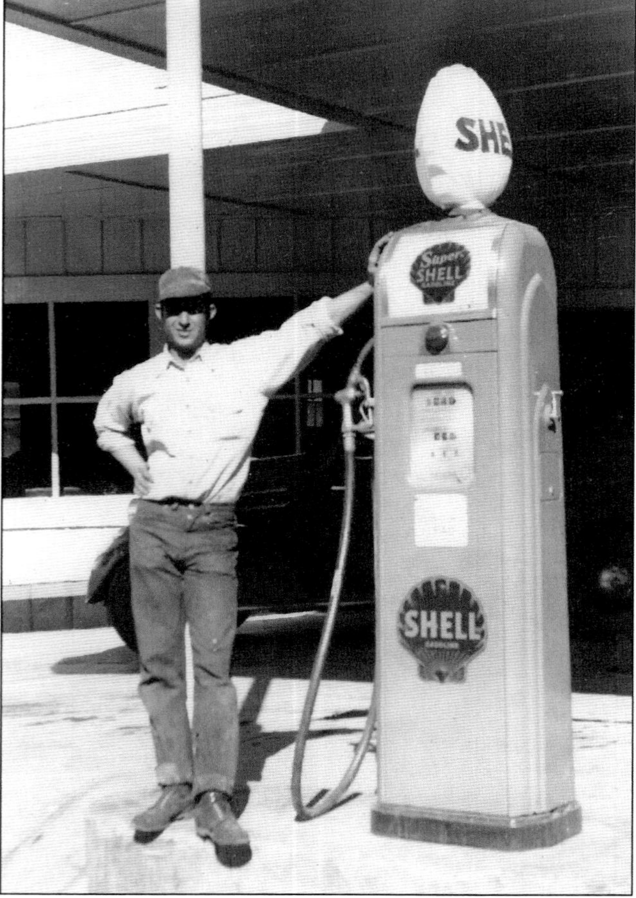

Bob Goff was owner of the Town Pump in its saloon and soda fountain days. Today, the building survives on as a saloon. (Courtesy of CC.)

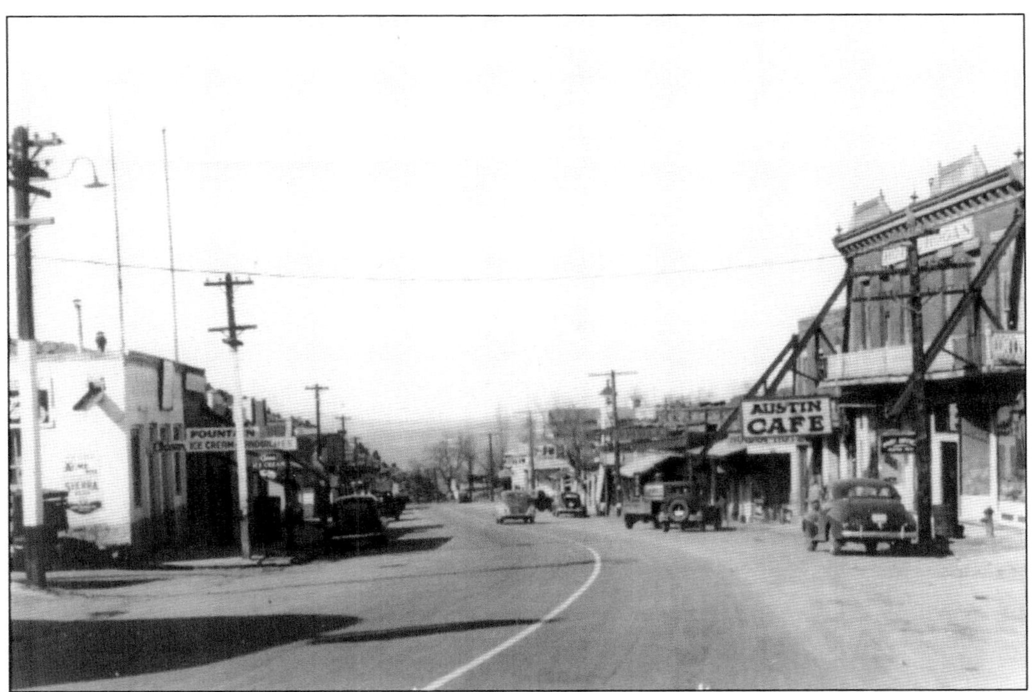

In this photograph, taken a few years later, the Town Pump saloon has become a soda fountain; Main Street has a new surface; and the Austin Café and Hogan Hotel have new signage. It is after World War II, and Austin looks prosperous. (Courtesy of JBC.)

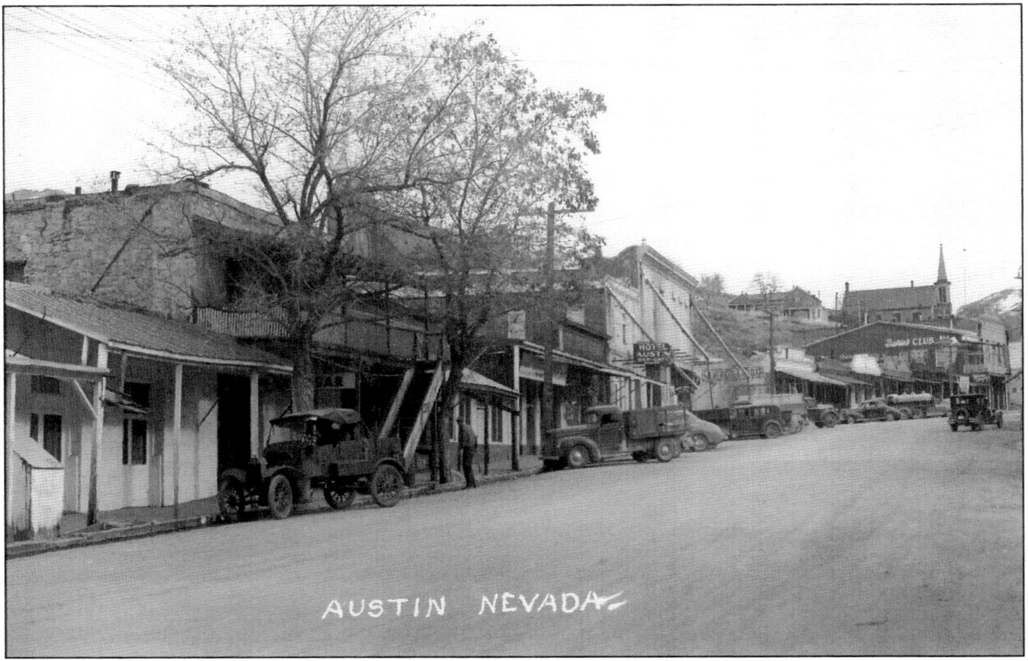

The Methodist church is clear in the background. The floods down Main Street have been pretty well tamed, but notice the old hinged steps leading to the second floor of the Silver State saloon (see pages 12 and 15). The Silver State, with its hinged stairs, is still there serving whiskey and beer. (Courtesy of SC.)

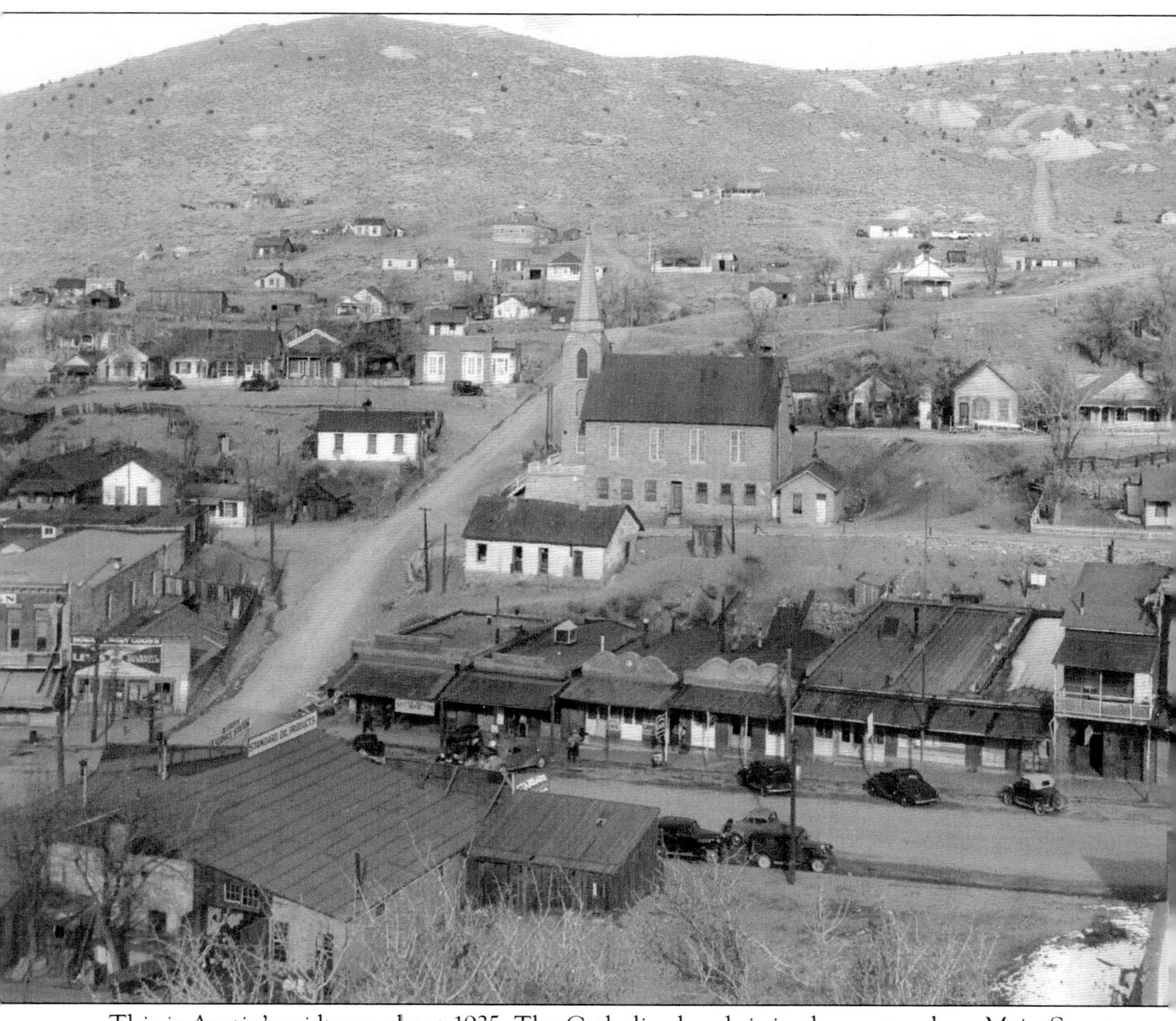

This is Austin's midtown about 1935. The Catholic church is in the center along Main Street, with the Hogan Hotel to the left and the Masonic hall to the far right. In the left foreground is the back of what will be named Celly's, then Cassidy's, and then Ramos's service station. (Courtesy of AHS.)

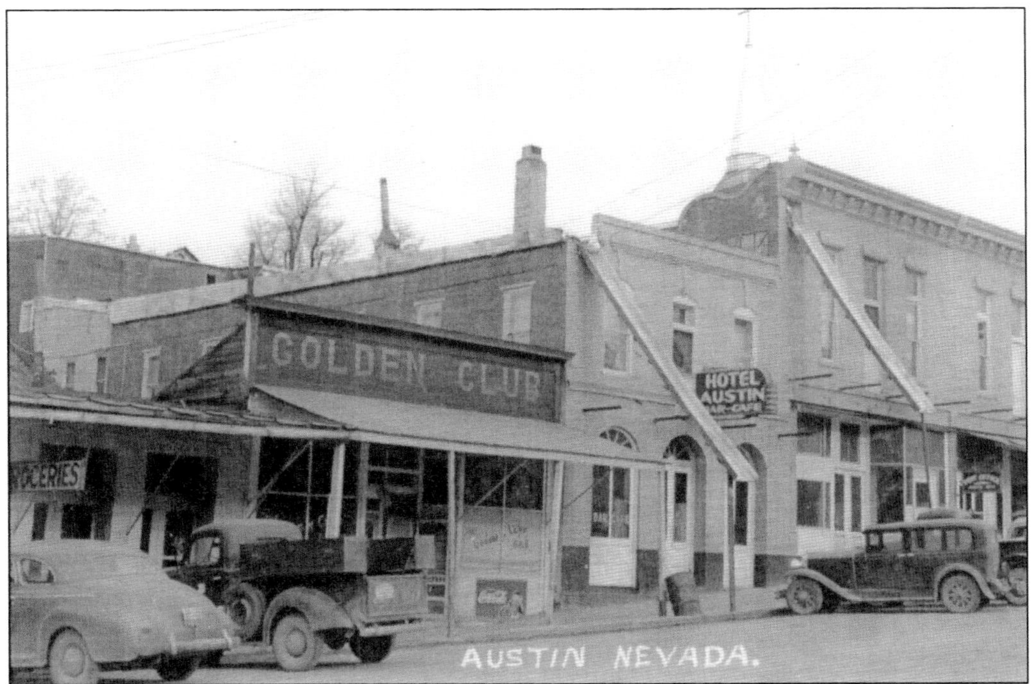

The Williams family owned the Golden Club, a saloon, for years. Clara Williams at 78 years old was the oldest licensed blackjack dealer in Nevada. She has since gone onto glory, and the building is in disrepair. (Courtesy of JBC.)

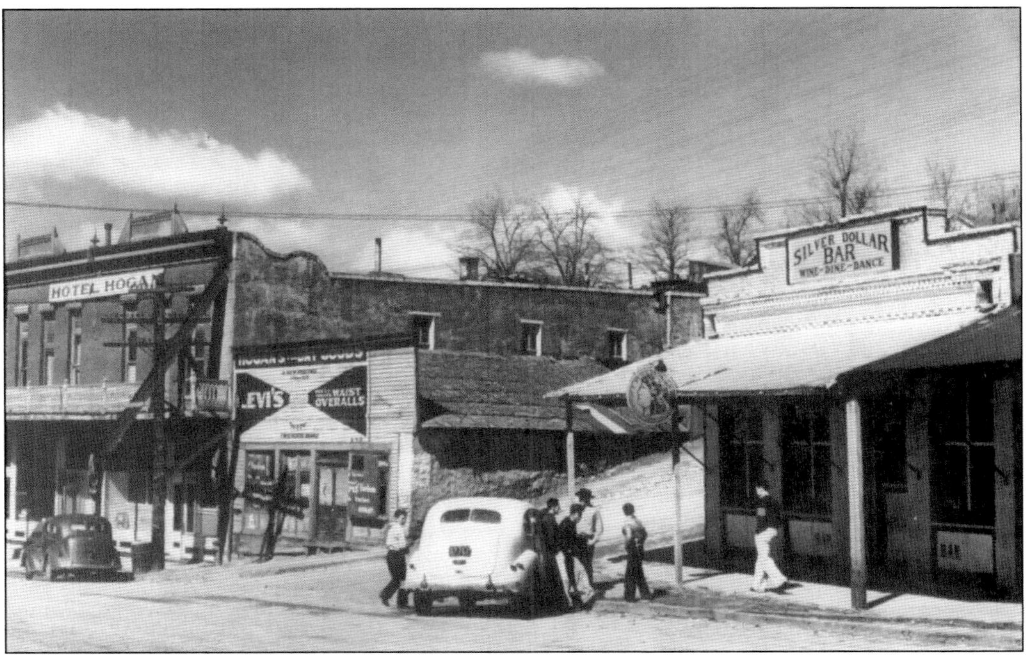

This image shows Virginia and Main Streets. The Silver Dollar Bar is no more, and a fire in the early 1980s destroyed the corner where Hogan's Dry Goods, Hogan Hotel, and Austin Café were located. The Hogan Hotel became the Austin hotel. The second floor had a dance hall that was the place to be on a Saturday night. (Courtesy of JBC.)

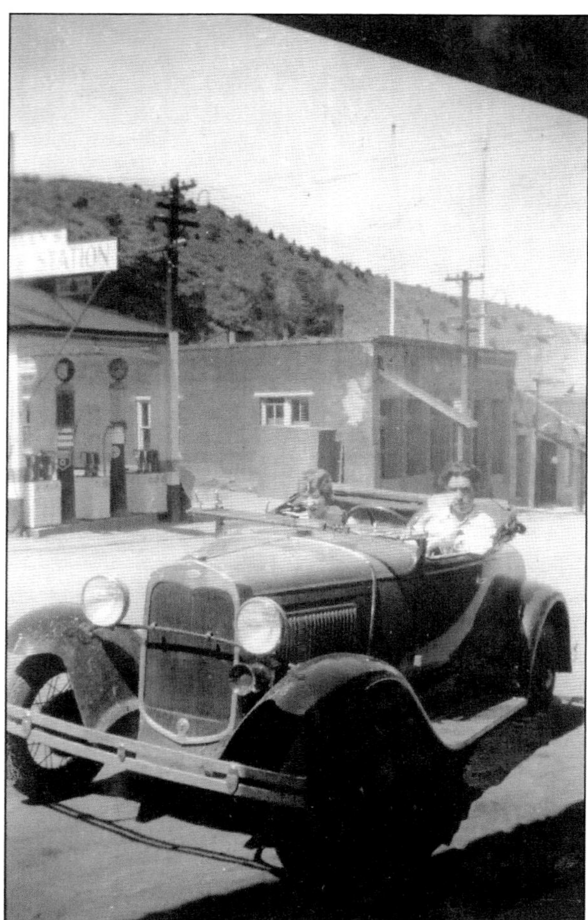

Paul Hogan is in a 1930 Model A Roadster with an unidentified companion. The old Telephone Exchange Office, which later became the Town Pump saloon, is behind him. Celly's service station is to the left. (Courtesy of SC.)

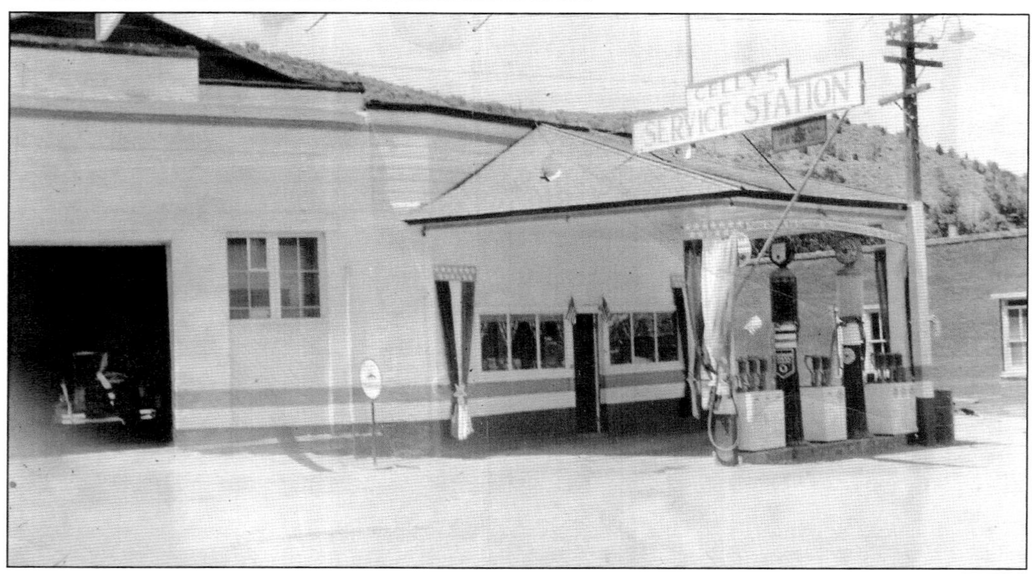

This Main Street Building was first a livery, then Celly's service station, then Cassidy Standard Oil, then Ramos's Chevron, and today is a rock and bottle shop. (Courtesy of JBC.)

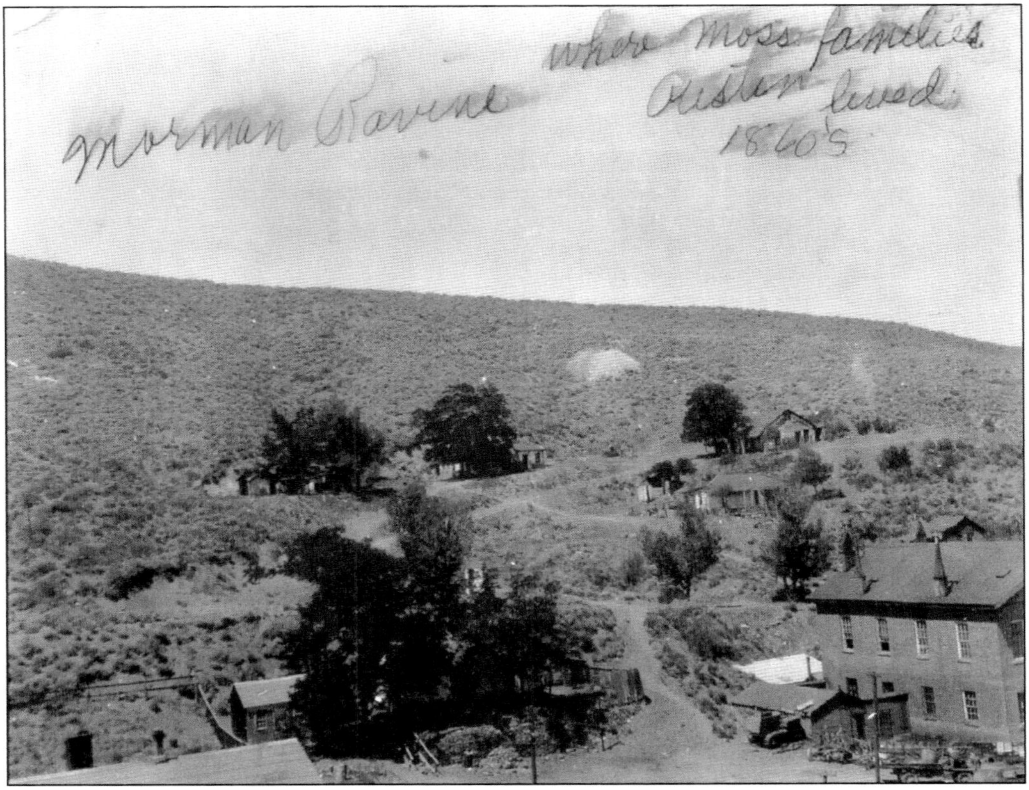

The area behind the 1878 Lander County Courthouse was originally known as Mormon Ravine. Right next to and connected to the courthouse, the fenced section was the exercise yard for the jail. The treaded vehicle parked just to the side of the wall was identified as an armored tractor. No other information could be found. Today, it is the site of the Lander County Sheriffs Substation. (Courtesy of SC.)

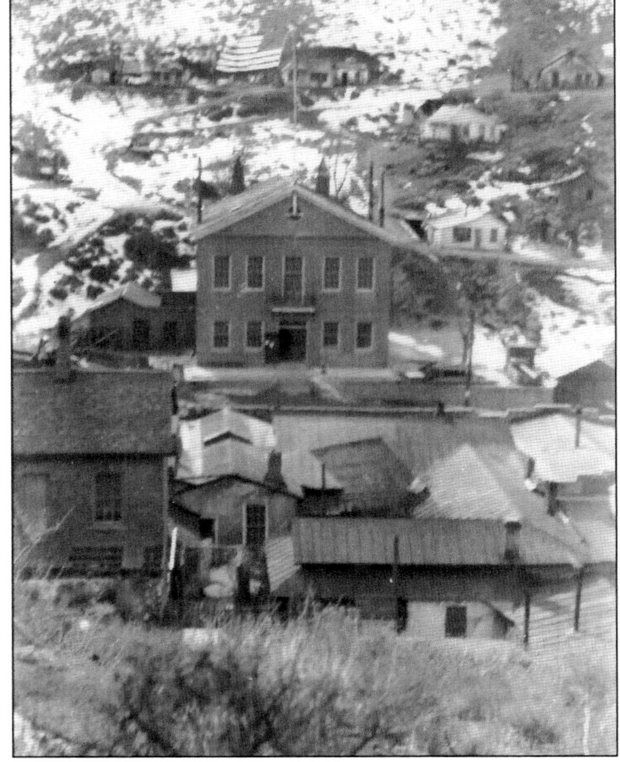

Looking across Main Street at the courthouse, the reader can get an idea for how tight Pony Canyon can be. The Potts and Berchams families, who were Native Americans, eventually settled the area behind the courthouse. (Courtesy of JBC.)

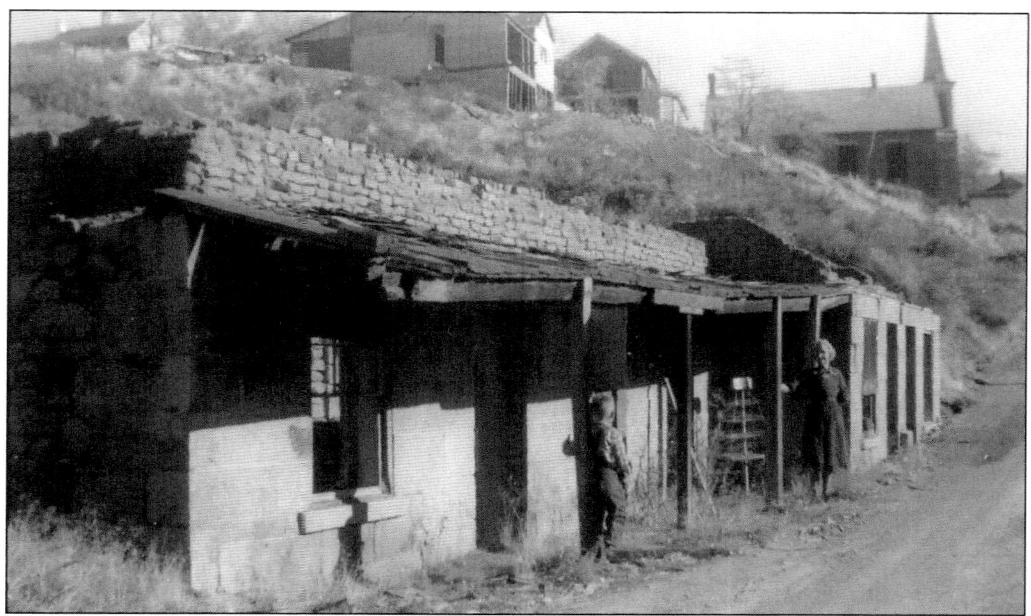

This was Austin's first courthouse, and by the time this photograph was taken around the 1930s, it had fallen into ruin. The street was named appropriately Court Street; the former site of this old courthouse is directly to the east of St. Augustine Catholic Church. It is said Austin's first hanging was on a tree directly up the hill and to the left. Nothing from the courthouse's existence remains today. (Courtesy of SC.)

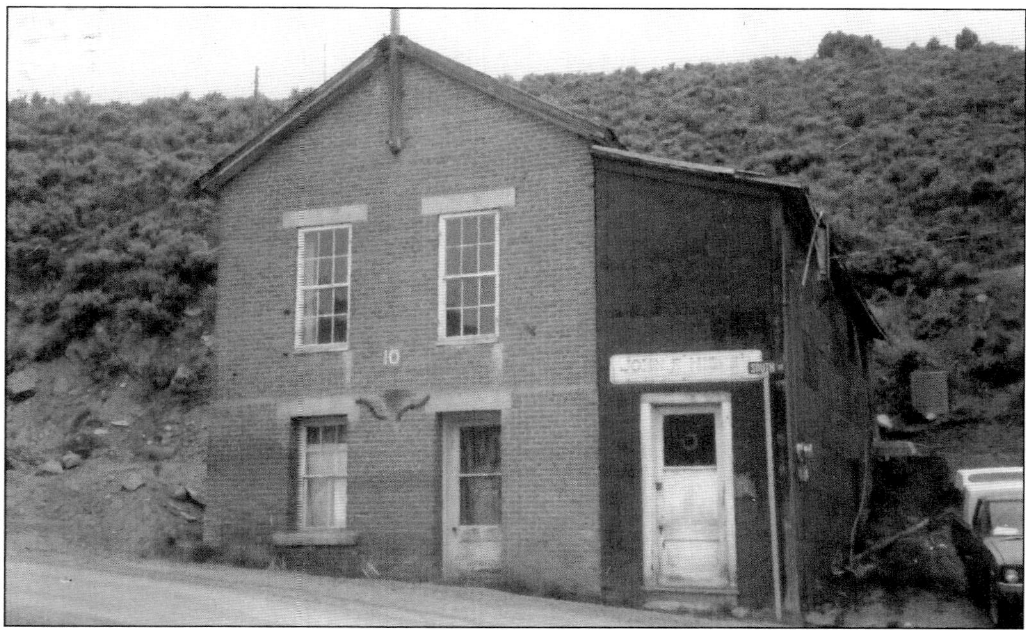

Austin's first town hall and jail still stands one block up from Main Street at South and Virginia Streets. Part of the lower building has the jail's original bars in the windows. Later, it became the Knights of Pythias Hall. The upstairs, being quite substantial, was used for balls and dances. Today, the building survives on as the John Hiskey Post 45 of the American Legion. (Courtesy of JBC.)

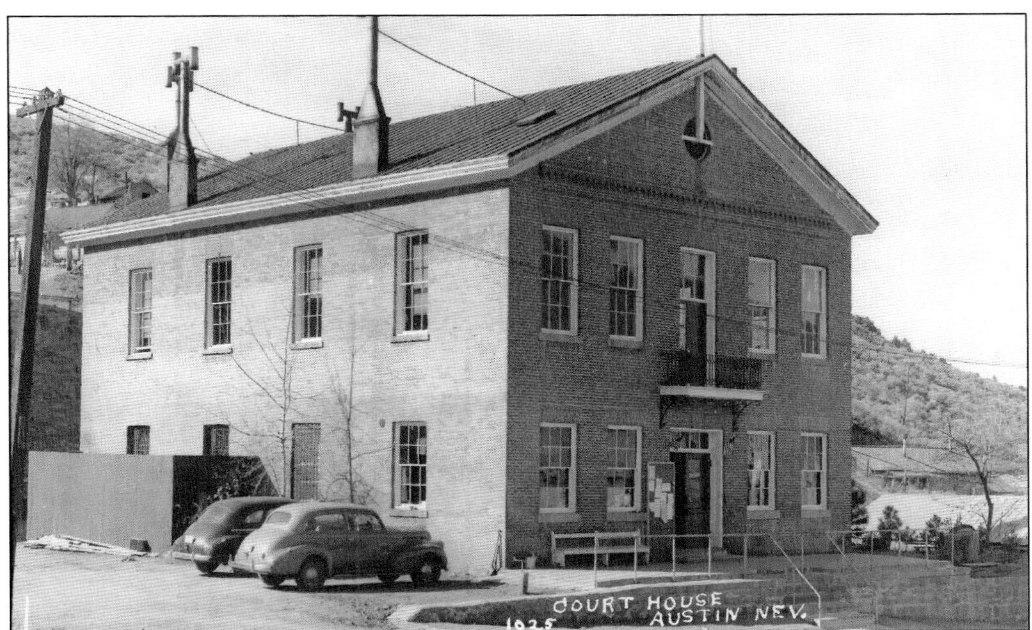

On December 14, 1881, Richard Jennings was hanged from the courthouse balcony, having shot and killed John Barrett the day before. Justice could be swift in those days. As the noose tightened, Jennings last words were "Oh my God boys, I guess I deserve this." Note the enclosed exercise yard on the left. The original 1878 jail is still in place inside the courthouse, located along this wall. (Courtesy of JBC.)

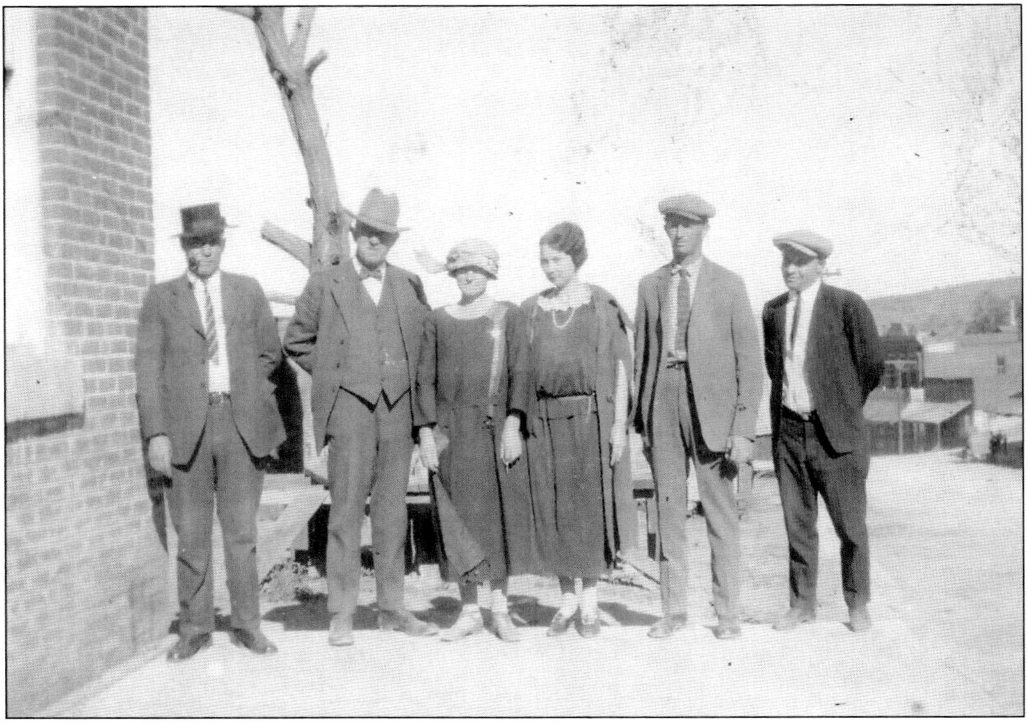

This photograph was taken from the east side of the courthouse. The man second from the right is a young John Spencer, and next to him is Lena Streshley. (Courtesy of JBC.)

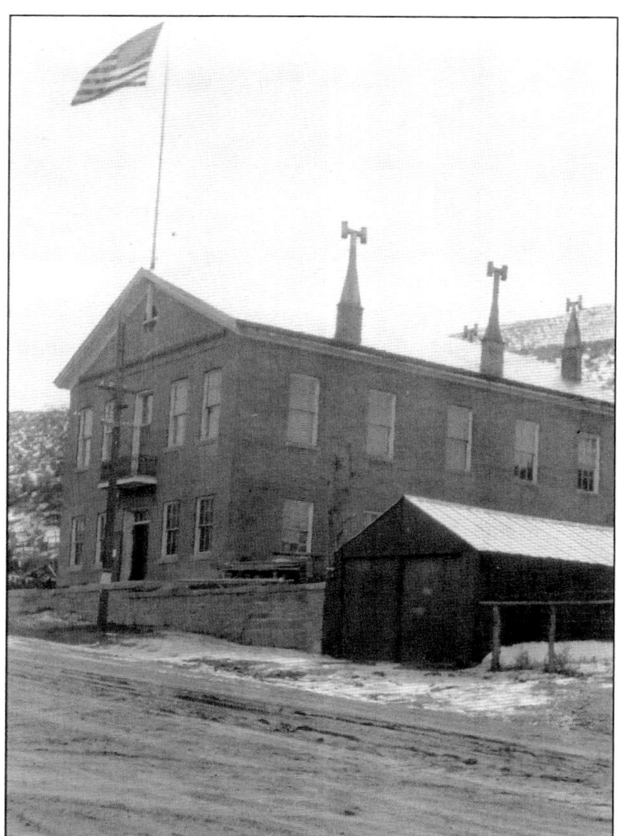

The old courthouse is still open today as offices for the Austin Water Department, the chamber of commerce, the county recorder, and the Department of Motor Vehicles. At the time of this writing, the Honorable Joe Dory holds court as justice of the peace upstairs. The stable to the right was owned by Lee Maestretti and was torn down to make way for a new volunteer firehouse. (Courtesy of JBC.)

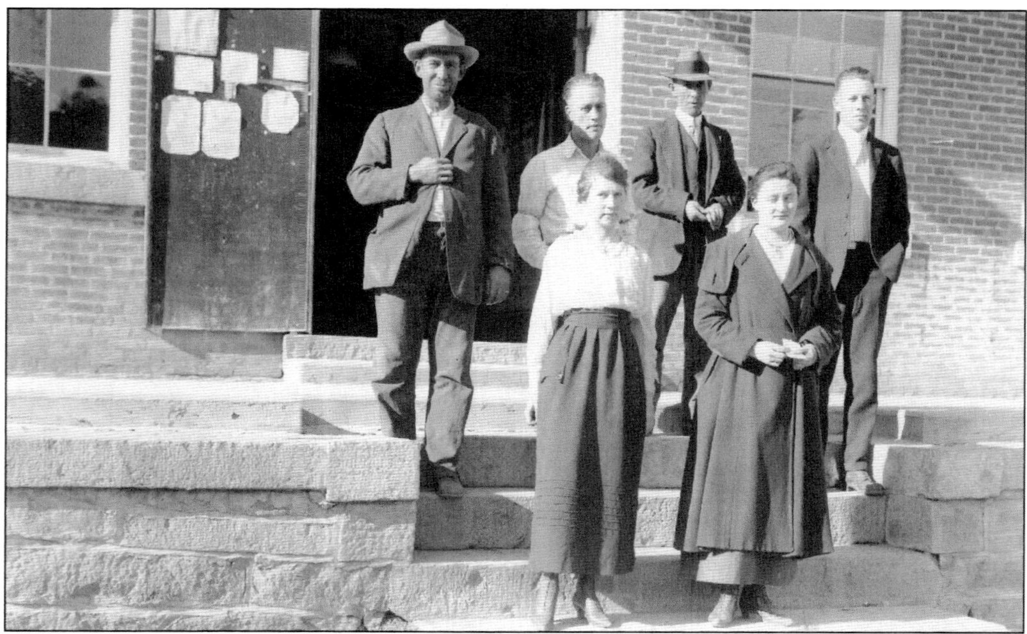

Those pictured in 1920s on the courthouse steps are, from left to right, (first row) Lena Streshley and Lena Scuichetti; (second row) John Spencer, county treasurer; Walt Collins; Thomas White; and Bert Acree, county recorder. (Courtesy of JBC.)

Two

MINING AND TRANSPORTATION

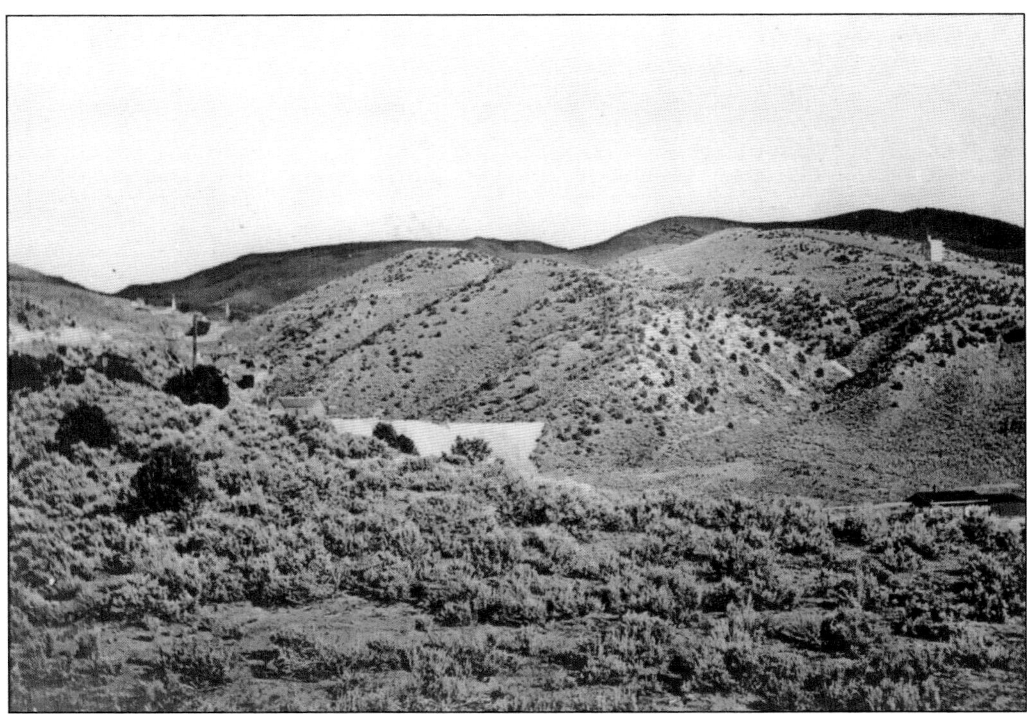

Here is Pony Canyon in the 1900s. Stokes Castle can be seen in the upper right. Directly below the castle is Clifton, the southern terminus of the Central Nevada Railroad. The light-colored berm in the center is mine waste from the Clifton Mill; the mine buildings are just above and to the left of the waste. Above the Clifton Mine, and up the canyon, is the town of Austin. The spires of the Catholic and the Methodist churches are visible. (Courtesy of NVHS.)

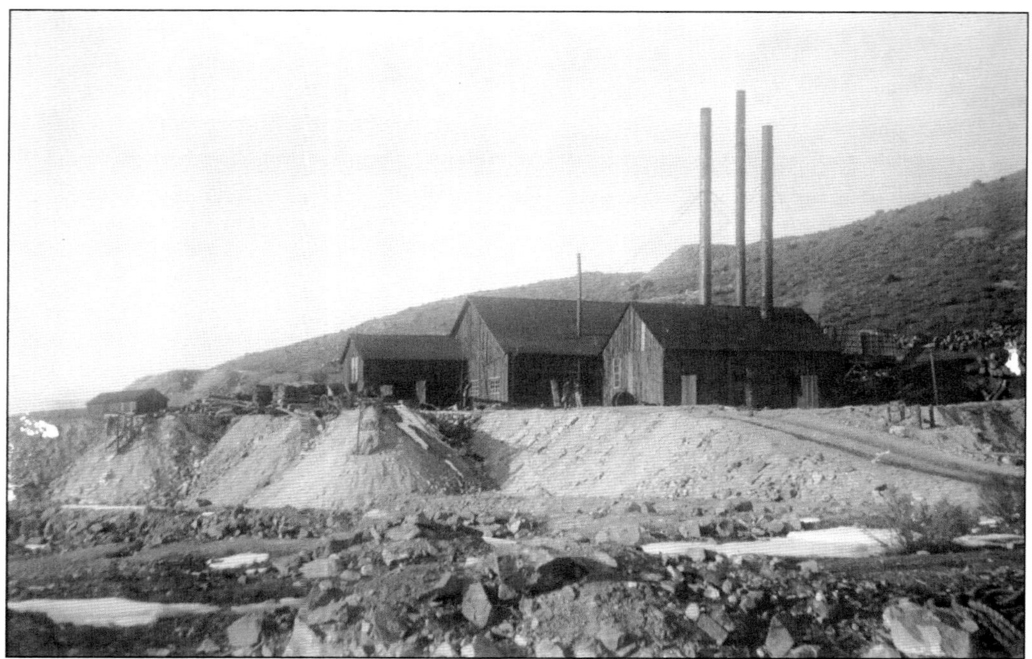

The Paxton Mine was an early producer. At 1,800 feet, it had the longest single incline of all the mines. Most of Austin's early silver production came from a one-acre square, which was located slightly above upper Austin on Lander Hill. Early mine records are incomplete, and Paxton's production is unknown. (Courtesy of NVHS.)

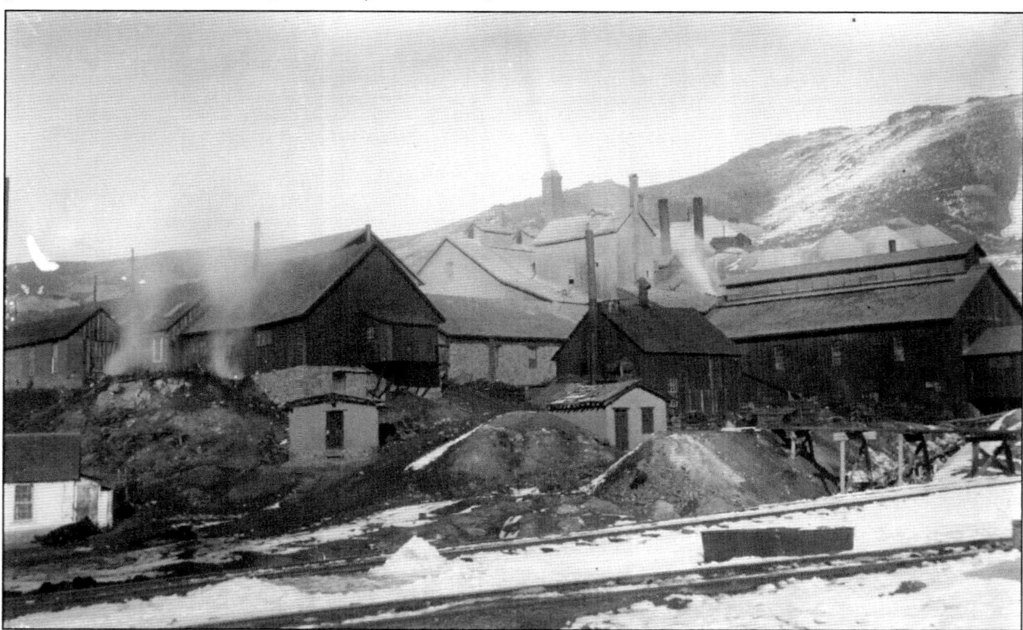

The Manhattan Silver Mining Company bought out the Oregon Mine and Mill (see page 2) in 1865 and had consolidated the mining efforts of upper Austin by 1870. This photograph of the Manhattan Mill and Concentrator is from around 1880. In the foreground are the tracks of the Austin City Railway, laid in August 1880 and pulled June 1893. From 1865 to 1887, the Manhattan Company's mines produced over 20 million ounces of silver. (Courtesy of NVHS.)

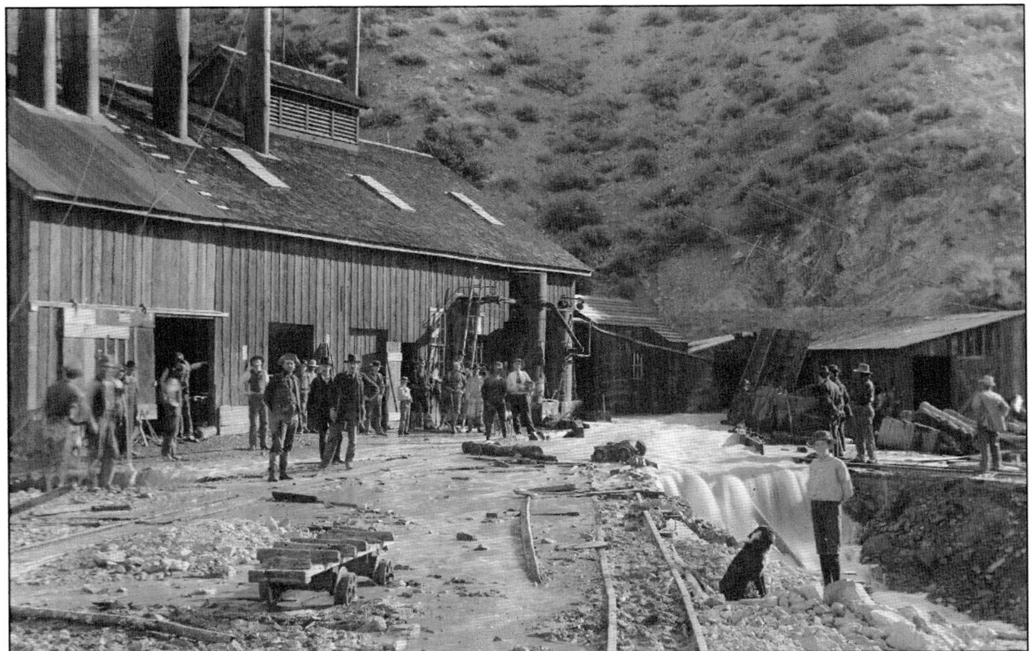

In 1891, the Austin Mining Company acquired the workings of the Manhattan Syndicate and further consolidated other mines in the area. An adit (tunnel) was punched from the canyon below Austin, 6,000 feet in length, underneath the town to the lower workings of Lander Hill. (Courtesy of SC.)

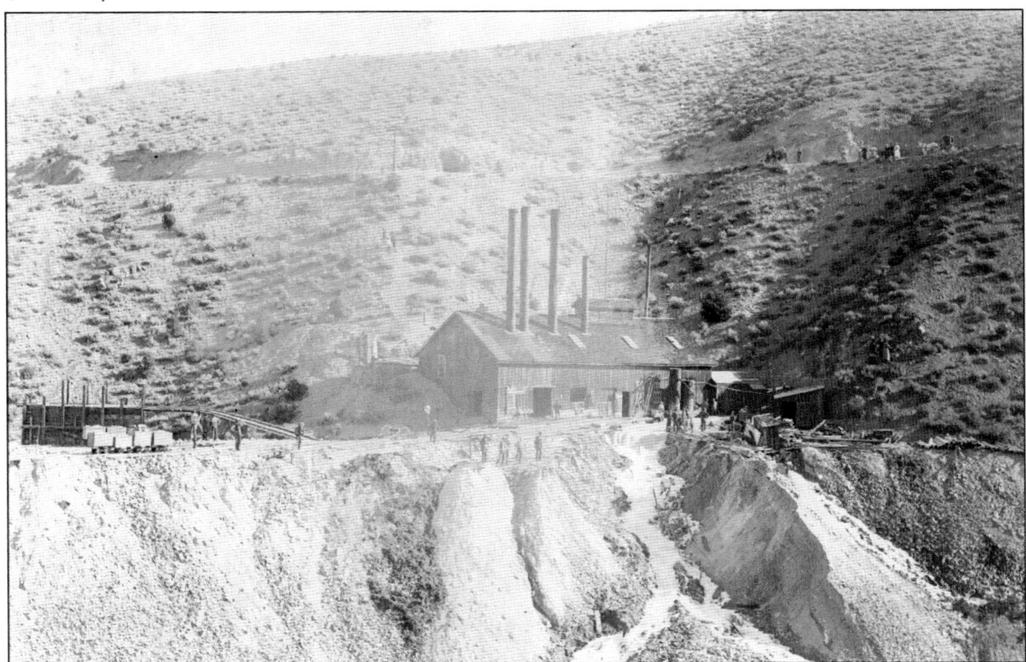

Breaking through to Lander Hill in 1896, the water drained the lower workings of the mines up the canyon. It was thought that with better drainage, improved ventilation, and with easier ore transportation the Clifton Portal would ensure the success of the Austin Mining Company. (Courtesy of NVHS.)

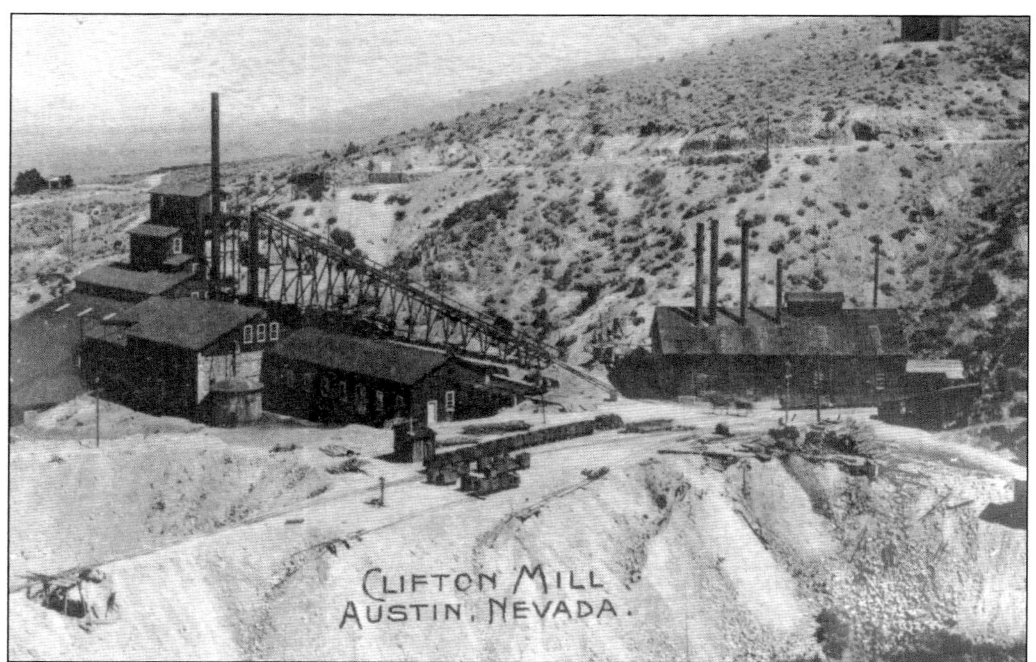

When the Clifton Mill was built, the price of silver collapsed, making it difficult to turn a profit. By 1902, the Austin Silver Mining Company had suspended operations. Mining continued, albeit, on a reduced scale under a system of lessors. The entrance to the Clifton Portal is to the right. (Courtesy of NVHS.)

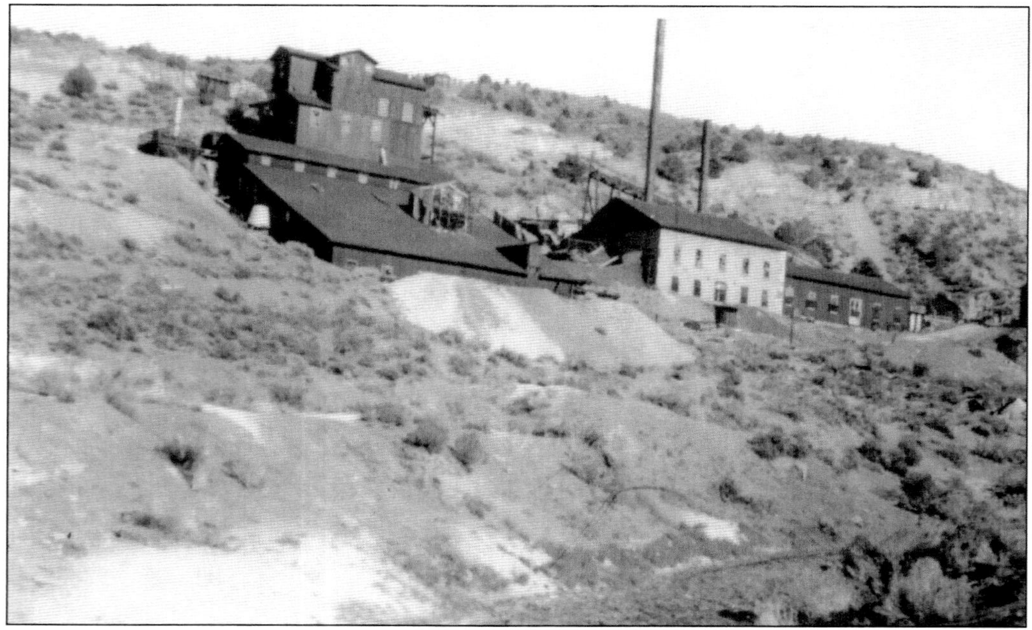

A new syndicate was formed in 1908, called the Austin-Hanopah Mining Company. After many renaming and reorganizations, the Clifton works fell silent. By 1920, only local miners and lessors picked over the area. A brief interest in the 1930s resulted, yet again, in failure. Today, the mill works still stand silently, and a trickle of water from the Clifton Portal is used to water a vegetable garden. (Courtesy of JBC.)

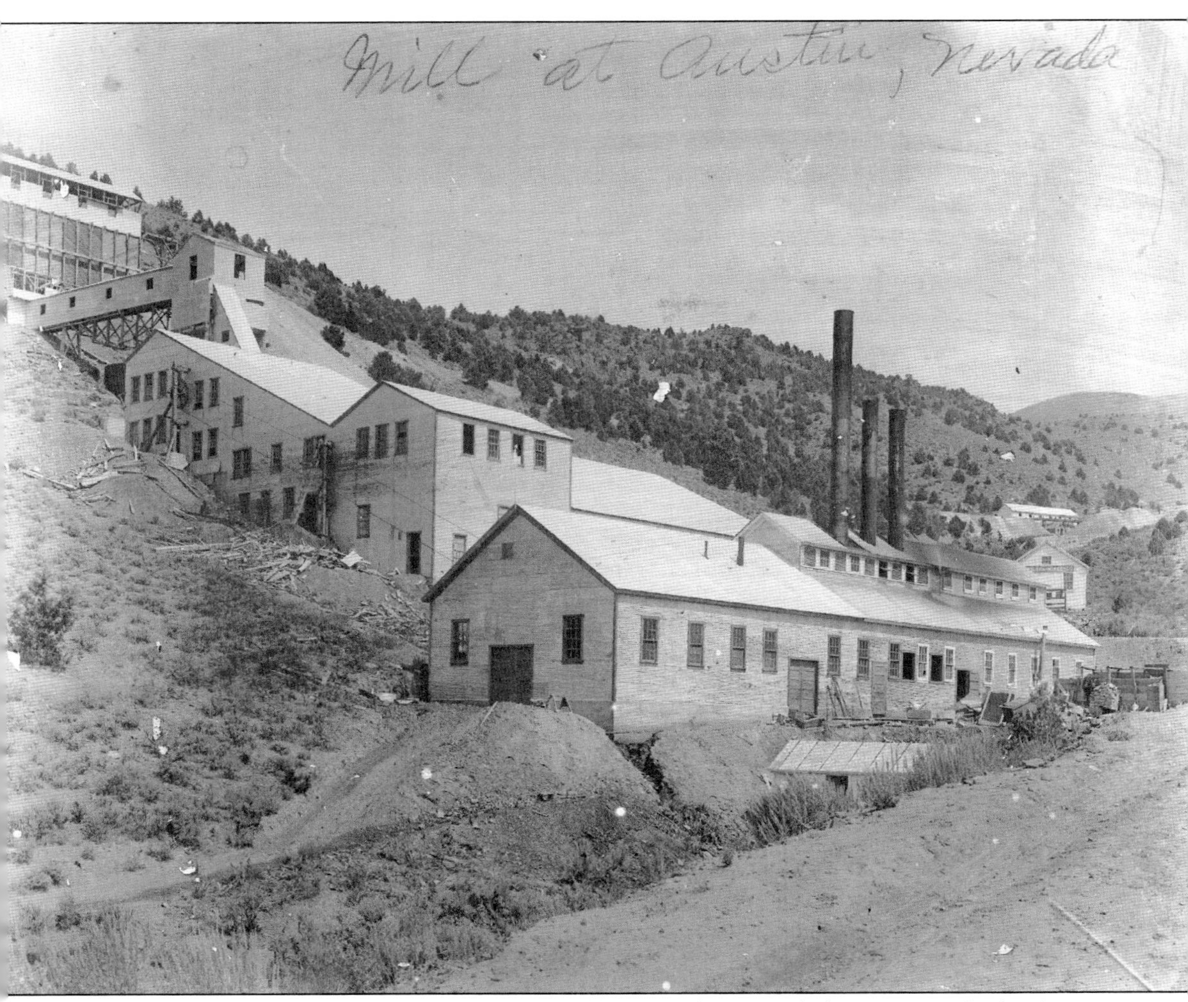

This photograph shows the Clifton Mine and Mill in new finery, including new methods of ore refinement, new ledges of silver, and new dreams of riches. But alas, a mine can also be just a hole in the ground to pour money into. (Courtesy of SC.)

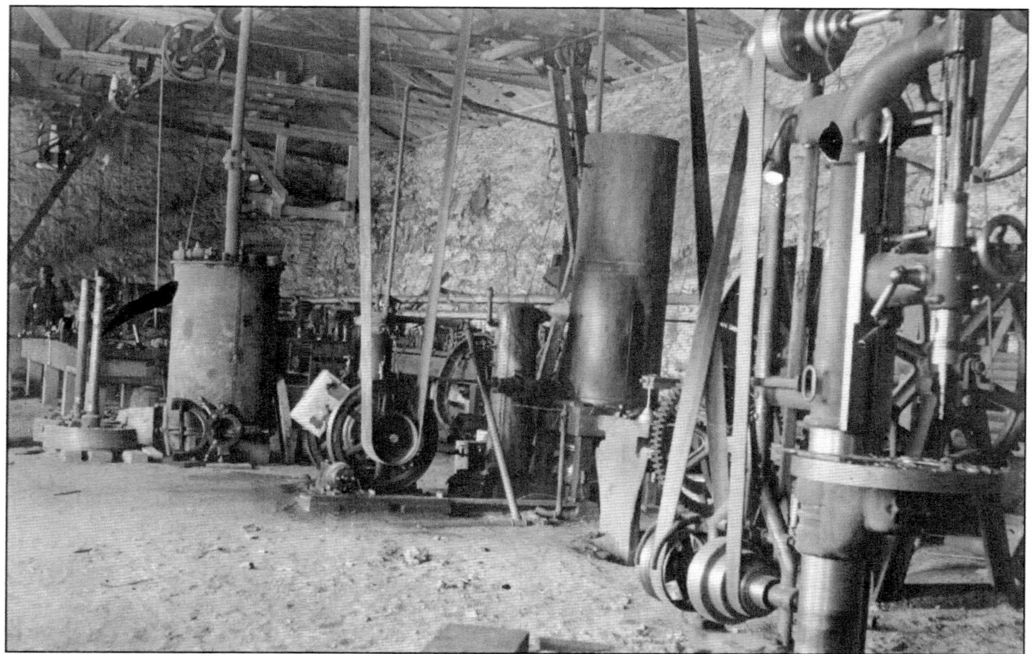

This scene has been identified as inside the Clifton Mill machine shop. A drill press or milling machine is to the right, and other machine shop tools can be seen, along with a workbench in the background. All power ran from belts connected to a common drive shaft in the overhead. (Courtesy of NVHS.)

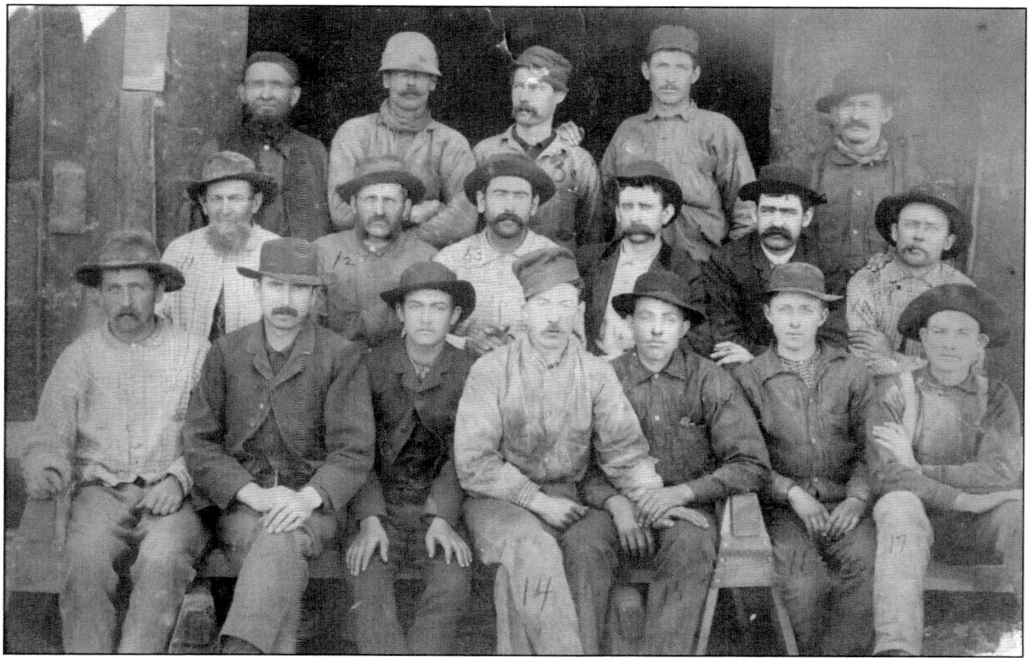

These workers pictured in the 1890s at the Clifton Mine and Mill are, from left to right, (first row) three unidentified, Fred Birchfield, unidentified, Willie Frost, and James Nagle; (second row) Billy Raymer, Ike Johnson, Frank Van Palters, unidentified, Jake Frost, and Julius Eidner; (third row) two unidentified, Sam McIntire, unidentified, and "Cox." (Courtesy of SC.)

Anson Stokes built this castle just outside the limits of Austin in 1897. Stokes was the owner of the Austin Silver Mining Company and the Nevada Central Railroad. The castle was used as a home for two summers, when Stokes and his family examined his Nevada interests. The castle still stands today silently over looking the Reese River Valley. (Courtesy of JBC.)

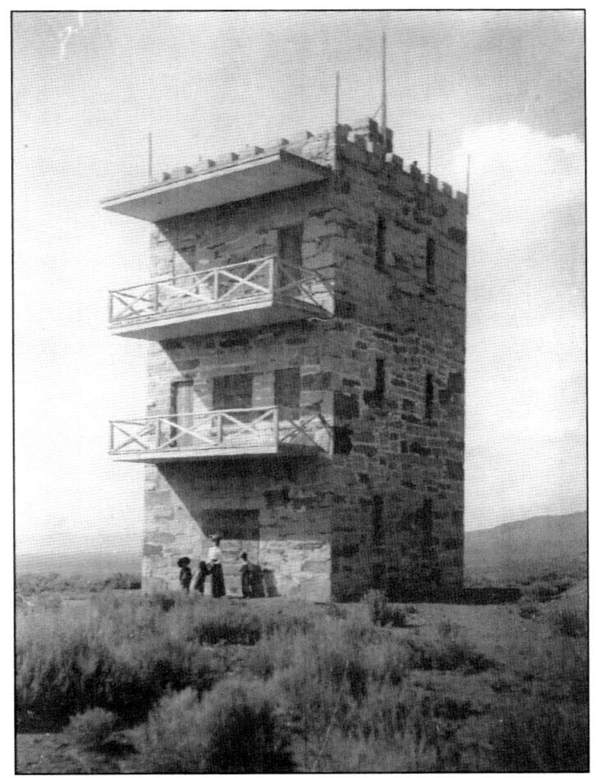

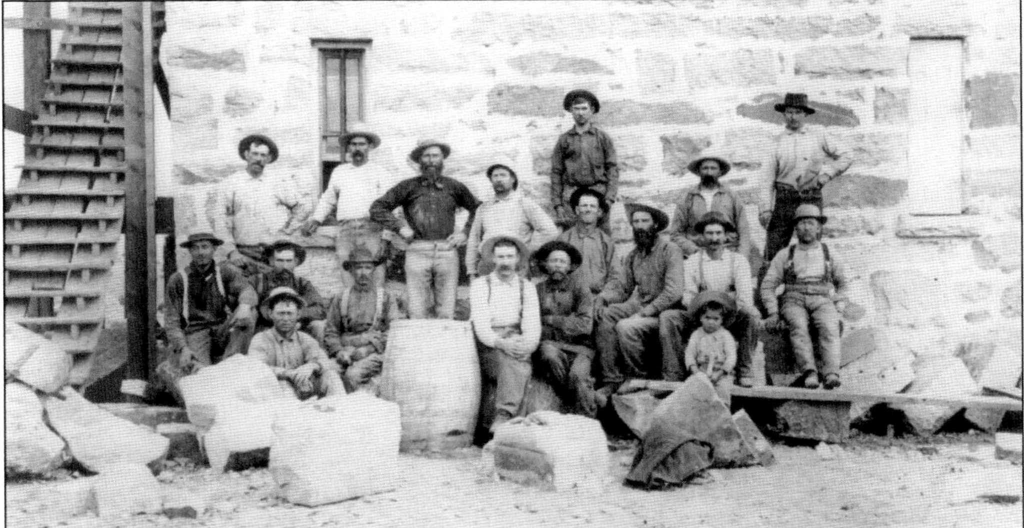

These stonemasons constructed the castle from locally hewn granite. Standing in back row are, from left to right, Louis Norris and Jack Timlin, and Frank Puffero is seated in between them. Those found in the full row sloping to the right, and immediately below the three men in the back, are, from left to right, Tony Gandolfo, Julius Barcelona, Joe Eason, John Latta, Mike Myles, John Wholey, William Trabert, and Jake Kunkle. Those sitting in the following row are, from left to right, Fred Luetjen, three unidentified men, and Alex Dron. Those seated in front are John Mullen and the youngest of them all, Frank Piffero Jr. Some of their descendants are Austin residents today. (Courtesy of JBC.)

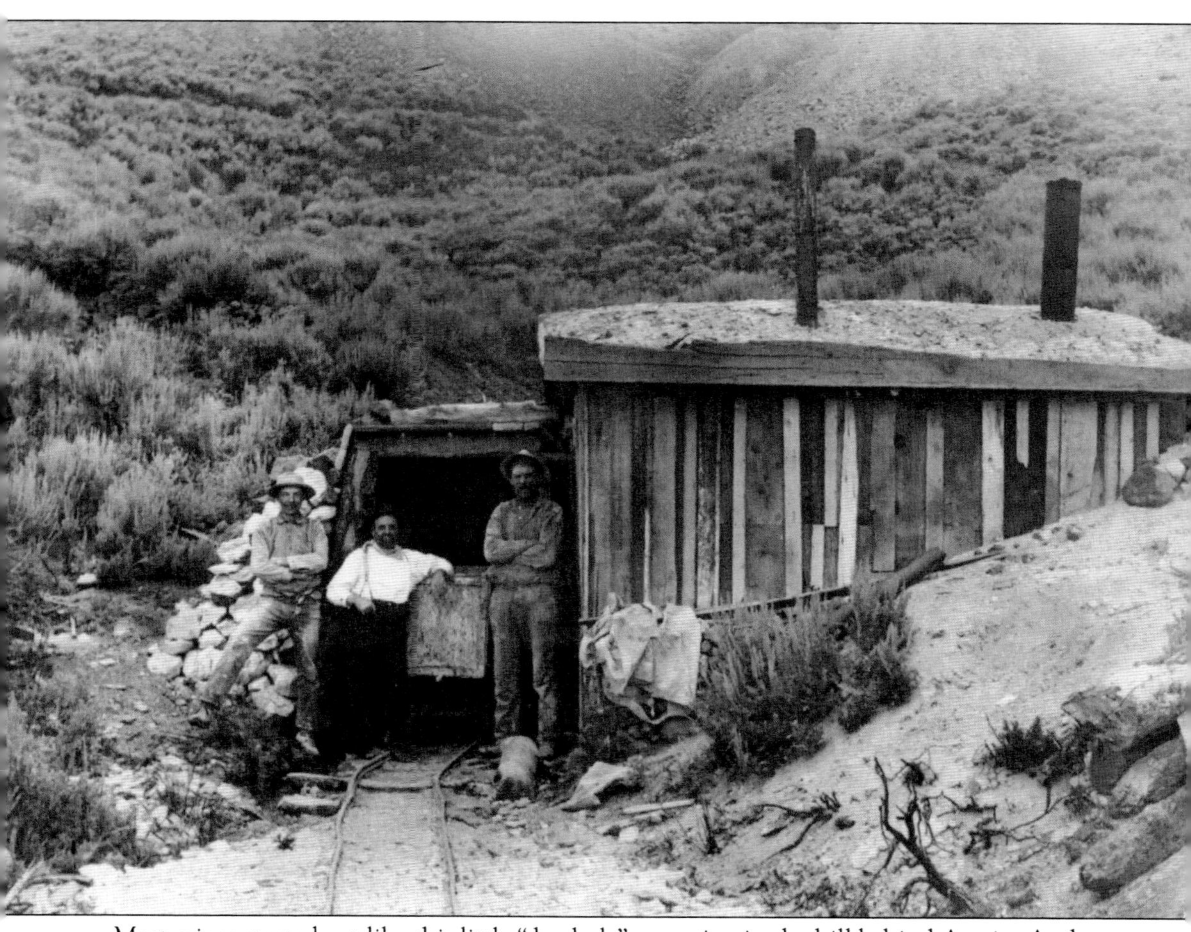

Most mines started out like this little "dog-hole" operation in the hill behind Austin. And most mines never expand beyond this size, with few miners cobbling out a living, searching for that vein of silver that will make them all rich. With a little luck and much hard work, rich ore in volume is occasionally found. Most miners, at this point, did not have the capital to develop their riches and ended up selling out to those who could. And so, the cycle starts again, strike, dog hole, hard work, and sell out. (Courtesy of AHS.)

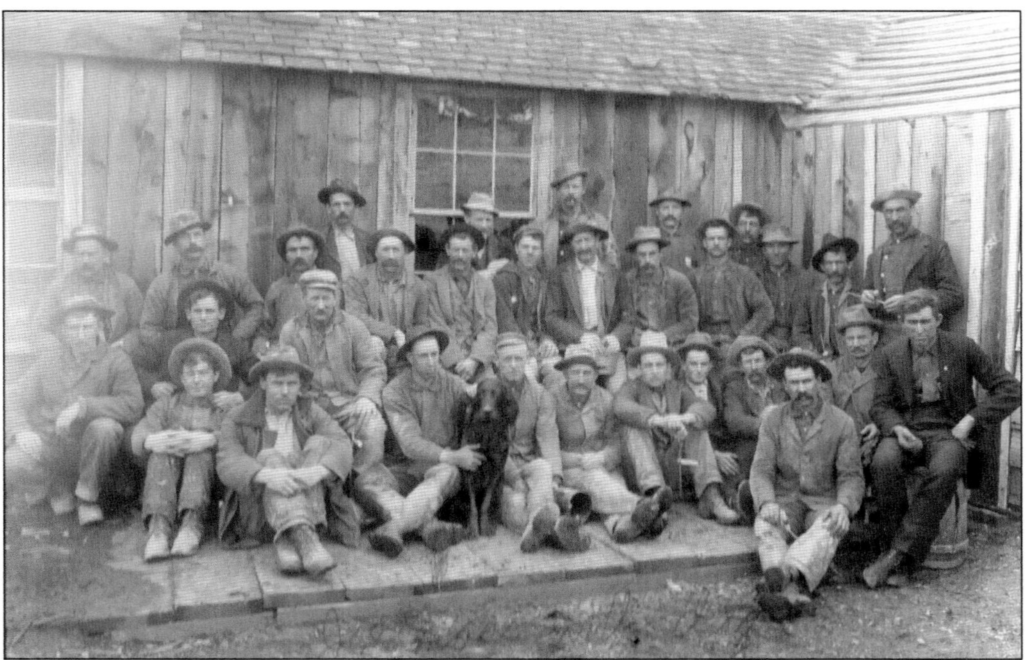

Miners and mill workers generally made good wages. Miners often earned $4 a day, and those with specialized skills could make up to $8 a day. Although mine workers were often "used up" by age 40, it was considered a good life. The man with the dog is identified as Austin resident Joe Moss. (Courtesy of SC.)

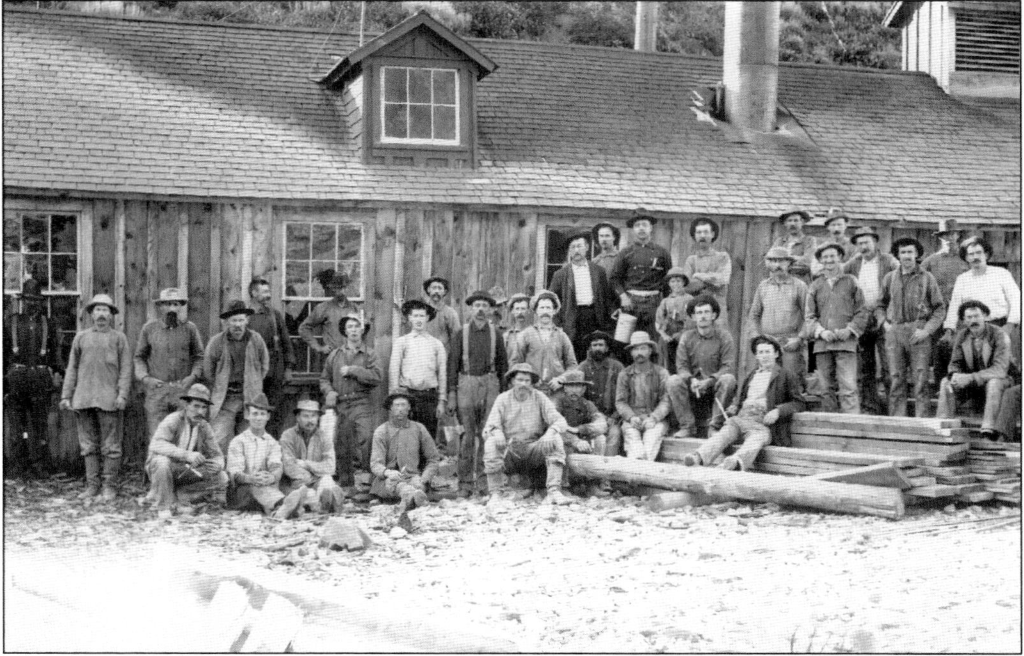

Many foreign-born people, such as Welsh, Italians, Bohunks, Slavs, worked the mines. But the best miners were from Cornwall, having learned their trade in the English tin mines. Their skills were respected wherever they worked throughout the Western mining camps. This group portrait was taken at the Clifton Mill. (Courtesy of SC.)

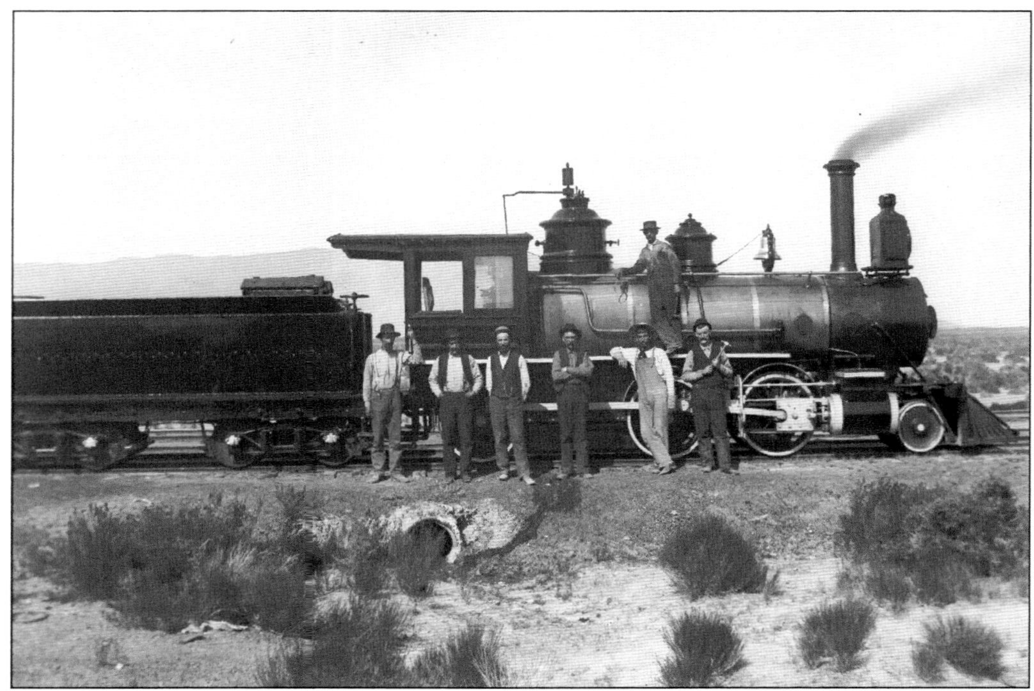

The Nevada Central Railroad was chartered in 1875. Austin's hope was with better transportation the mines could be worked more efficiently, and lower grads of ore could be utilized. The Nevada Central Engine No. 1 is pictured. (Courtesy of NVHS.)

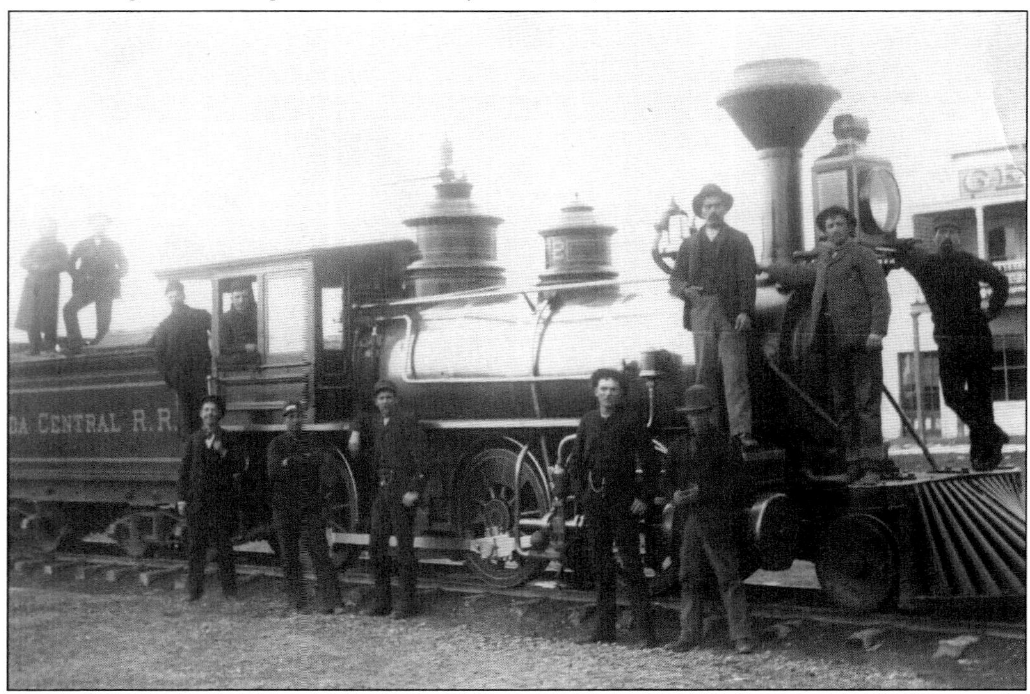

Performance bonds where issued to expire February 9, 1880, and the railroad was completed just 10 minutes before midnight. Austin was now linked to the Central Pacific, which was 90 miles to the north. The Nevada Central Engine No. 2 is pictured. (Courtesy of NVHS.)

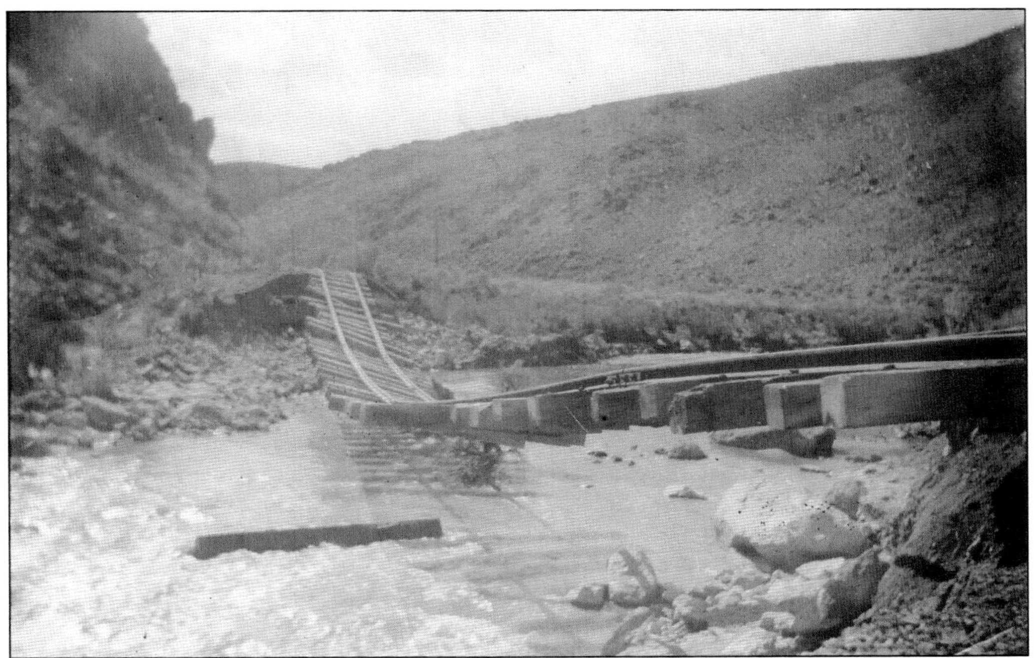

The Nevada Central ran from Clifton, which was located just below the canyon from Austin, 90 miles north to Argenta (Battle Mountain). Unfortunately, with declining silver prices and ore values, the line never really prospered. Hastily built and poorly maintained because of a lack of working capital, washouts like this could eat up a whole year's profits. (Courtesy of JBC.)

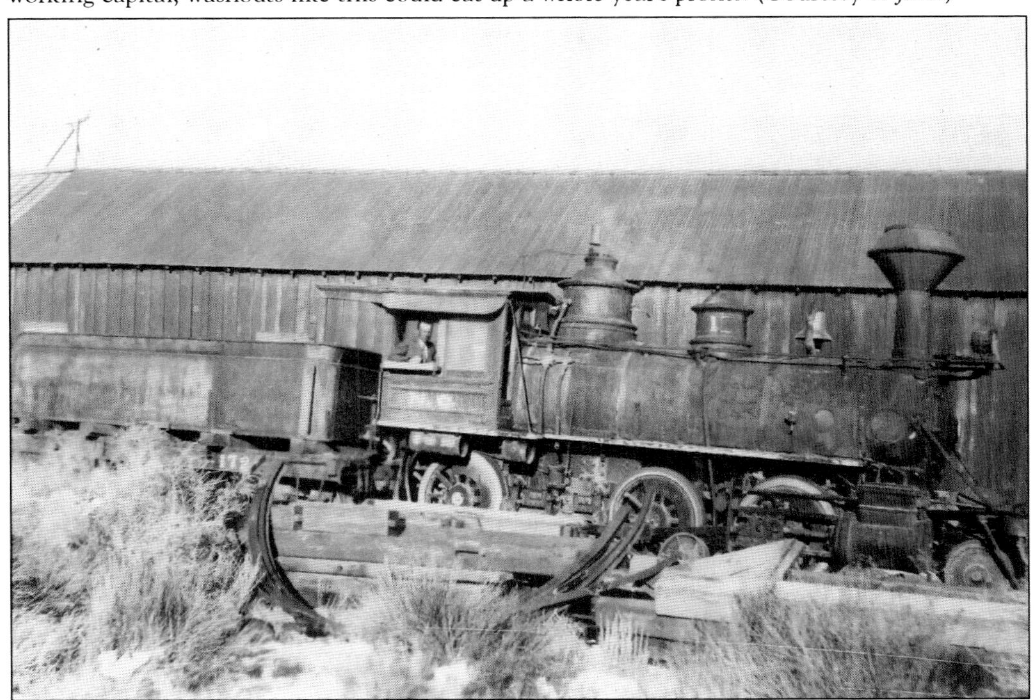

A few boom years interspersed with declining revenues sealed the Nevada Central's fate. By the 1930s, revenue had dropped below $30,000 a year, and on February 1, 1938, the line passed into history. Easton Scoggin is shown in the cab. (Courtesy of SC.)

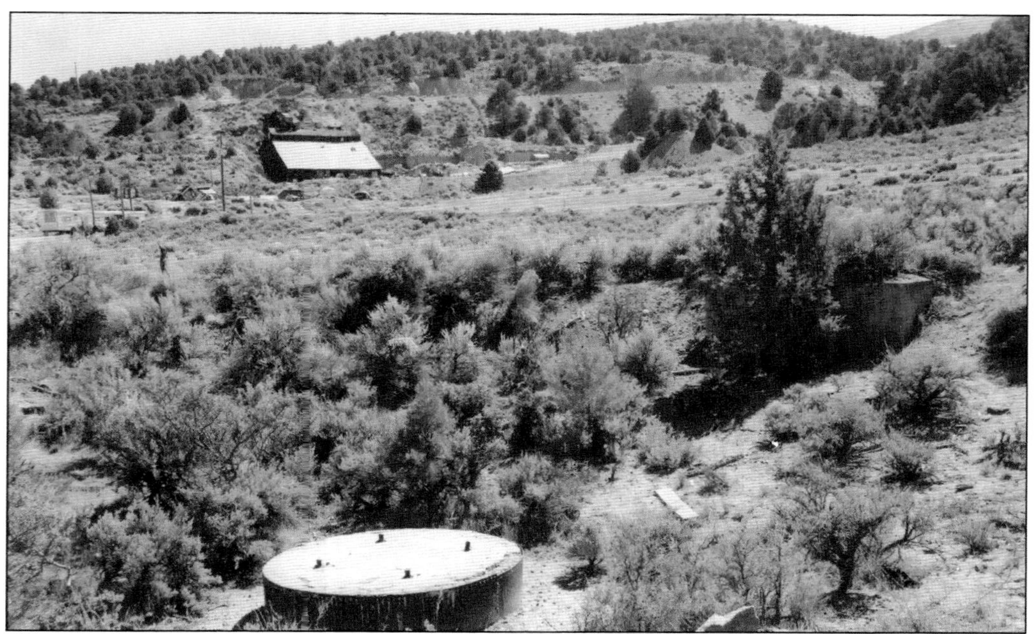

Not much can be found today of the old Nevada Central. Some of the grade is there. The turntable foundation and rock works marks the Clifton yard. And behind the turntable are the remains of the Clifton Mill. An outhouse was moved into Austin and is used as a shed today. Fortunately, the California Railroad Museum in Sacramento has preserved several pieces of rolling stock. (Courtesy of JBC.)

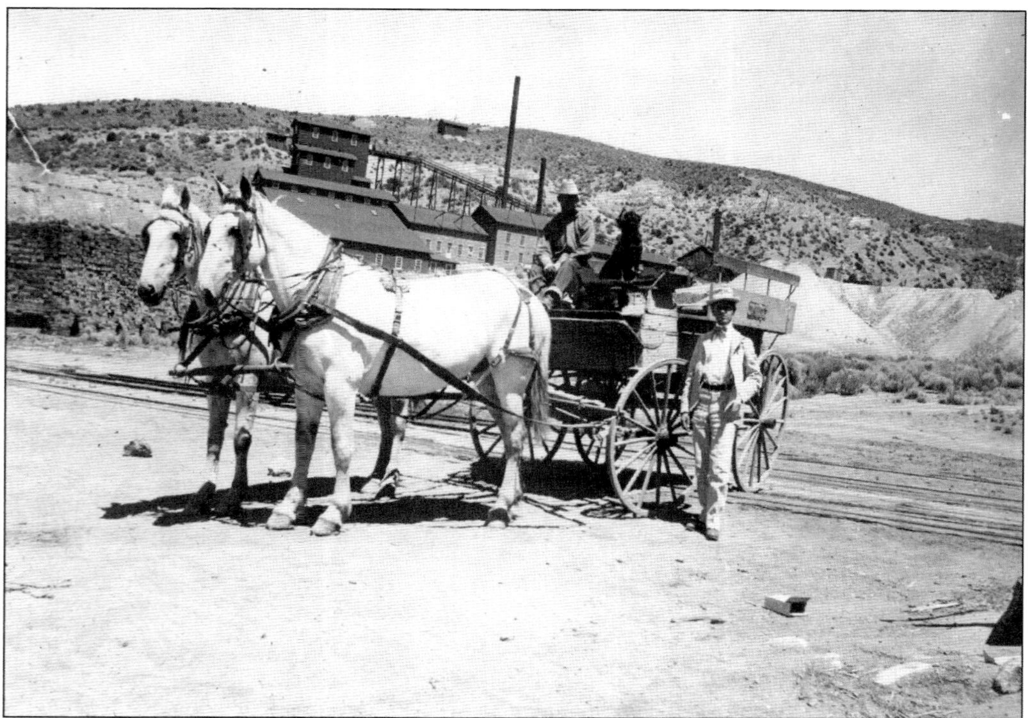

A wagon and driver await the Nevada Central. The Clifton Mill is in background, and the rails are from the Austin City Railway. The photograph is from the 1900s. (Courtesy of NVHS.)

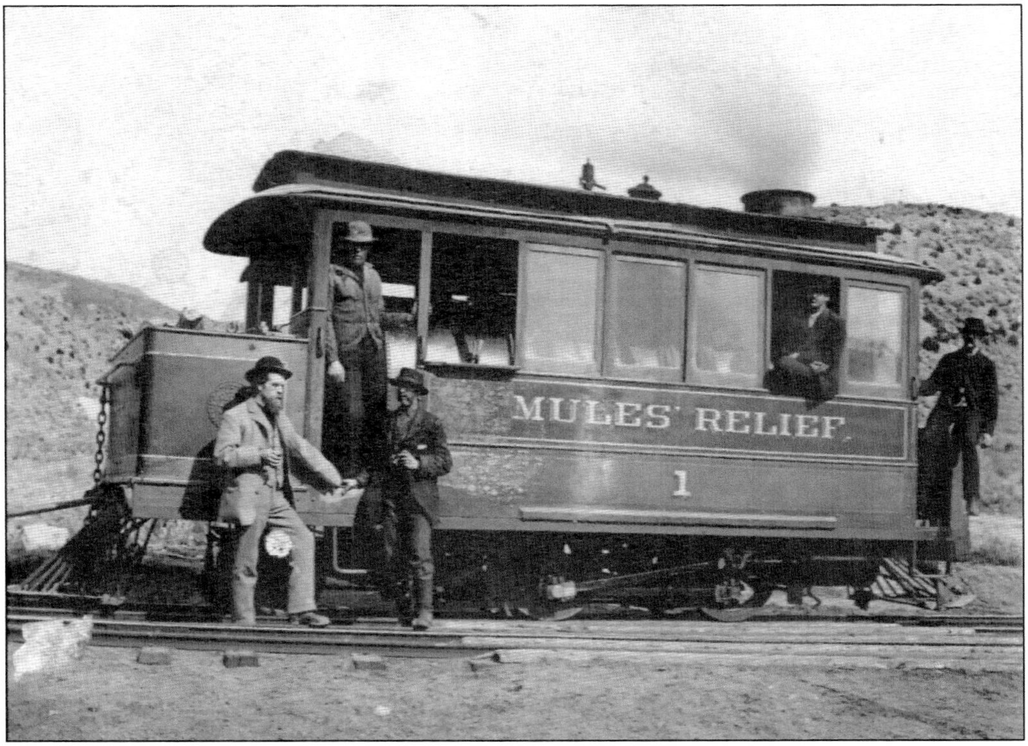

A few months after the Nevada Central was completed, a short line of 2.8 miles was laid up the canyon, linking the mines of upper Austin to Clifton. Officially named the Austin City Railway, it was locally know as the Mules Relief. (Courtesy of JBC.)

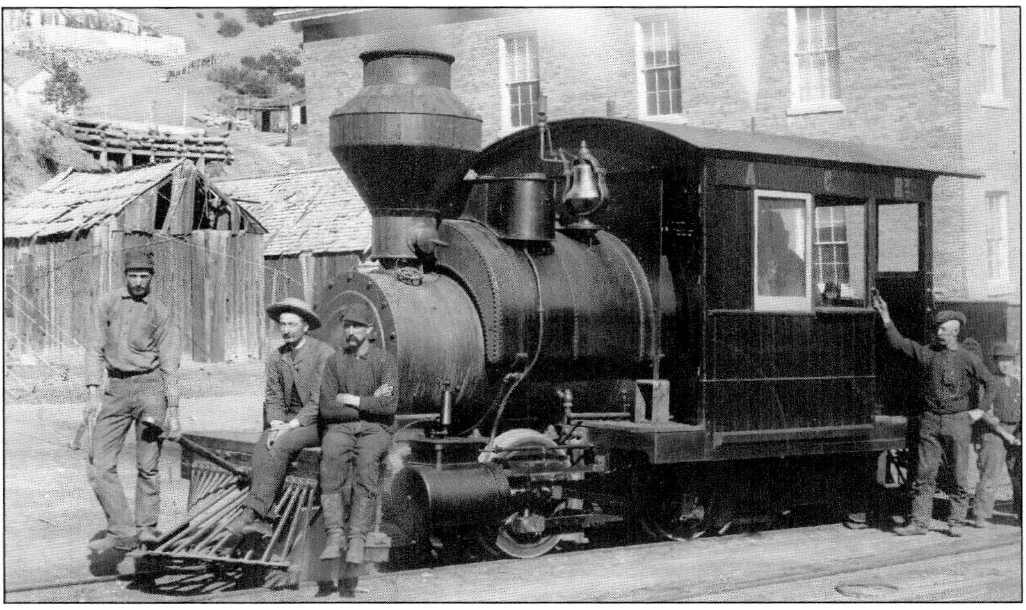

In 1882, while navigating a grade of seven percent, the Mules Relief jumped the tracks going downhill and was later rebuilt in this configuration. Pictured from left to right are Frank Dixon, George Alsopp, Dan Marrigan, Mr. Hale, and Gus Mcintire. The courthouse is behind the engine. (Courtesy of SC.)

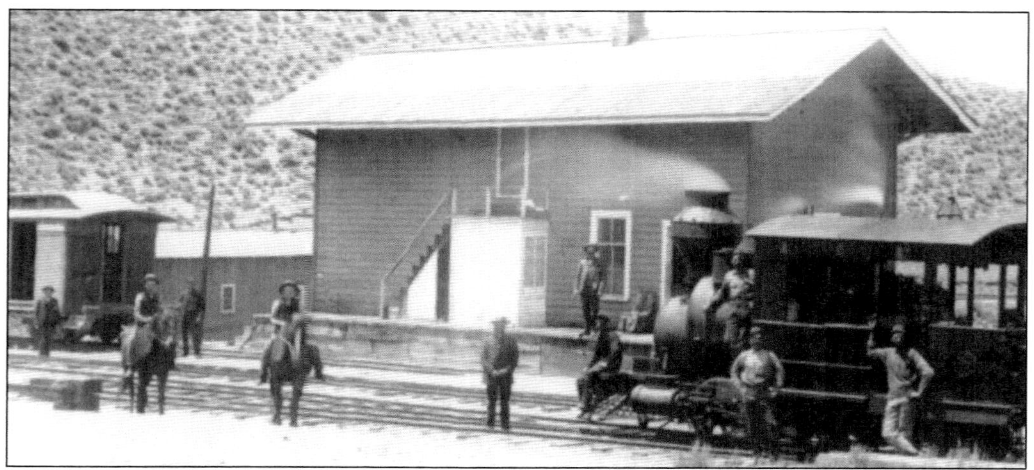

The Mules Relief was often pressed in to switching duties at the Clifton station. (Courtesy of JBC.)

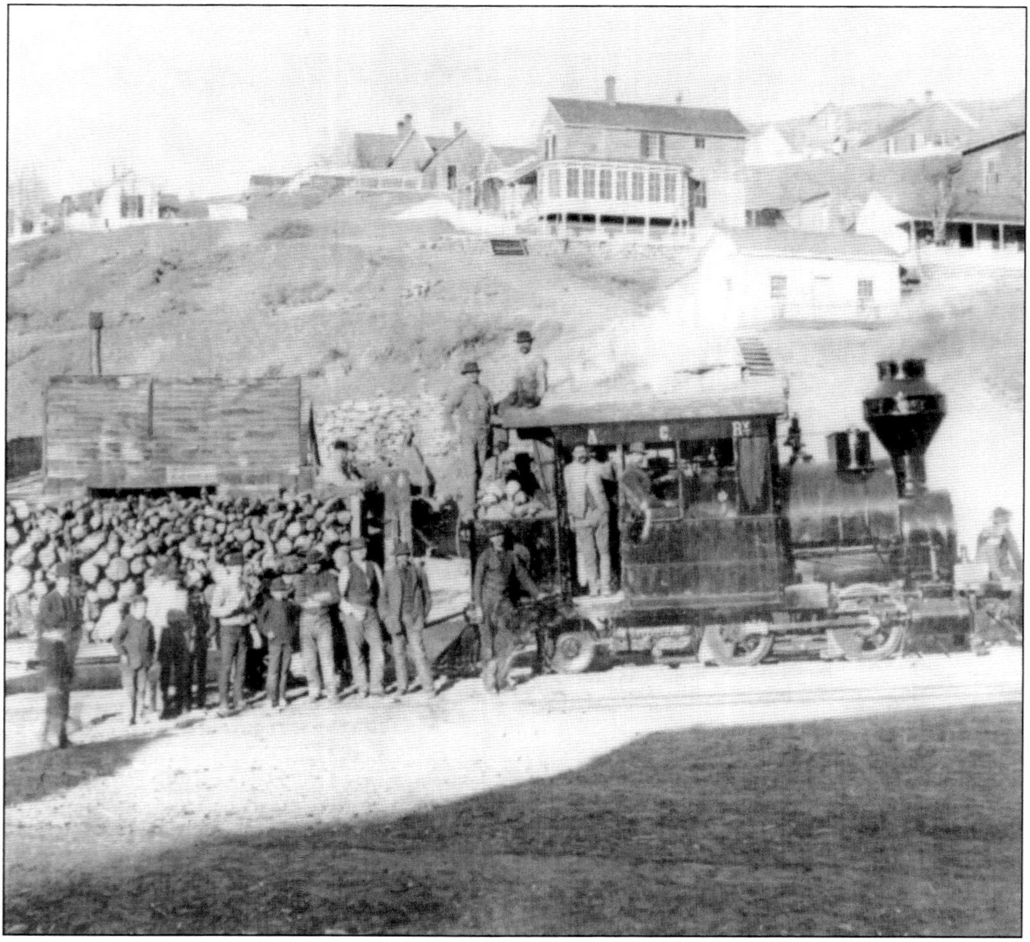

The Austin City Railway track ran right up Main Street. With a load of cordwood bound for the mines' boilers, the Mules Relief has stopped in the vicinity of the Austin Station. (Courtesy of JBC.)

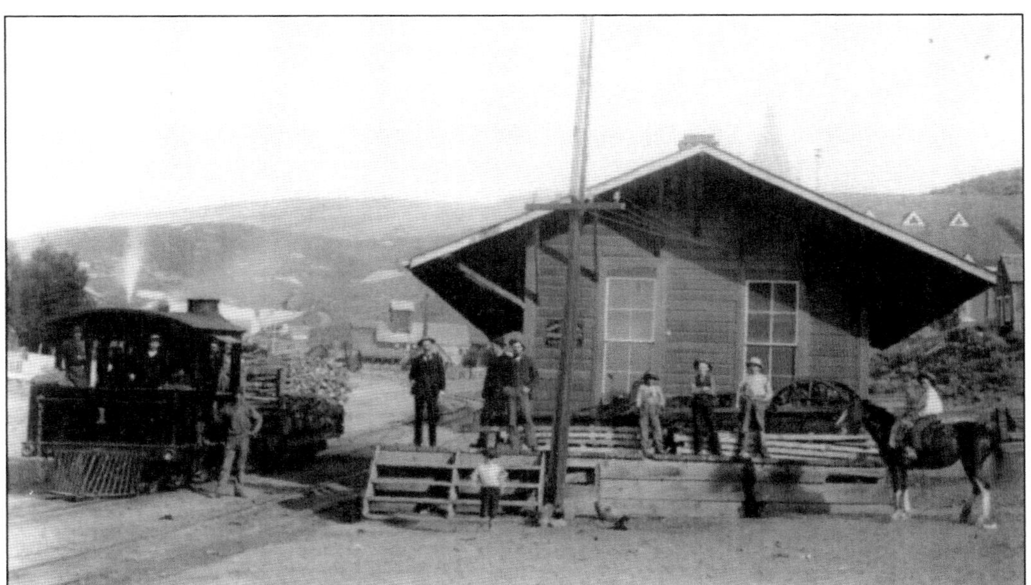

The Mules Relief is shown stopping at the Austin Station. In the background, part of the Manhattan Silver Mine complex can be seen, and behind the station is St. George Episcopal Church. Compare this photograph with the image on page 27. (Courtesy of JBC.)

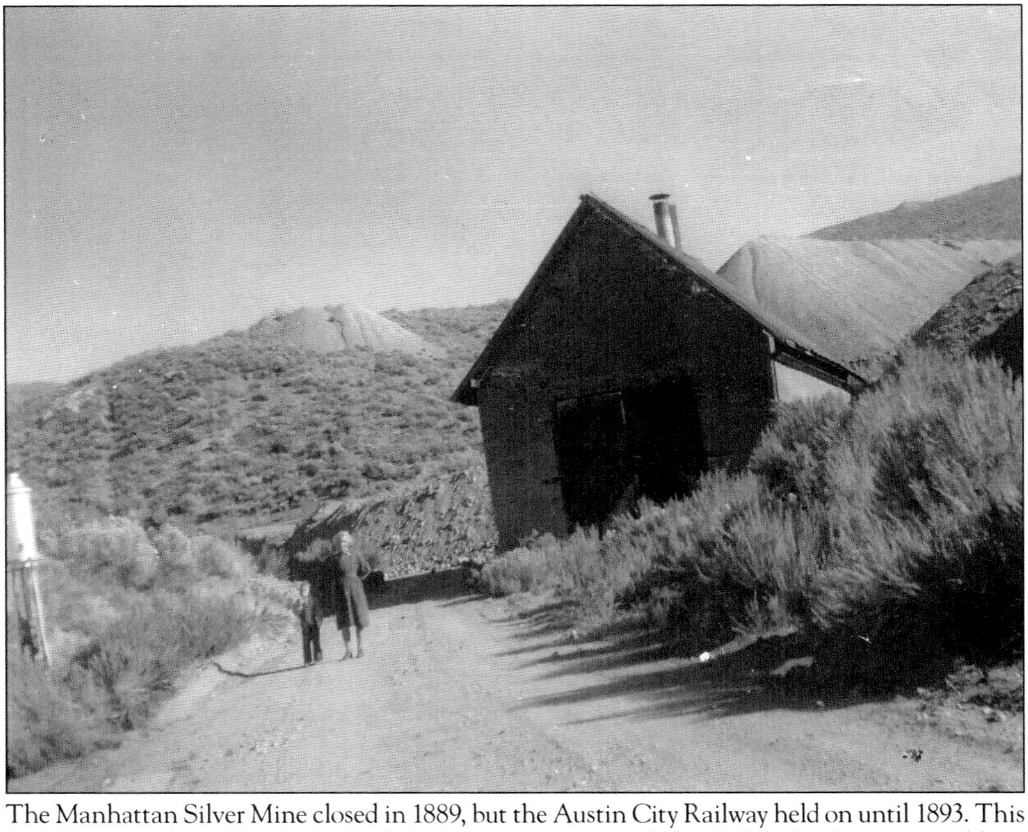

The Manhattan Silver Mine closed in 1889, but the Austin City Railway held on until 1893. This was the engine house for the Mules Relief in upper Austin. Made of adobe brick, it was unable to with stand the elements and came down in the early 1970s. (Courtesy of SC.)

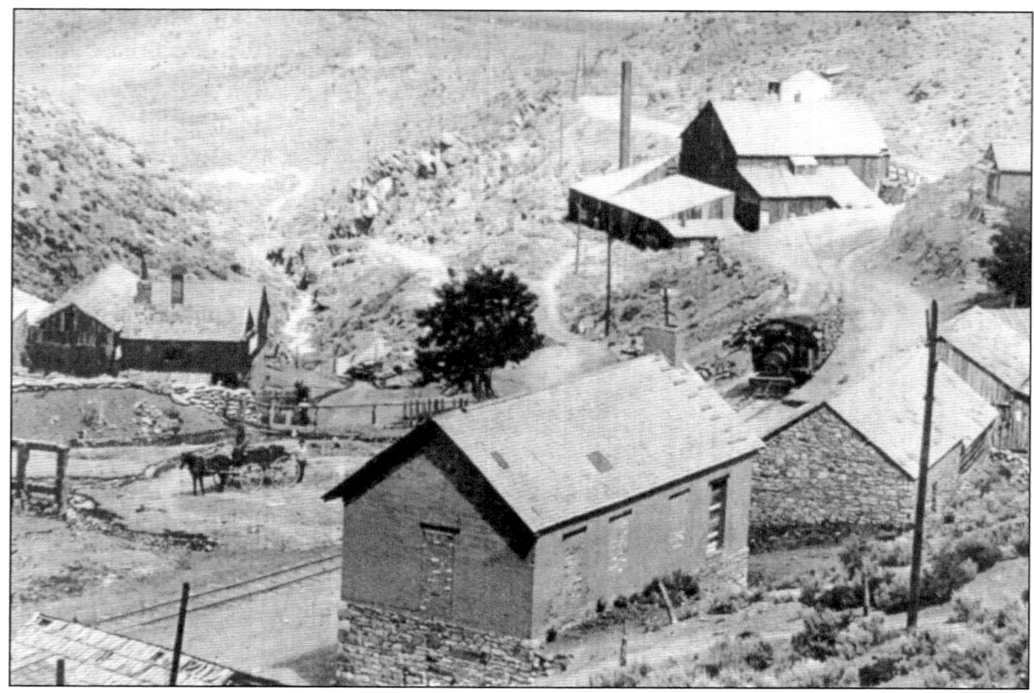

This 1880s image is of lower Austin, looking west. The Mules Relief has worked its way uphill with a load of firewood for the mills. The building to the left is a brewery; the foundations can be seen today. The small mill was know as the Peoples Mill and no longer exists. (Courtesy of AHS.)

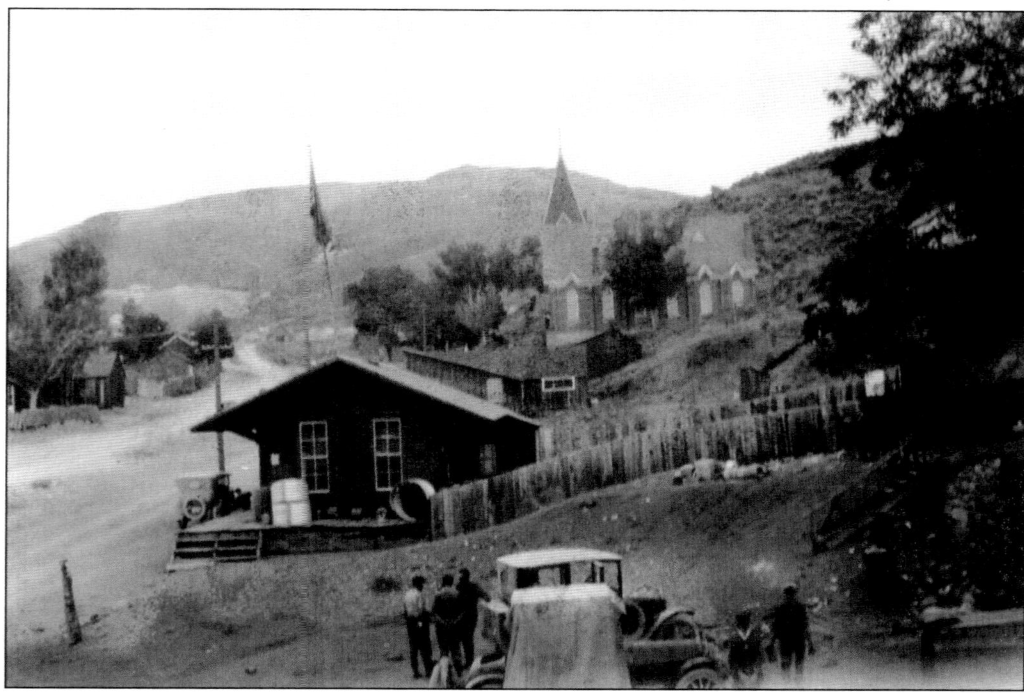

The Mules Relief is gone, and the track has been pulled up, but the Austin City Railway Austin terminal on Main Street is still used as a freight way station. Up the hill is St. George Episcopal Church. (Courtesy of AHS.)

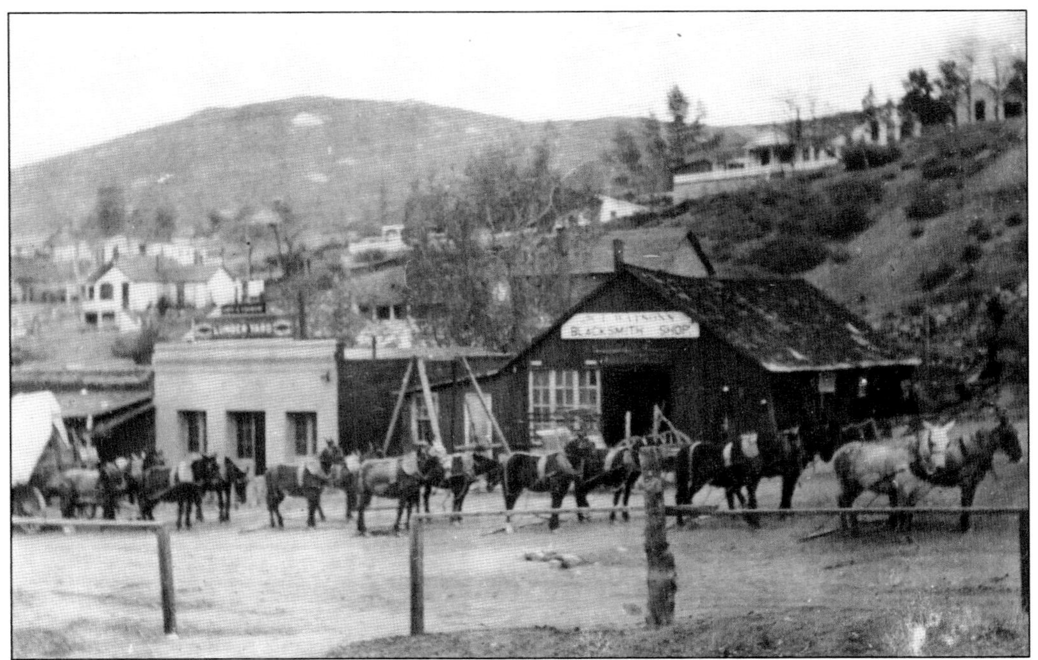

Austin was the commercial and freighting center for much of central Nevada until silver was found in Tonopah in 1901. Teamsters and freight wagons were a common sight along Main Street, hauling mining and milling equipment and even ore from the surrounding mines. (Courtesy of NVHS.)

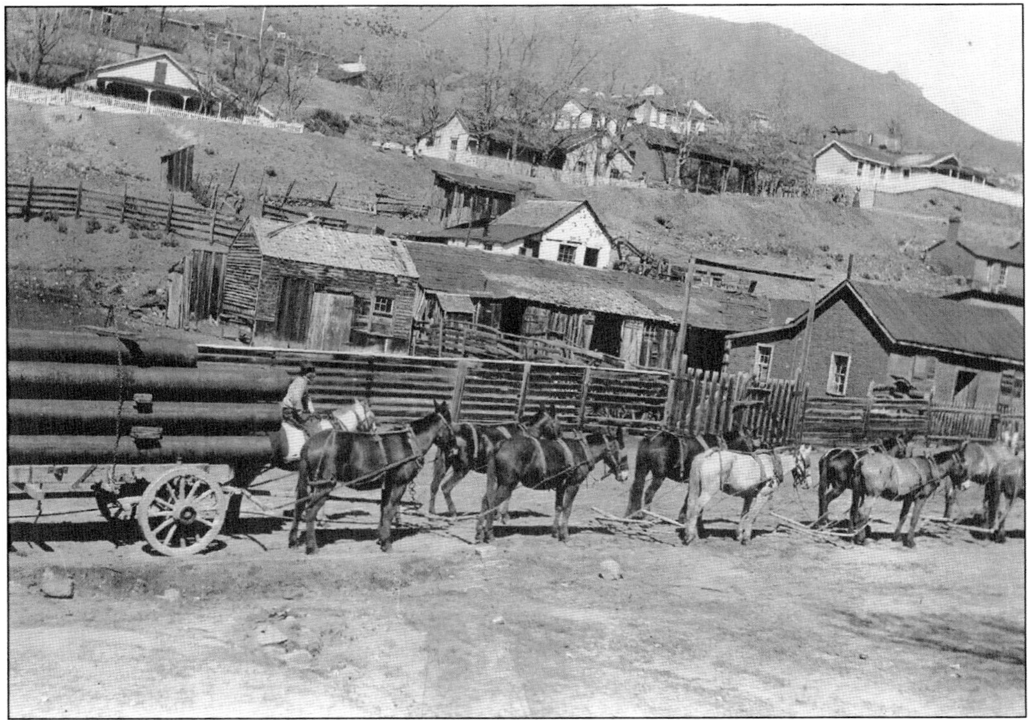

Although not all visible, this team of 11 horses is making its way up Main Street and over Austin Summit (about 7,500 feet). (Courtesy of JBC.)

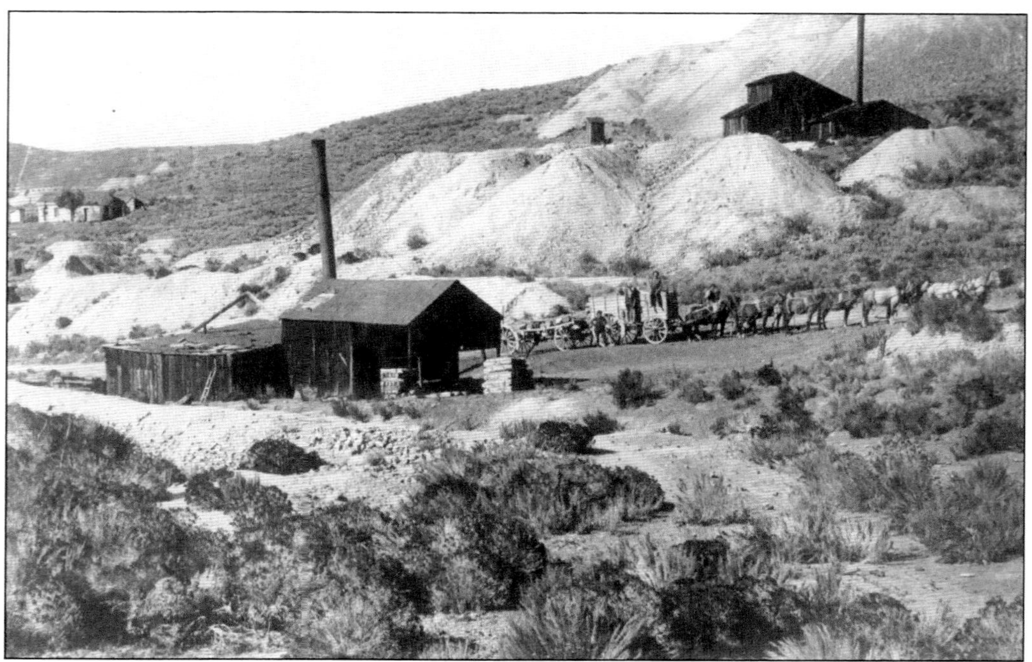

This team is making way in upper Austin, pulling a large freight or ore wagon that is capable of holding several tons. In the foreground is the old sawmill, used to cut Reese River lumber sawed from local pinion pine. At the top right is the shaft house of the Great Eastern Mine. (Courtesy of NVHS.)

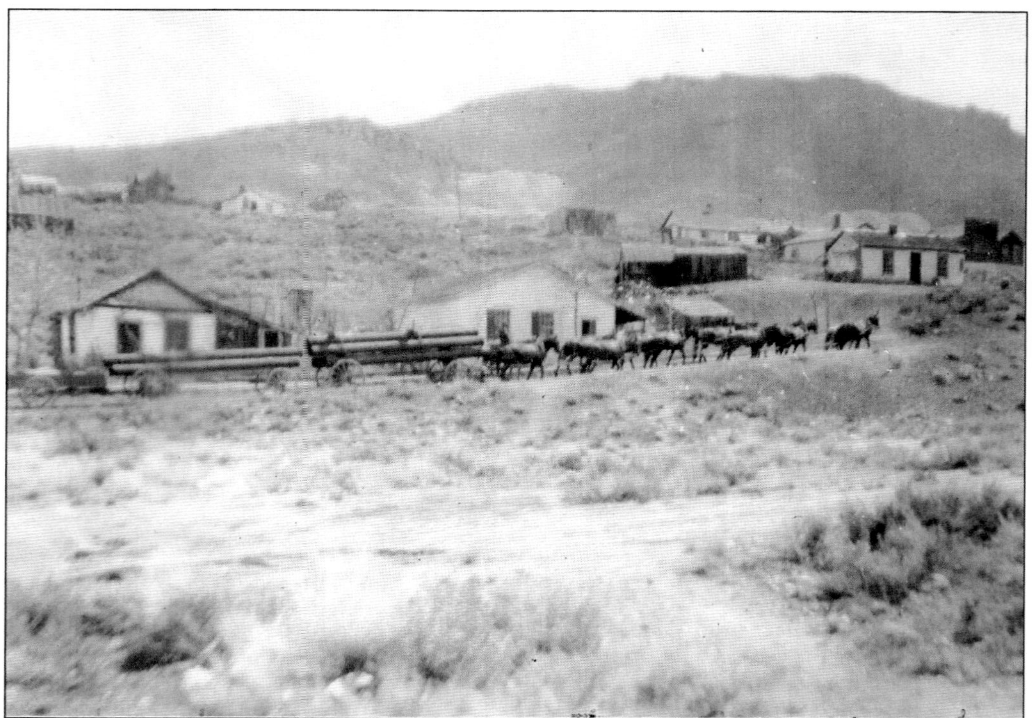

Shown in 1900, another load of pipes is heading up and over Austin Summit. Residential upper Austin is seen in the background. (Courtesy of SC.)

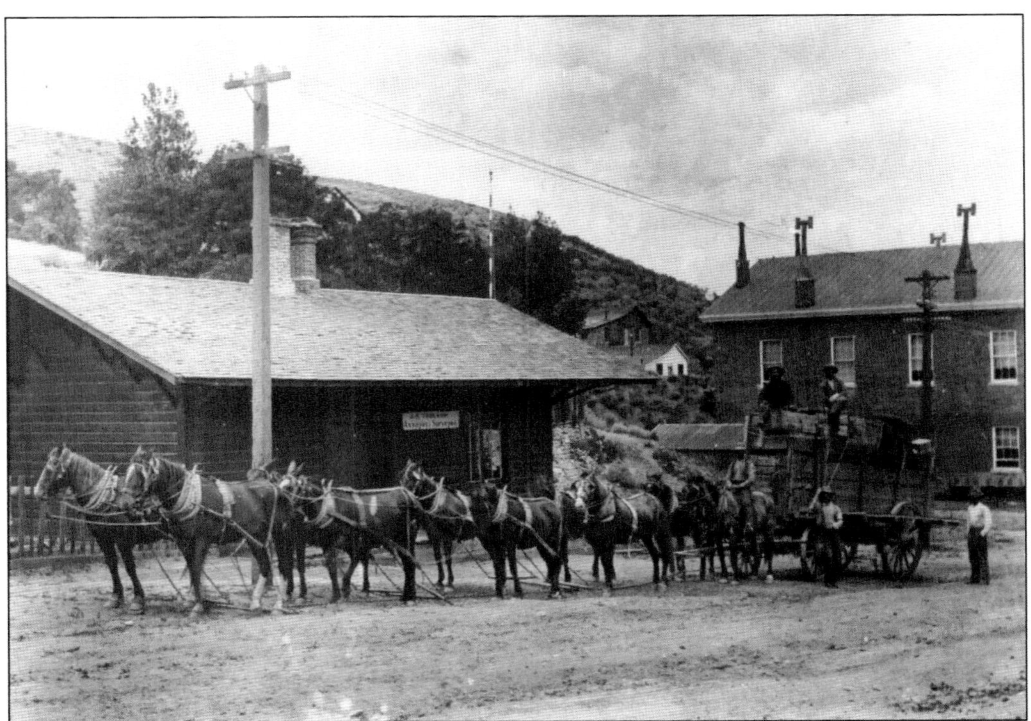

This freight wagon, shown around 1905, takes a pause in front of the old Austin City Railway Station. The Lander County Courthouse is to the right (see page 55). (Courtesy of NVHS.)

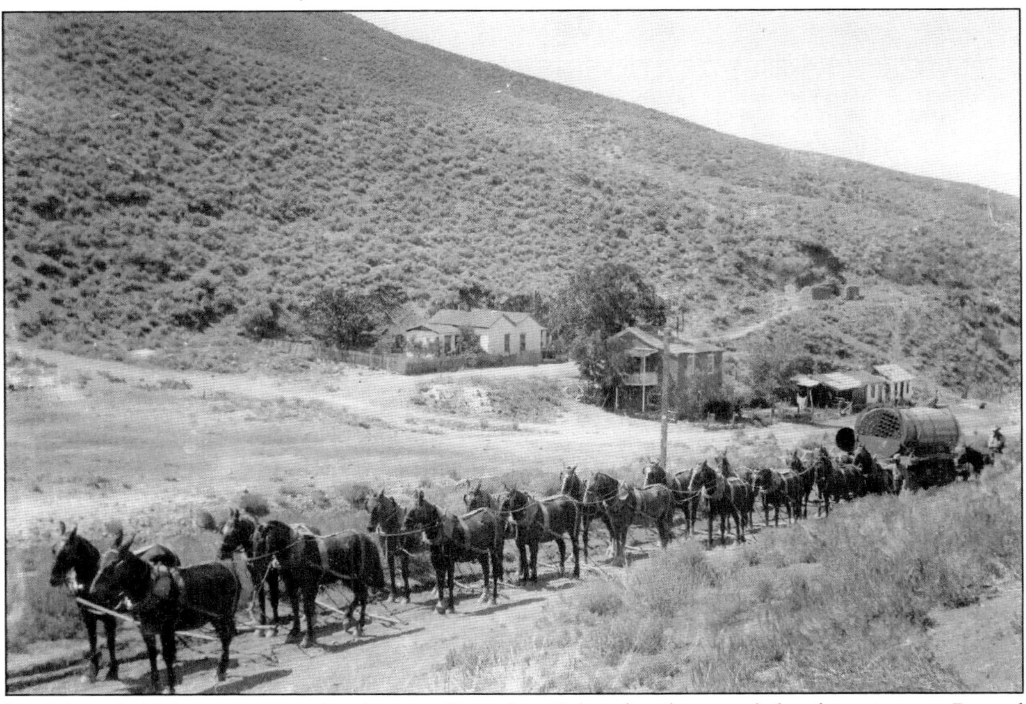

Joe Morris's 18-horse team is hauling an "anaeliner" (used to heat ore) for the mines at Round Mountain, located 80 miles to the south. The large house in the background is today the sight of Austin's Latter-day Saints church. (Courtesy of SC.)

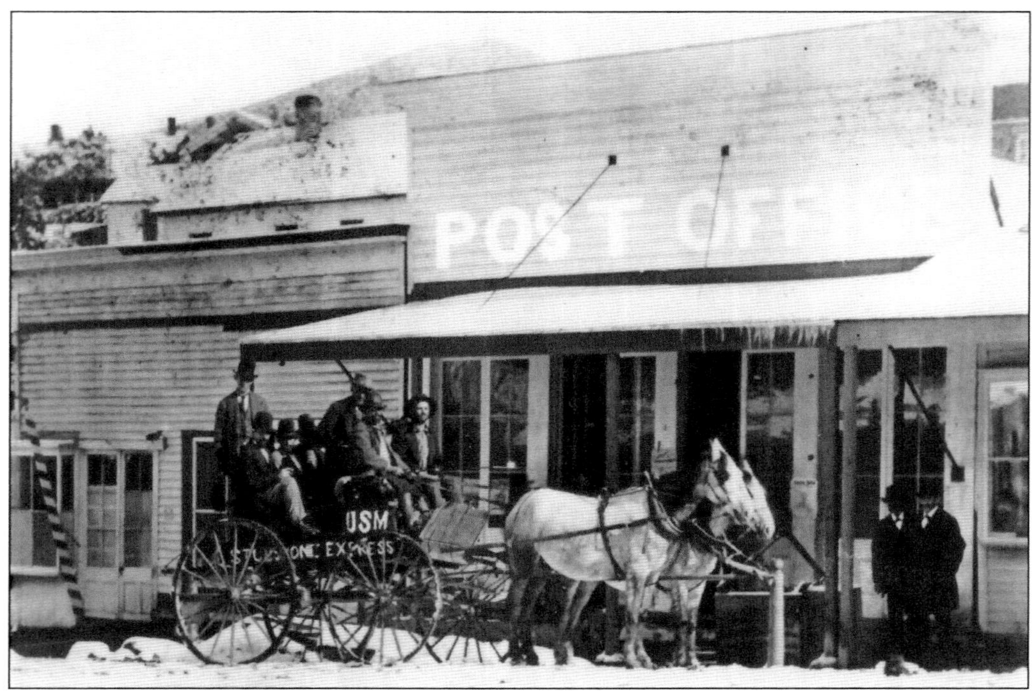

This image shows winter in Austin, and a mail stage is about to depart the post office on Main Street. Mail-delivery contracts helped to subsidize passenger and small freight services to many outlying camps. (Courtesy of AHS.)

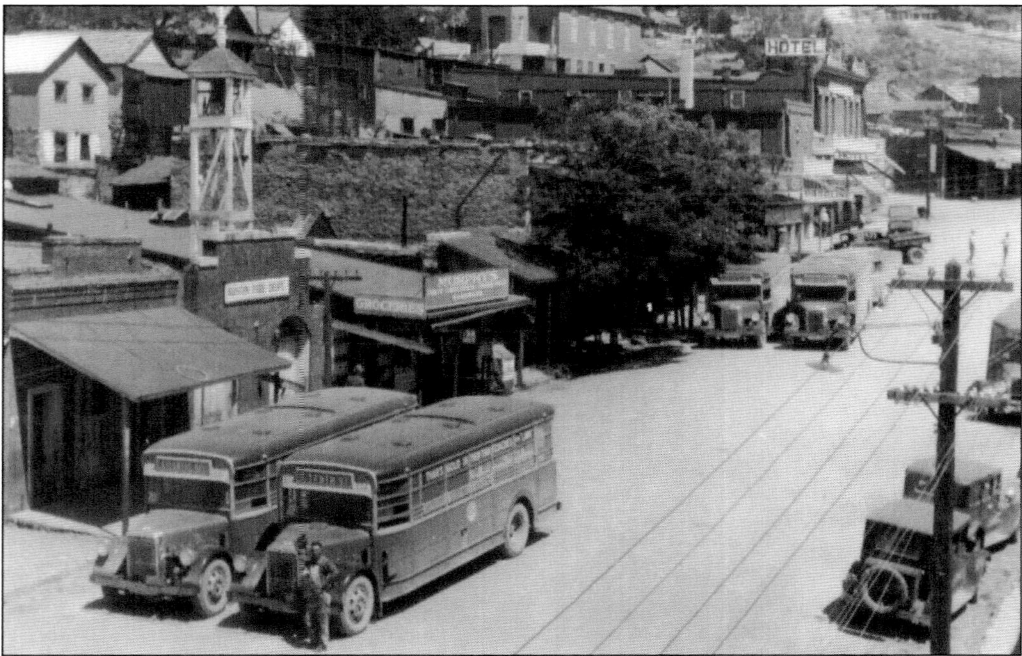

By the 1930s, transportation was pretty much the domain of the horseless carriage, now much refined. This busy Main Street scene shows five buses parked for a lunch brake. Compare this picture with the one on page 12, and note the bell tower for the fire department. The bell still stands and rings. (Courtesy of AHS.)

Three

SCHOOLS, CHURCHES, SALOONS AND MERCANTILE

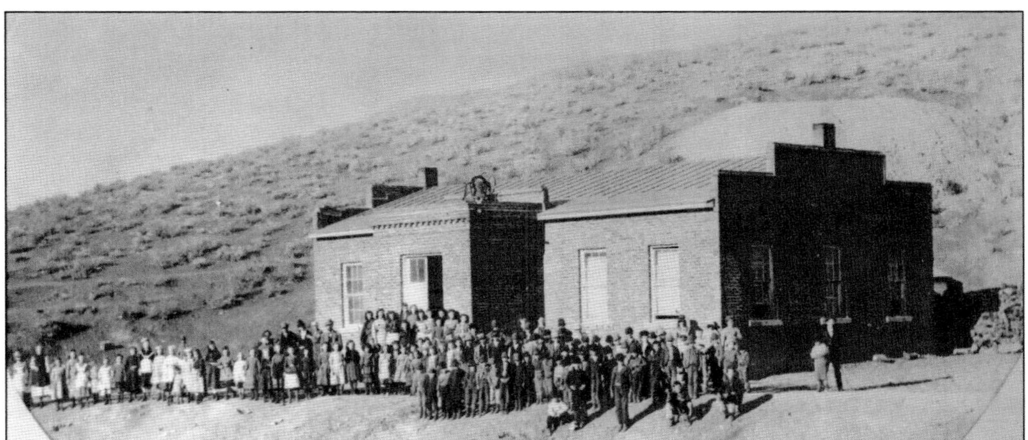

Austin's public school history began in 1863 when the first class was held in a tent. After several other locations, this building was erected in the 1880s. Expanding a few years later, the grammar school was to the right. Many families from the outlying mines and ranches would board their children in town for part of the year in order to have access to higher education. Depending on the booms and busts of the mines, enrollment varied greatly. This building was located several blocks north of Main Street and no longer stands today. The site is now a private residence. In 1926, a new building was built 100 yards to the west and was last used as a grammar school in 2003. Today, Austin's education system carries on in a new complex, built in the 1980s, with all grades under the same roof. The high school graduating class of 2010 had a total of four students. (Courtesy of SC.)

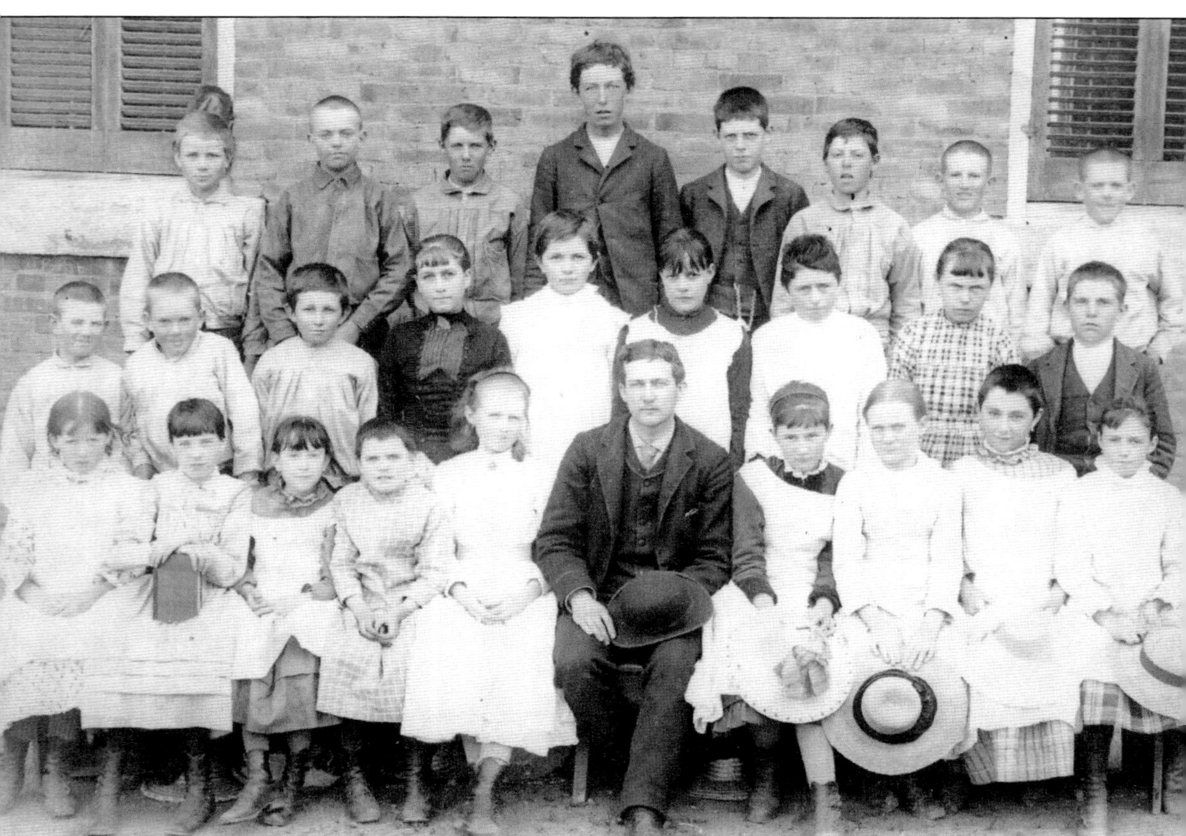

Pictured in the 1890s, students are, from left to right, (third row) Leon Wallace, Jack King, Ed Tremuaw, Tony Mastretti, Albert Shivley, Nick Pearce, George Thorpe, and John Hennessey; (second row) Louis Norels, A. Henaussey, Leon Ott, Annie Baker, Grace McKerney, Lizzie Arndell, Hannah Variston, and George Polkinghorne; (first row) Emma Tremeuaw, Minmete Keough, Ethel Price, Katie Lynde, unidentified, Jim Fleming (teacher), Belle Thorpe, Lily Rodgers Stocks, Maggie O' Rourke, and Clara Gandolfo. (Courtesy of SC.)

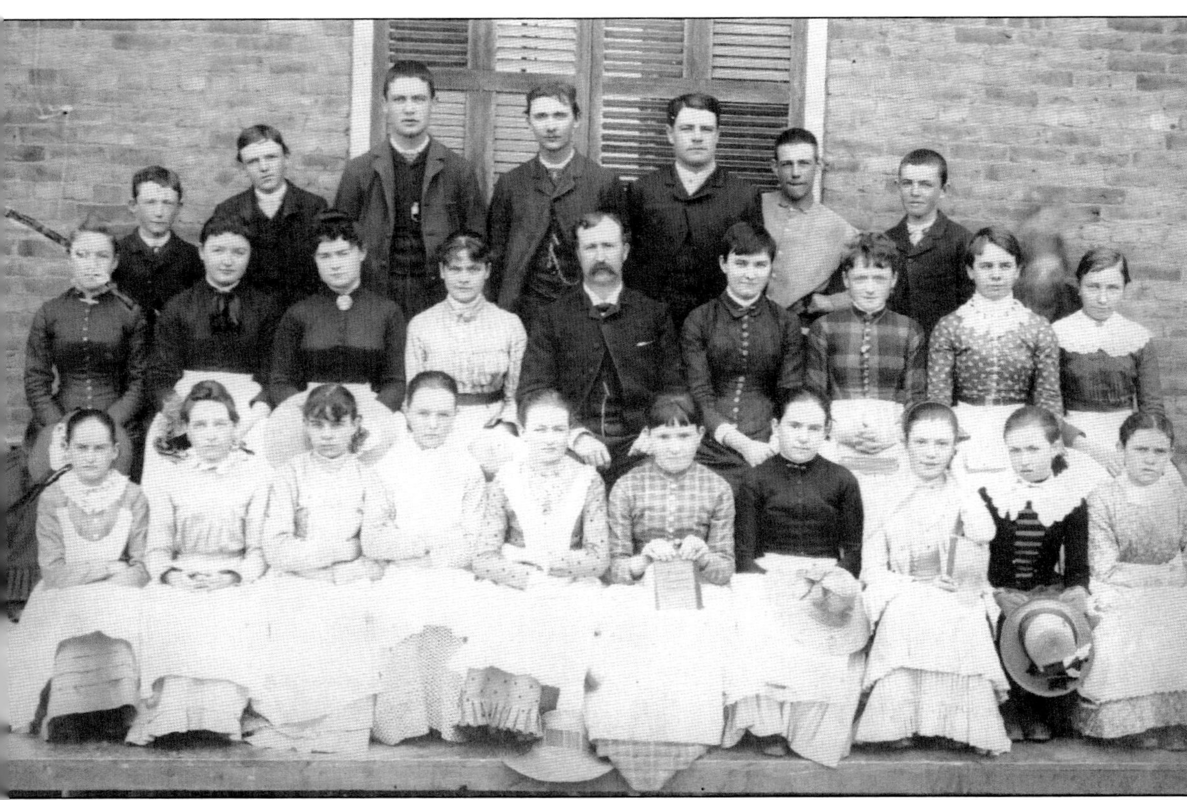

Members of this class from the 1890s include, from left to right, (third row) George McIntire, Sam Reufree, John Pringle, Adolberd McIntire, John Willianisou, Tony Gandolfo, and Jim Lynch; (second row) Charlotte Balderston, Nina Grey, Nina Huser, Mamie Egan, Mr. Whartae (teacher), Nellie Nagle, Minnie Mitchell, Bessie Taylor, and Regina Smith; (first row) Grace Crockett, Stella Price, Hattie Woolcock, Annie Cummings, Amy Soule, Mamie Hennessey, Maggie Hennessey, Lizzie Gallagher, Katie O'Brien, and Clara Bozett. (Courtesy of SC.)

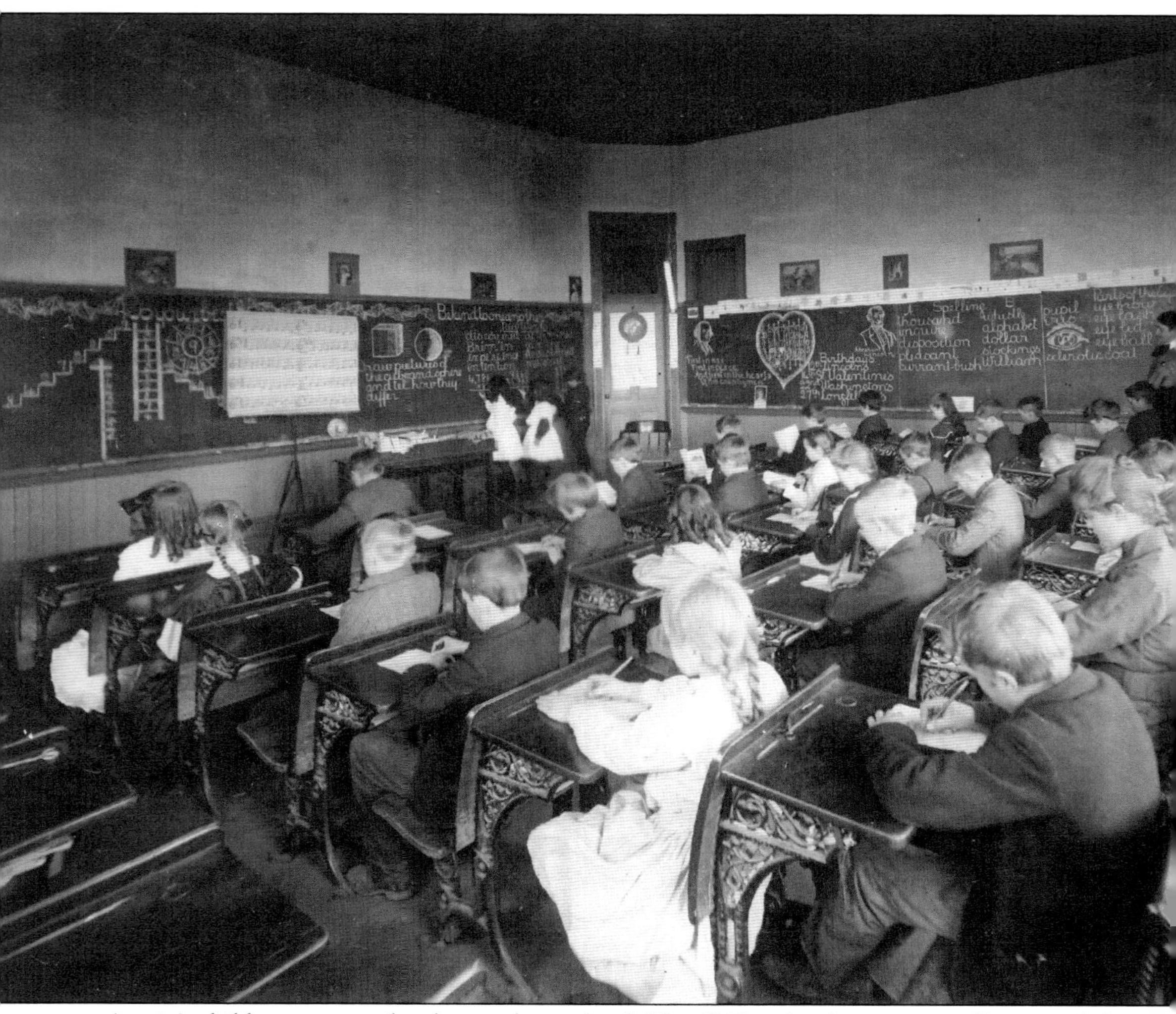

Austin's children are seen hard at work in school. The 1880s school was eventually expanded, with elementary students on one side and secondary students on the other. In 1926, an even larger facility was built 100 yards to the west. It would appear that there is a single teacher for 30 pupils. (Courtesy of AHS.)

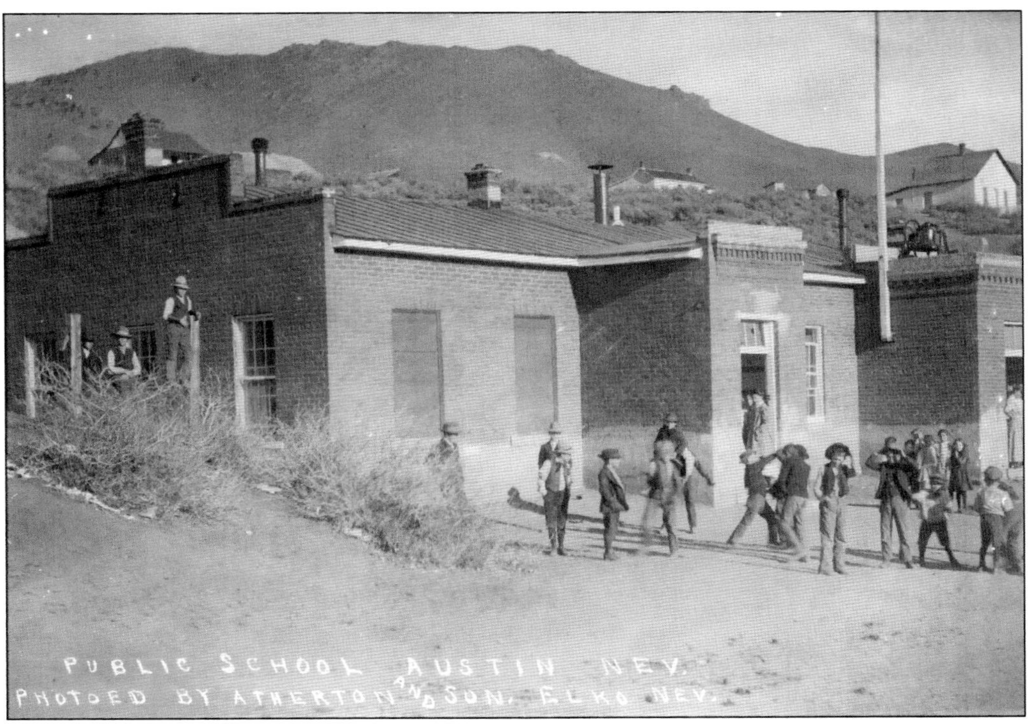

During recess on the schoolyard, children are "playing" while the teachers watch over them. (Courtesy of Mueller Collection.)

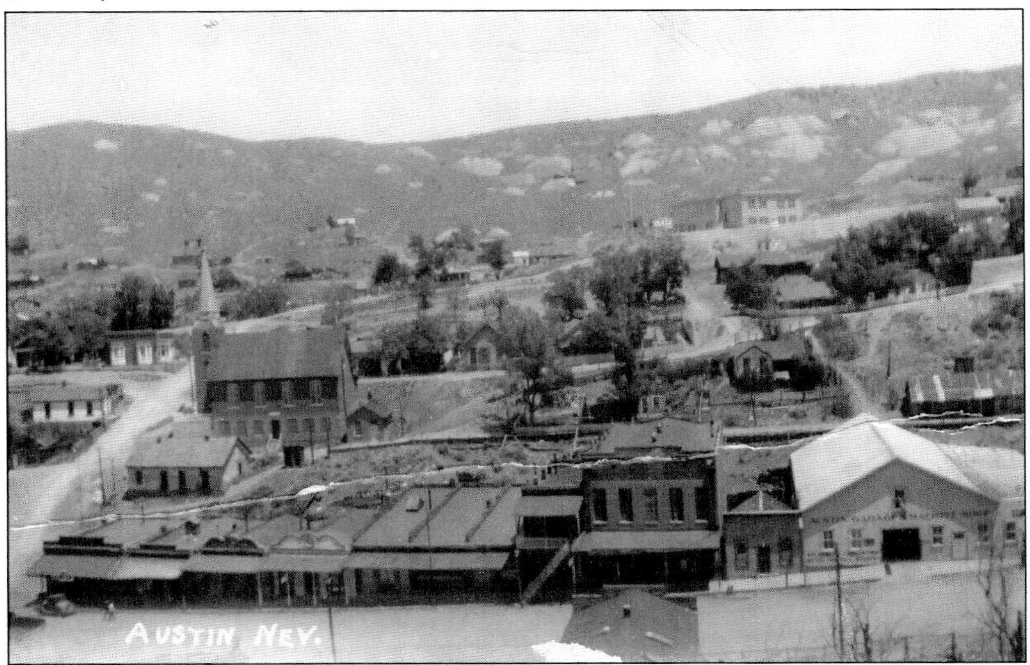

A newer school was built in 1926 and it is the large two-story brick building located on the hill. Main Street is in the foreground; the tall two-story Masonic Building is next to the garage; and St. Augustine Catholic Church is to the right. Old mine tailings dot the high hill. (Courtesy of JBC.)

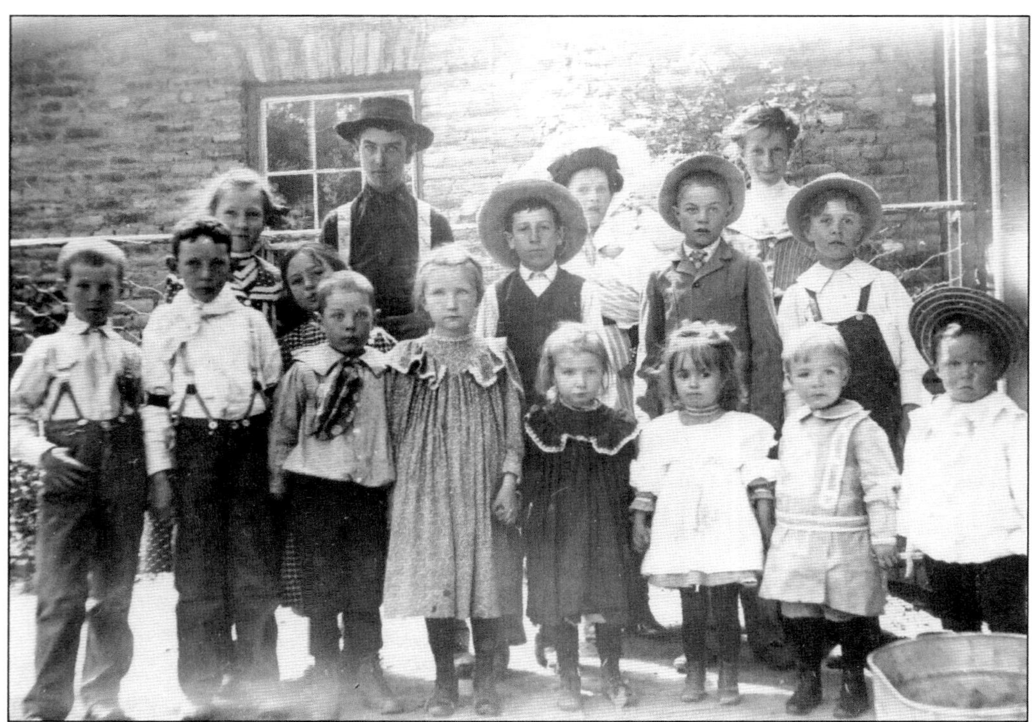

For a few years around 1905, St. George Episcopal Church also ran a private school. (Courtesy of NVHS.)

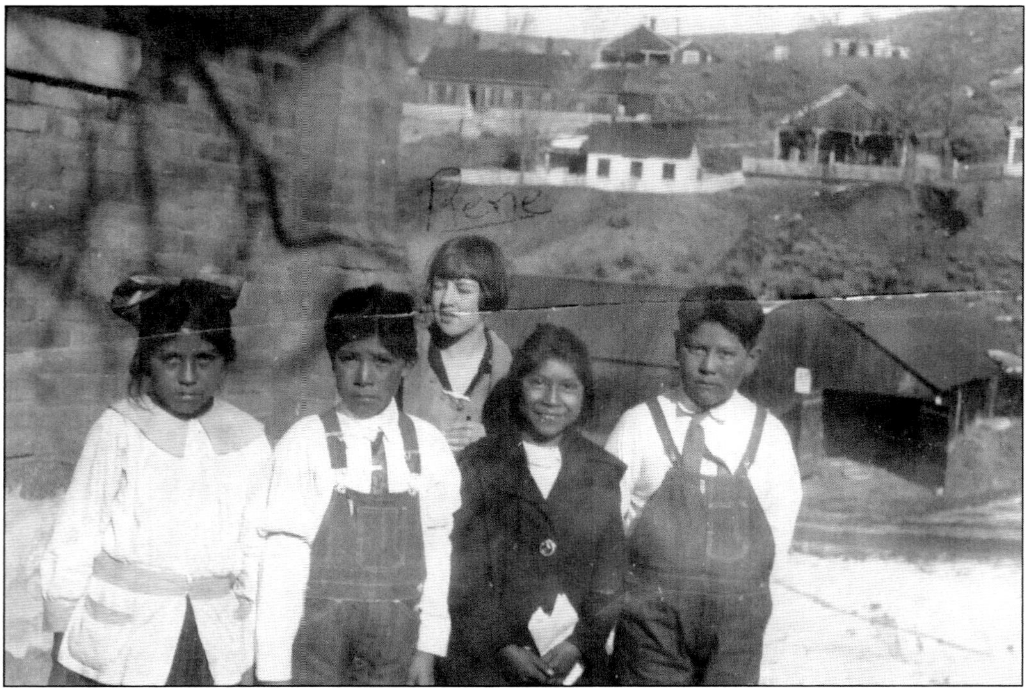

This is St. George's Sunday school in the 1920s. Four Native American children and Rene Acree stand on the east side of the church. Main Street is below, and the house midway up the right is the vicarage. (Courtesy of CC.)

This is St. George Episcopal Church around 1883. The congregation was founded in 1863 and built this magnificent church in the Gothic Revival style in 1878. The church was financed by pledges in one pass of the collection plate. The church bell was poured with a total of 400 ounces of Austin silver, which was said to give it a more pure tone. The Mules Relief tracks running on Main Street are seen in the foreground. (Courtesy of NVHS.)

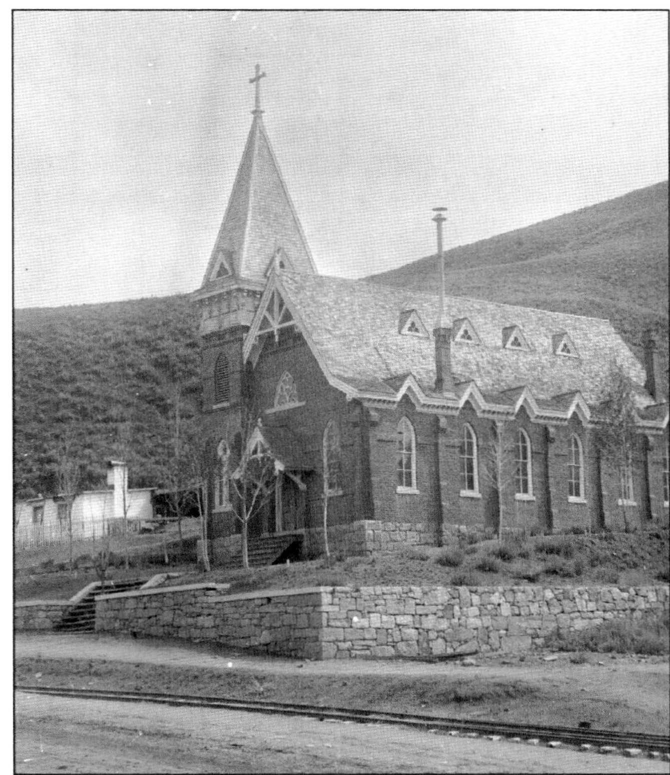

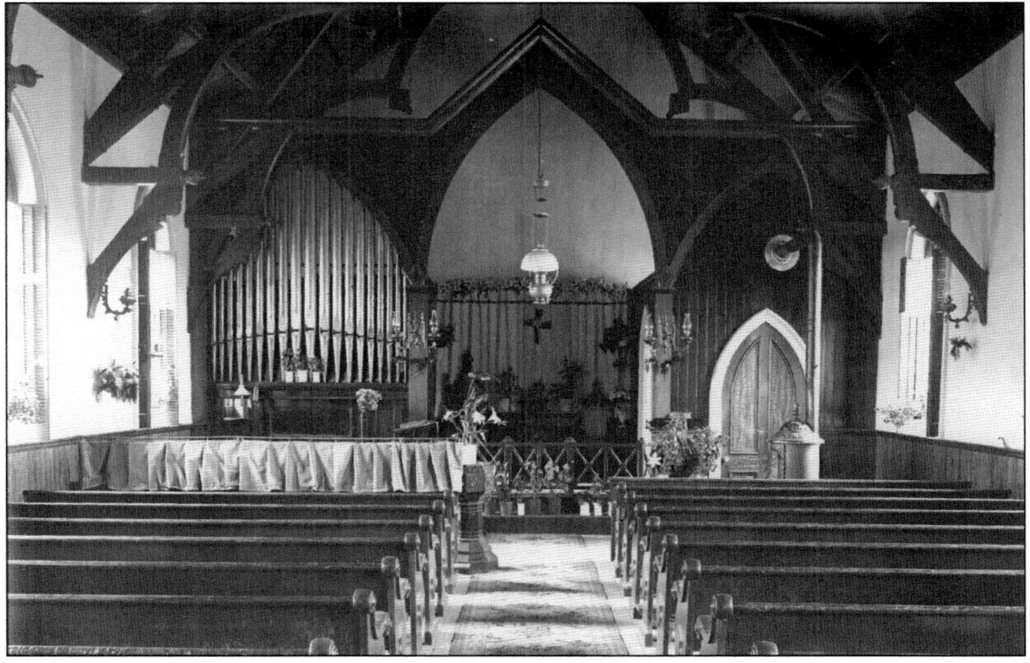

The interior of St. George looks much the same today. The heavy beams are cut from red wood; the altar rail, the pews, and fount are all still there. Although, the coal stove is gone. The original Mill's pipe organ from New York still plays; however, it was modified in the 1980s and no longer has to be hand pumped. (Courtesy of NVHS.)

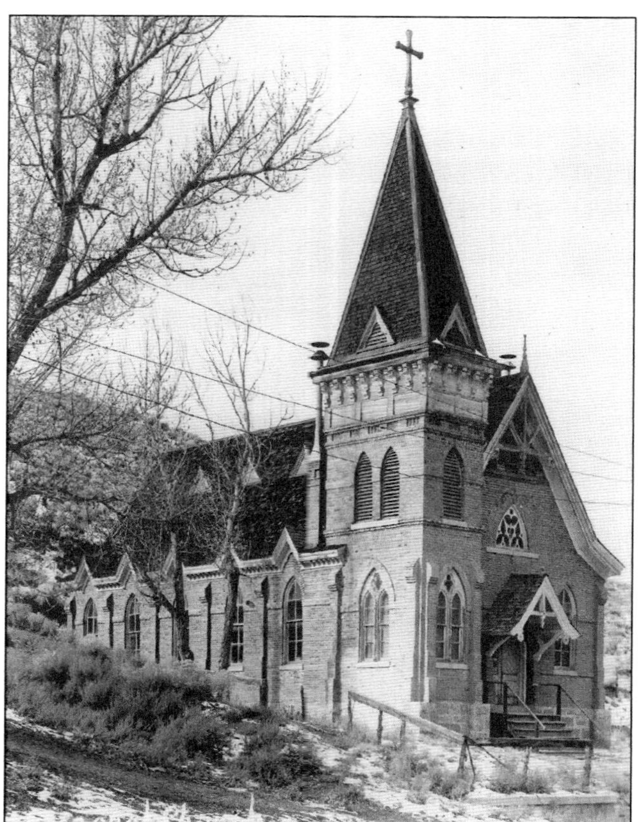

Services are still held, and a small congregation meets each Sunday. A few efforts at modernity have been completed. The bathroom has been moved inside, and running water was installed. In fact, the bell can be rung while sitting on the commode. (Courtesy of CC.)

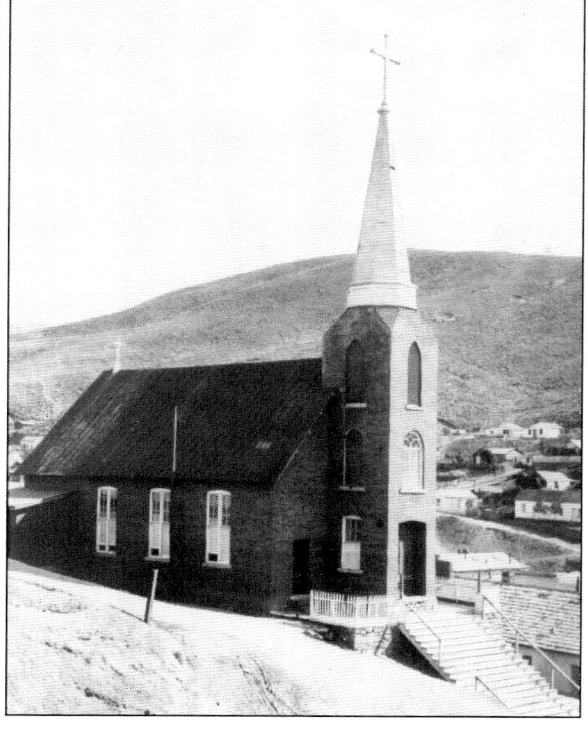

Built in 1866, St. Augustine Catholic Church is the oldest standing Catholic church in Nevada. This photograph is from 1889, and the church still looks much the same, perched on the side of Virginia Hill. Congregations rose and fell along with the fortunes of the mines. Eventually, services were held once a month and then no more. Today, St. Augustine has been purchased by a nonprofit and is slowly being historically restored to its past splendor. Future plans call for a cultural center where meetings, concerts, and weddings can be held. (Courtesy of NVHS.)

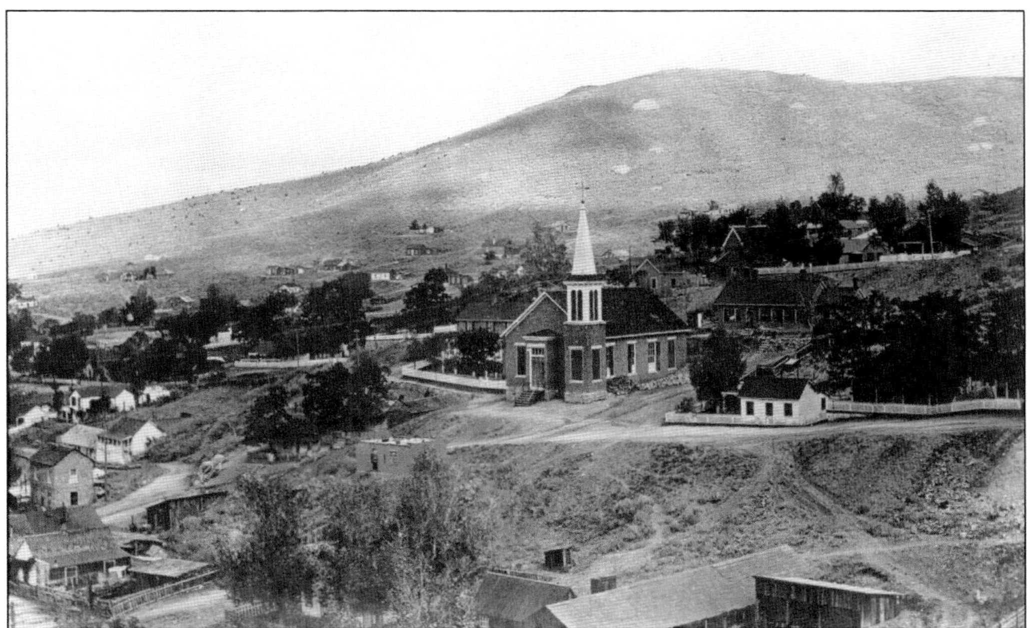

Austin's Methodists raised the capital for their church through a mining stock subscription, the Methodist Mining Company. A pool of silver claims were bundled together, and shares sold to Methodist churches back East. Austin was booming, and with God's direction, one could help raise the church and get rich to. Fortunately, the church was built before the entire scheme collapsed due to sallow deposits. God's work was done. (Courtesy of NVHS.)

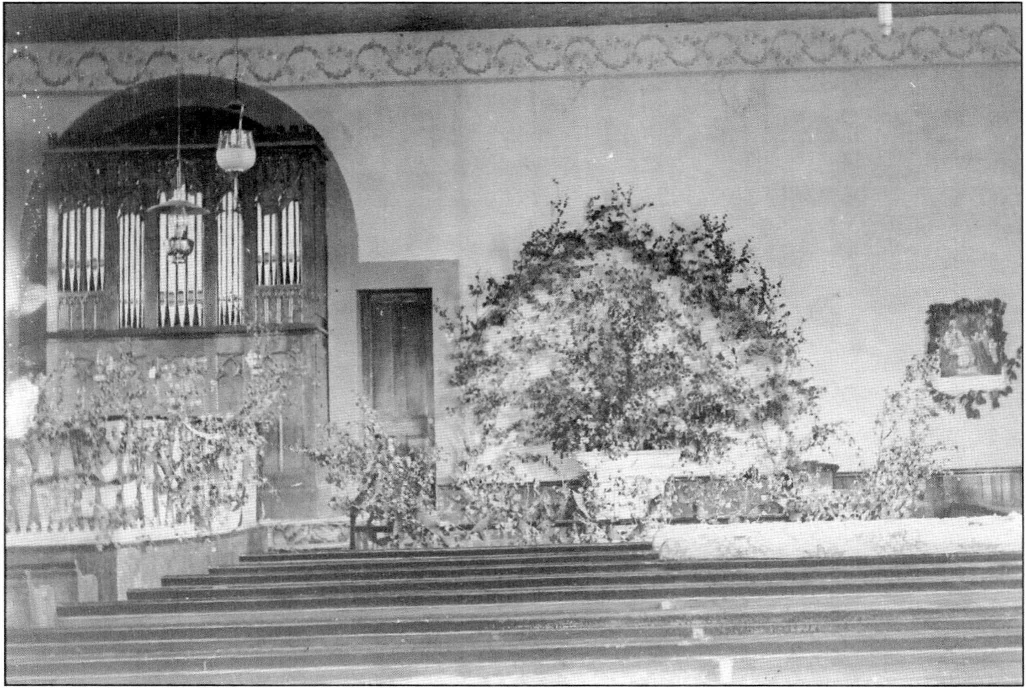

With over $35,000 spent, the church was one of the largest buildings in Nevada in 1868. This interior photograph shows the organ to the left and the period stenciling on the walls. Spacious, yet plain by the standards of the day, it could hold over 200 souls on Sunday. (Courtesy of JBC.)

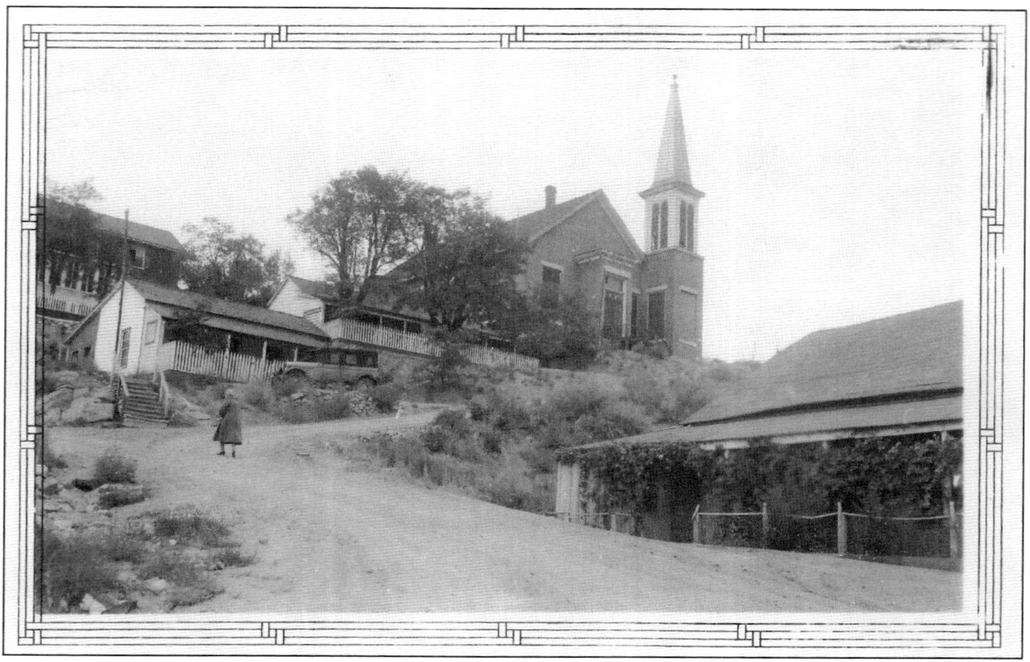

This is Austin's Methodist church, shown in the 1920s. The Leland House is to the right. Brothers Bill and John Hickerson owned the next two houses on the hill. They were well known for their ranch interests outside of town. (Courtesy of SC.)

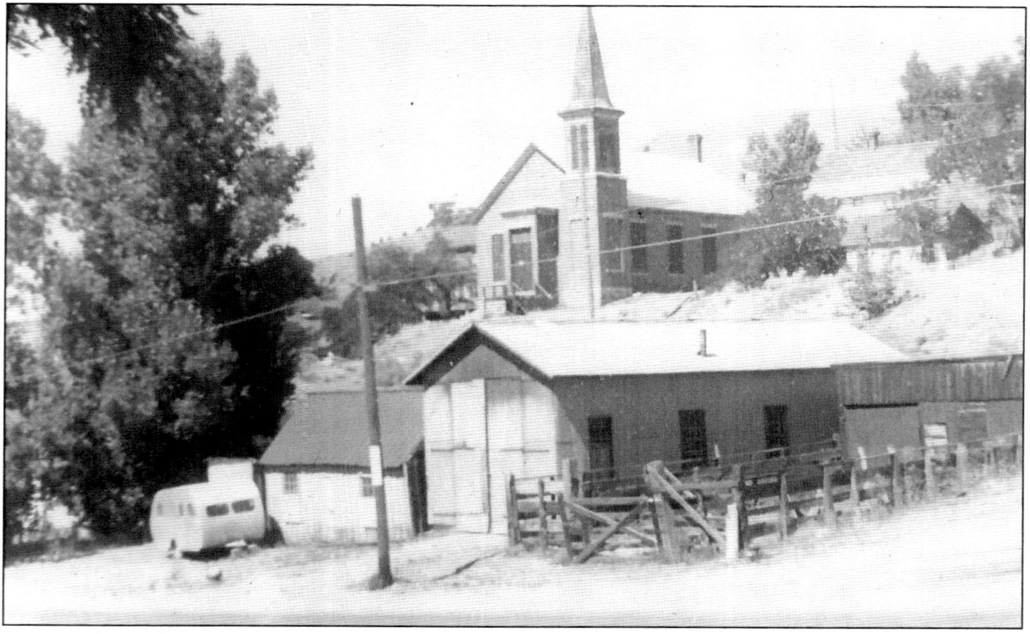

As seen from the Episcopal church across the street, here is the Methodist church in 1956. The tall garage below the church is the old engine house for the Nevada Central, which was brought up from Clifton. Like the silver mines that faded away, so nearly did the old church. In the 1950s, Bell Roberts started a campaign to save the old building. Today know as the Emma Nevada Town Hall, it is able to hold almost all of the residents of Austin. Weddings, funerals, and political debates are held instead of church services. (Courtesy of SC.)

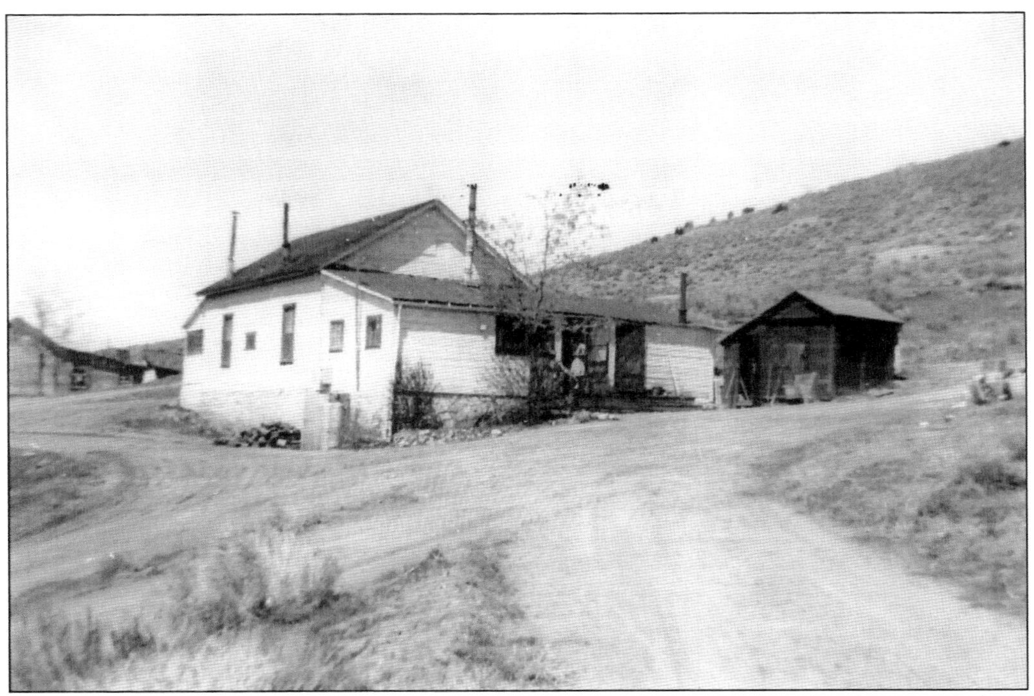

The Lander County Hospital was located at the top of Cedar Street, above and to the East of China Ridge. This photograph is from around 1900, when the cellar was use as the morgue. The building is abandoned today; rumor has it that a coffin still awaits use in the cellar. (Courtesy of SC.)

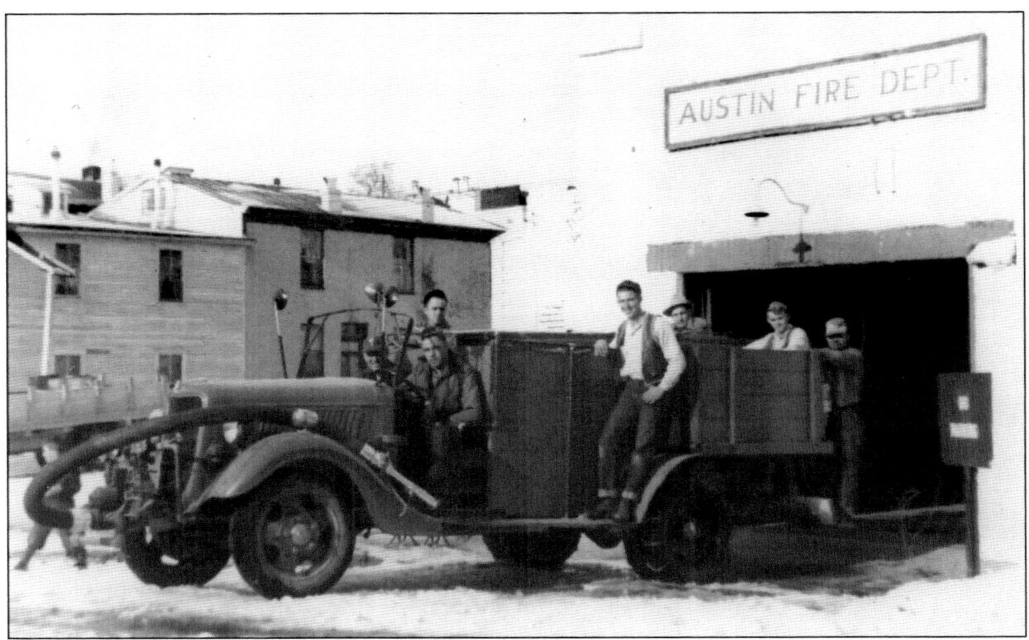

Here are members of the Austin Volunteer Fire Department with a 1938 Ford fire truck. The pump was run by a power take-off on the engine. William Brandt is the driver. Ralph King and Percy Dory are standing on the back of the truck. This old fire engine was used, until recently, in town parades and is now being restored (see pages 12 and 16 for earlier views). (Courtesy of NVHS.)

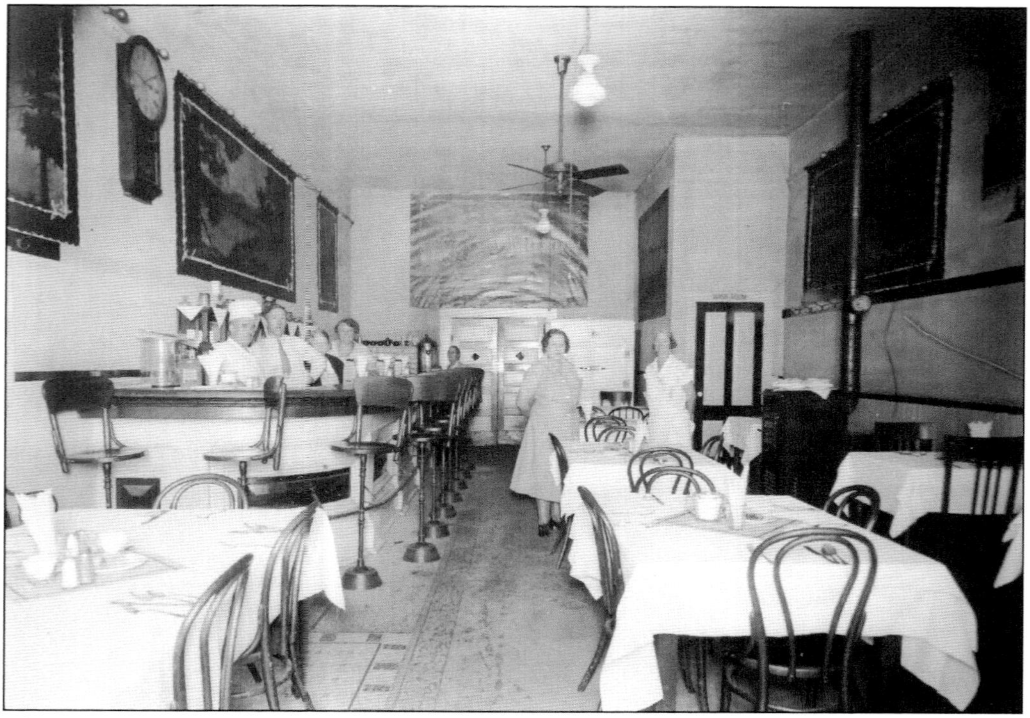

The Magnolia Café was located just down from the Masonic hall. Today, the old café is used as an occasional sandwich shop and gift store. (Courtesy of SC.)

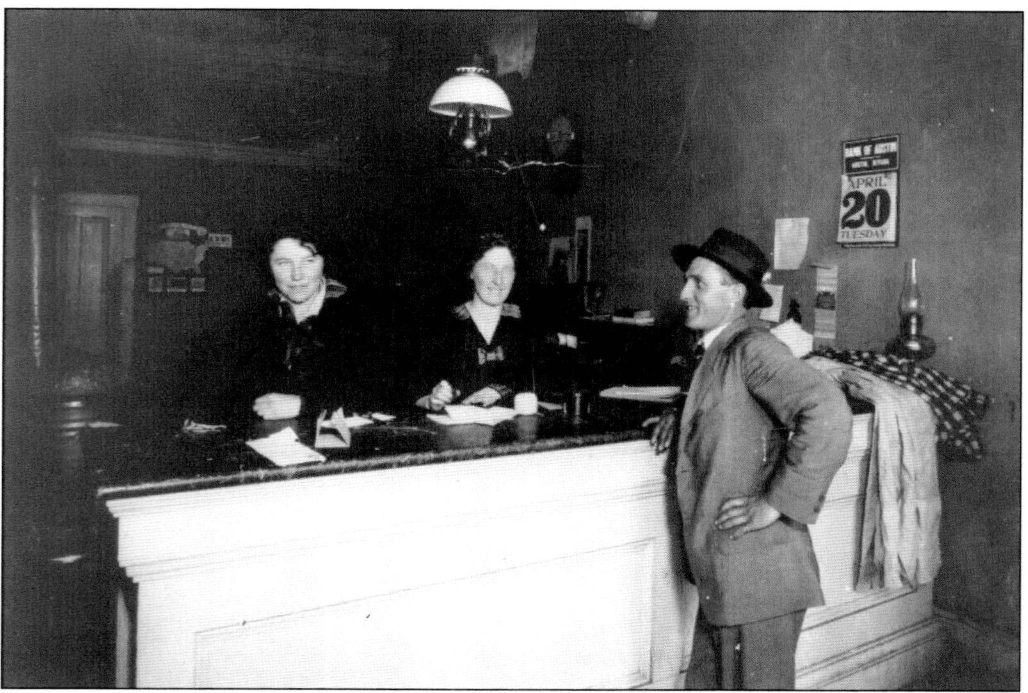

The inside of Austin's Telegraph Exchange Office is shown on April 20, 1909. These two women have some sort of uniform on. Clerical work was becoming increasingly open for women in the West. (Courtesy of NVHS.)

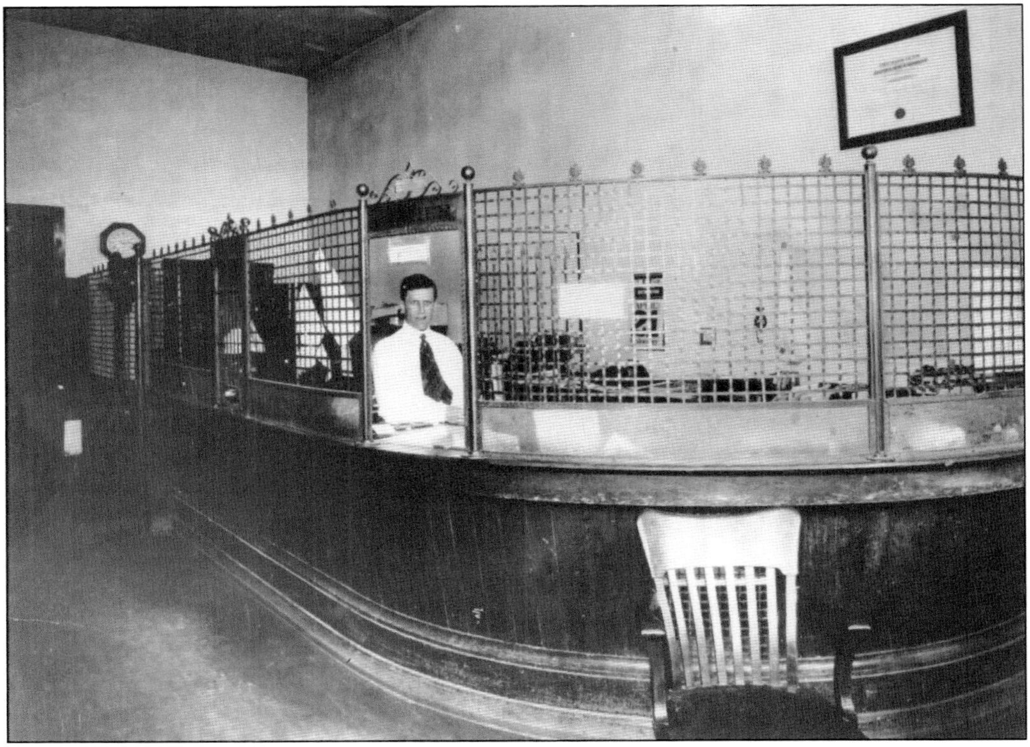

Pictured in 1909, this is the Austin State Bank on Main Street, which later became the Nevada Bank of Commerce. Never robbed, it remained solvent through the Depression. Today, it houses the Austin Library. (Courtesy of NVHS.)

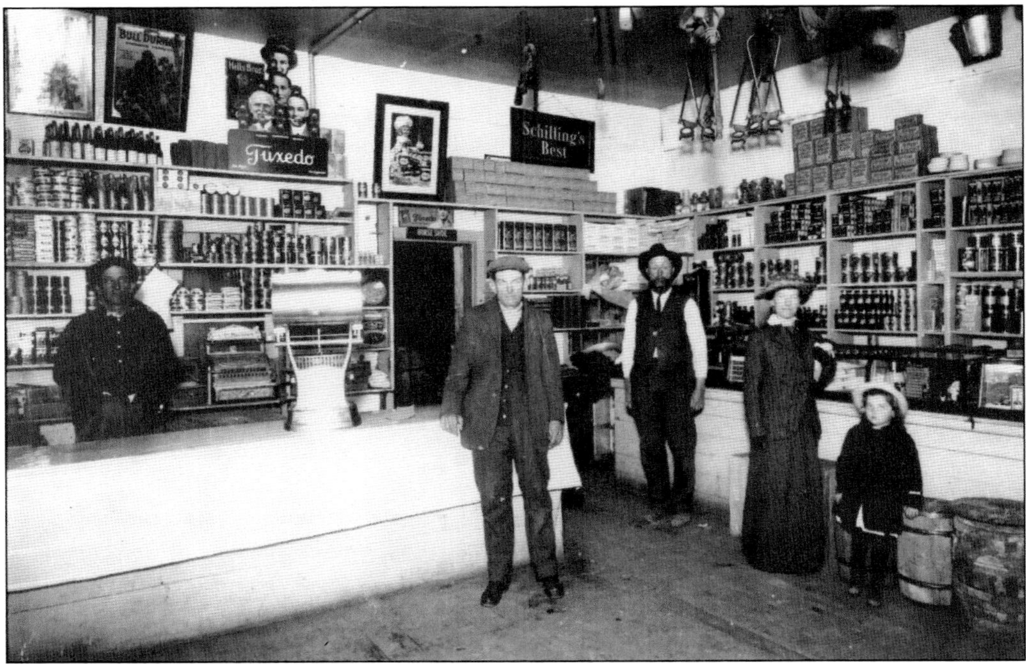

Seen here is the interior of an Austin dry goods and grocery store on Main Street in 1909. (Courtesy of NVHS.)

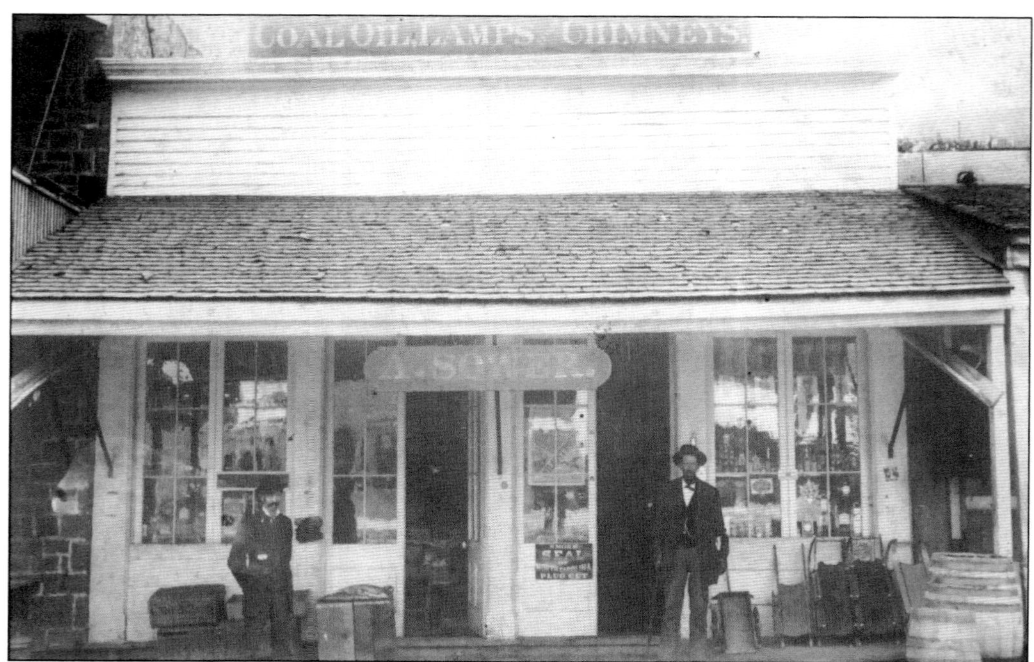

The A. Sower store sold "coal oil, lamps, and chimneys." Abe Sower had arrived in Austin by 1868. This store was next to the Silver State Saloon on Main Street, and this image was taken around 1890. The building was known as the Commercial Building and it later home to the Austin Commercial Company. (Courtesy of NVHS.)

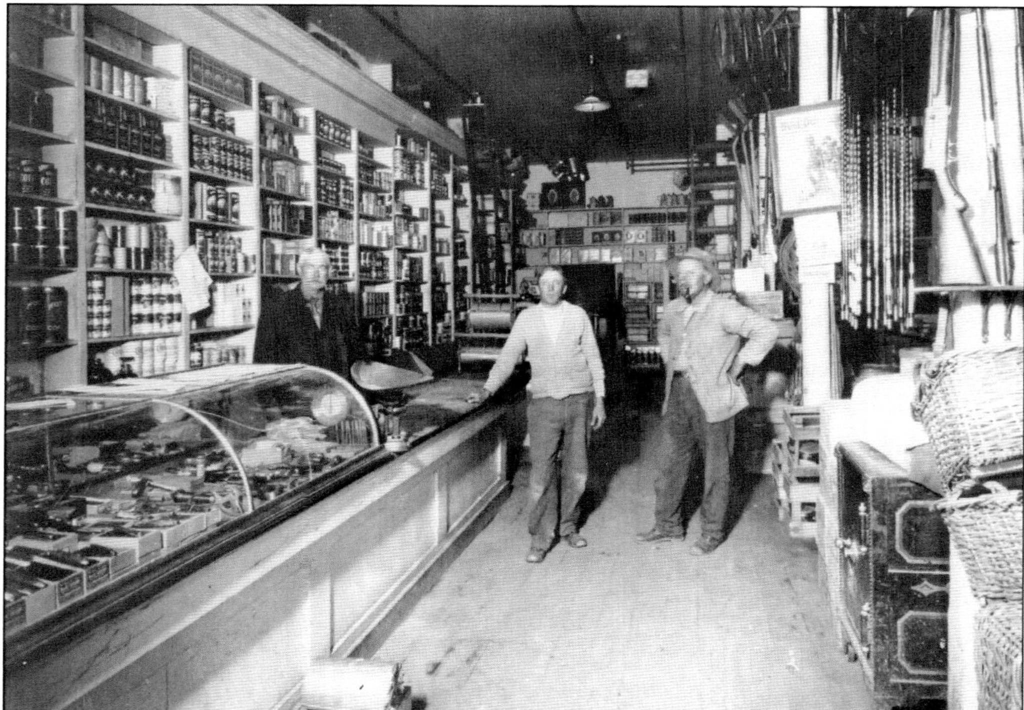

Billy Christian owned the Austin Commercial Company on Main Street in 1909. (Courtesy of NVHS.)

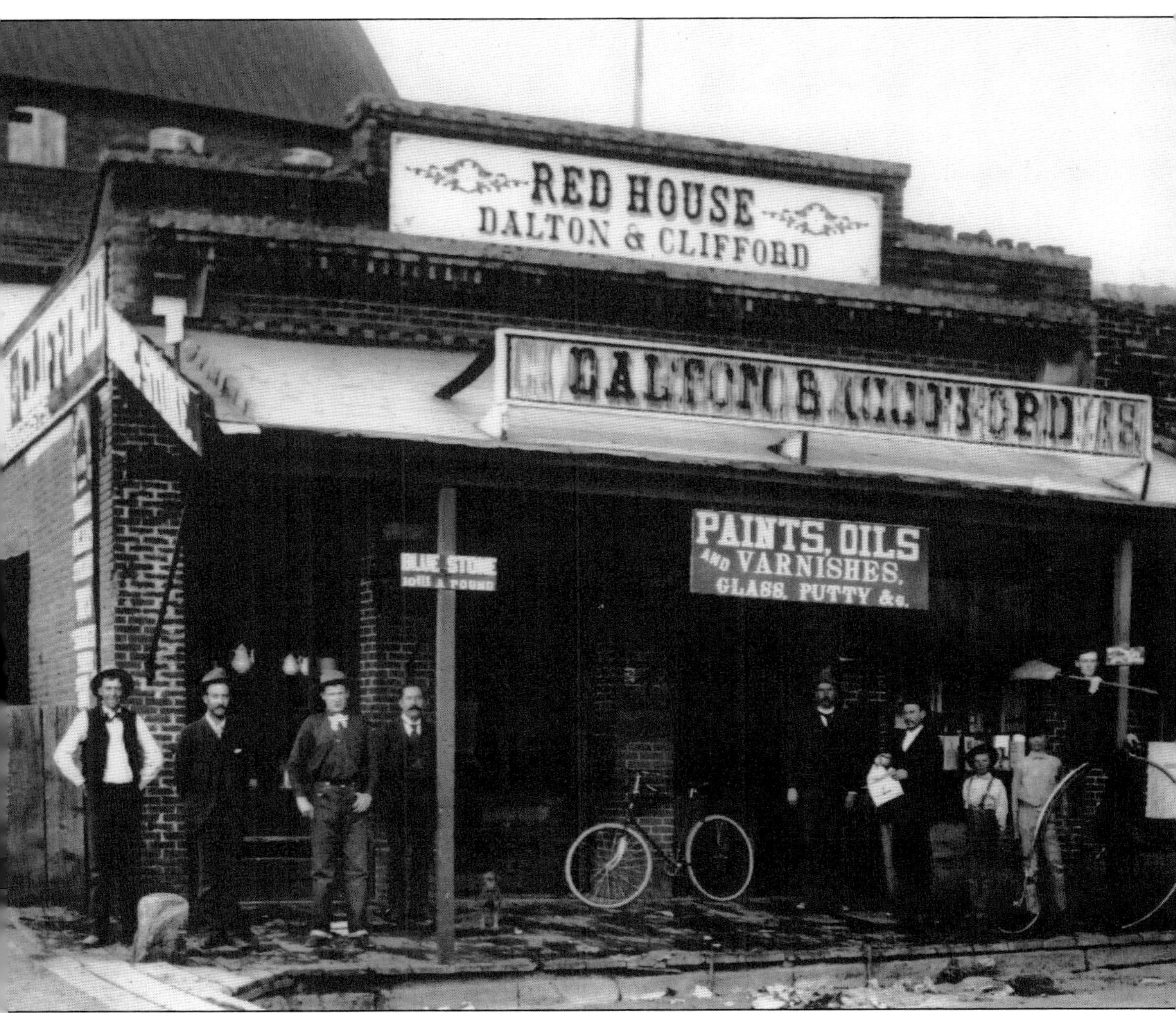

Dalton and Clifford was located at the corner of Main and Virginia Streets. Part of St. Augustine can be seen in the background. In this c. 1895 photograph, two different styles of bicycles are visible. Paint was made, in those days, by adding not just the pigments but also the oils, dryers, and so on. (Courtesy of AHS.)

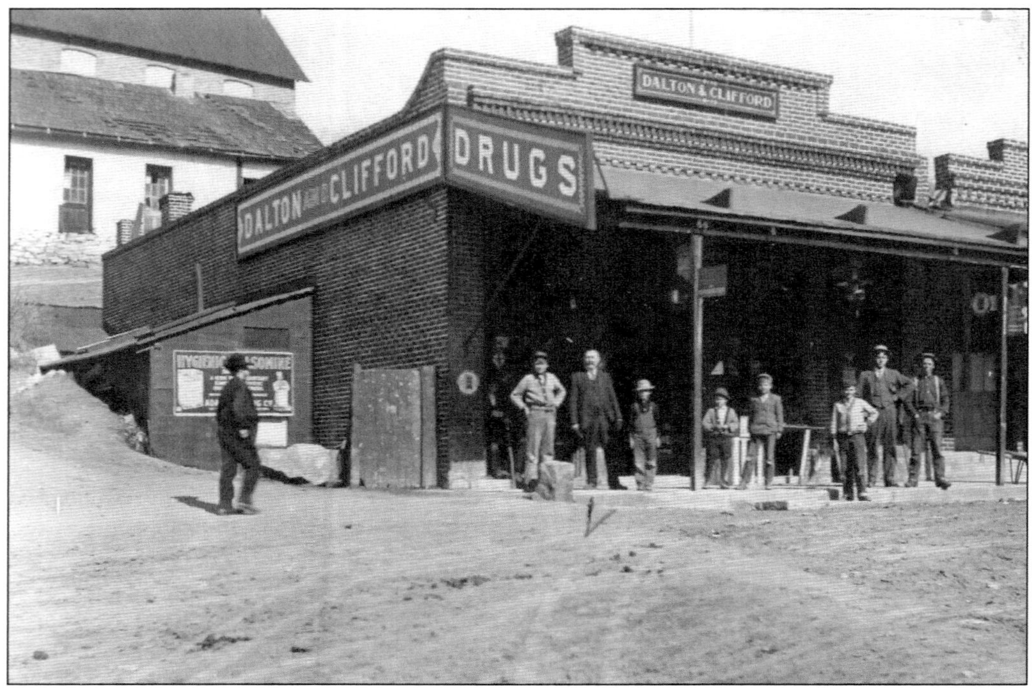

Dalton and Clifford was located at the corner Main and Virginia Streets. St. Augustine is barely visible in the left-hand corner. This photograph is from around 1910. Dalton and Clifford are now selling drugs. (Courtesy of SC.)

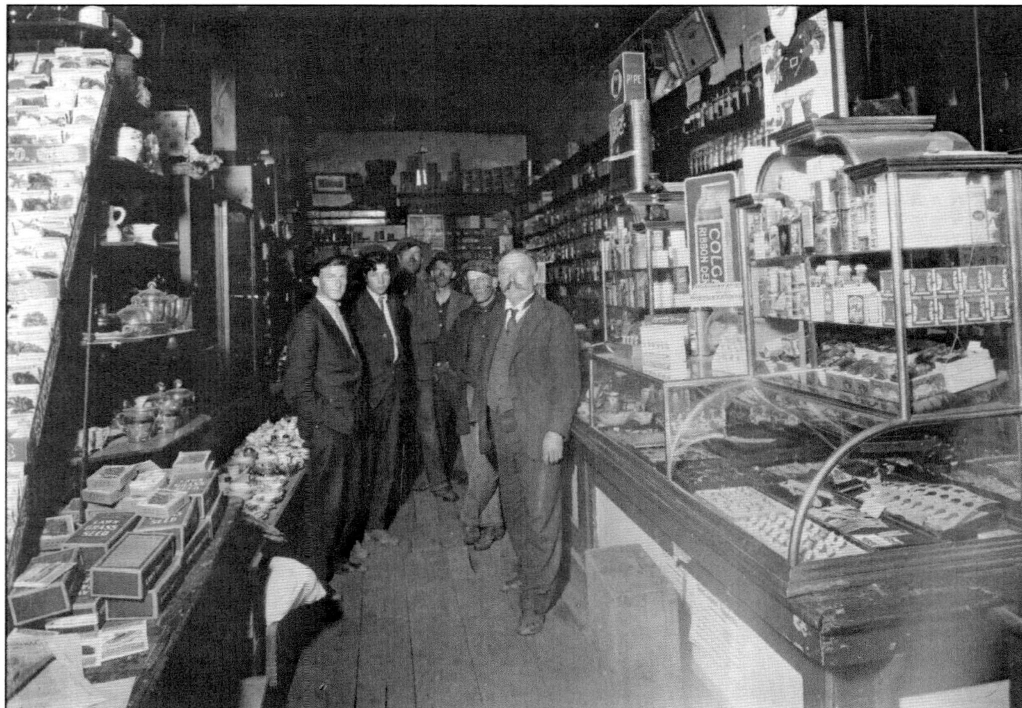

This is the interior of Dalton and Clifford in 1909. This building and the one next to it are no longer standing. (Courtesy of NVHS.)

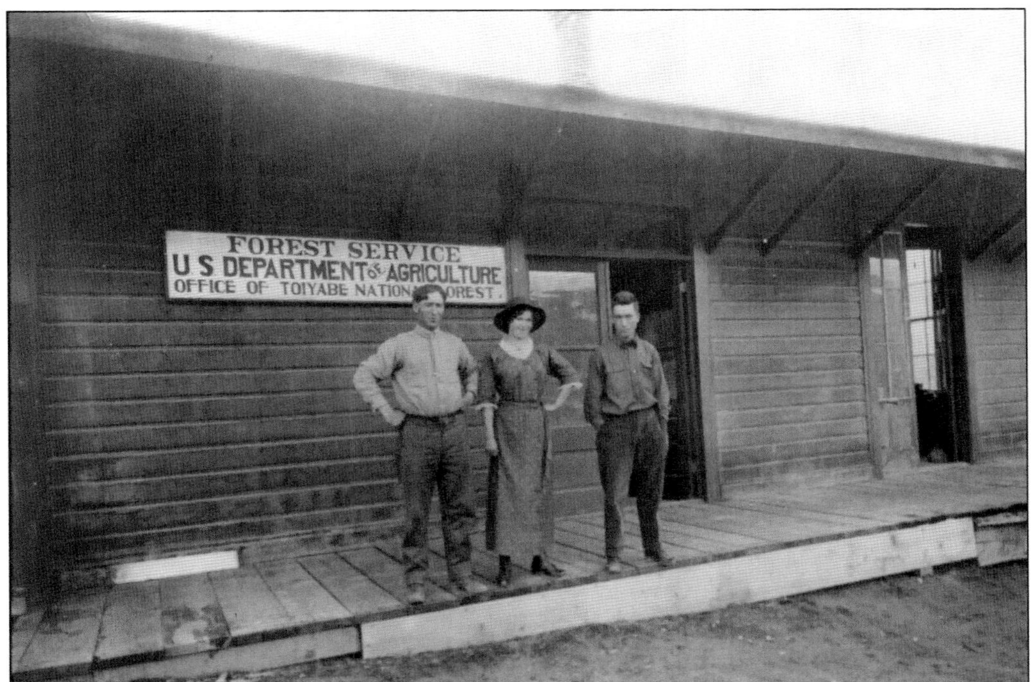

This photograph of the US Forest Service Office in Austin is dated 1909. Those pictured are, from left to right, Jim Cahill, Margaret Dyer, and Clyde Gsoim. Nevada was an open range state; early duties were to protect the forest from over grazing and to suppress fires. (Courtesy of NVHS.)

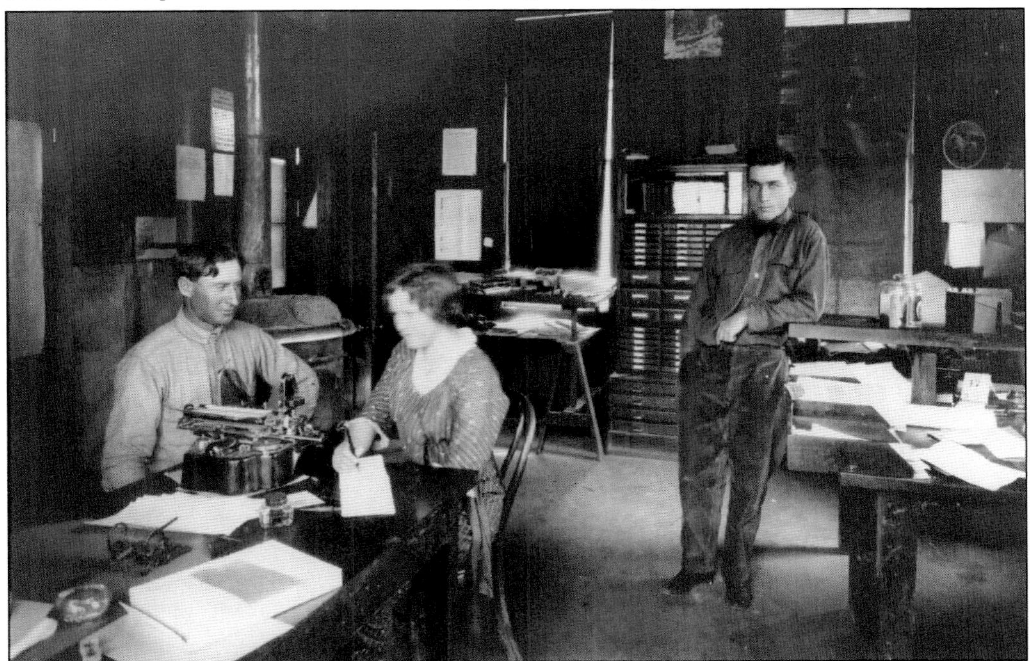

This interior view of the Forest Service Office shows the same people as above. Today, the Forest Service continues to have an office staffed in Austin. The town nestles on the western flank of the Toiyabe Mountains and is part of the largest National Forest in the contiguous United States. (Courtesy of NVHS.)

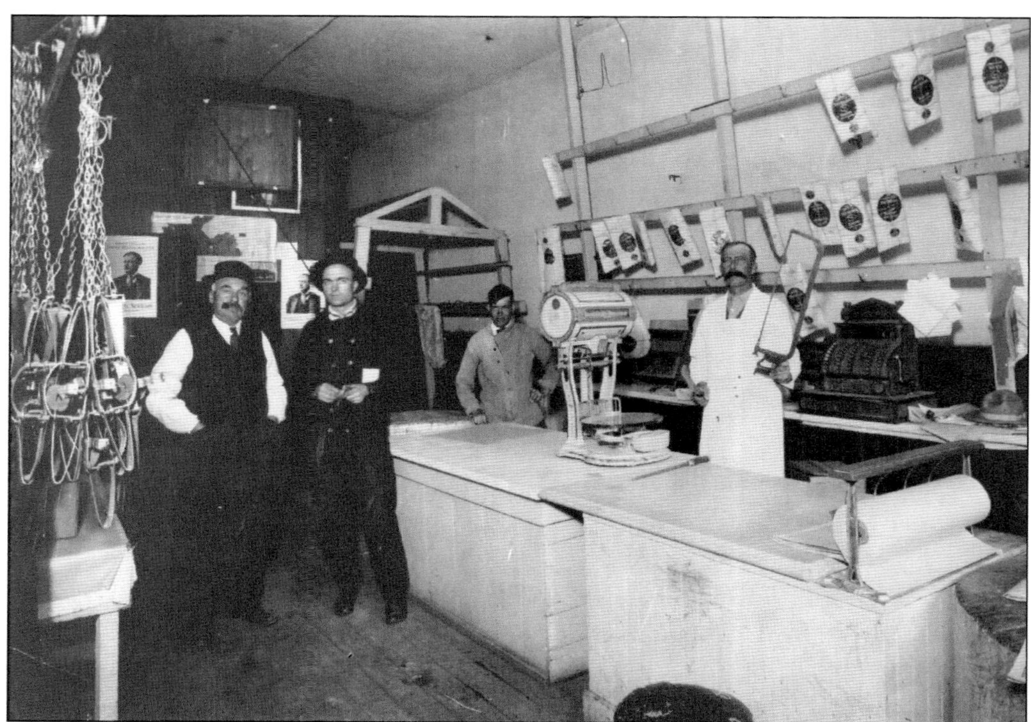

This is Murphy's Butcher Shop on Main Street in 1909. Herbert Rast is holding the saw. Notice the traps to the left. (Courtesy of NVHS.)

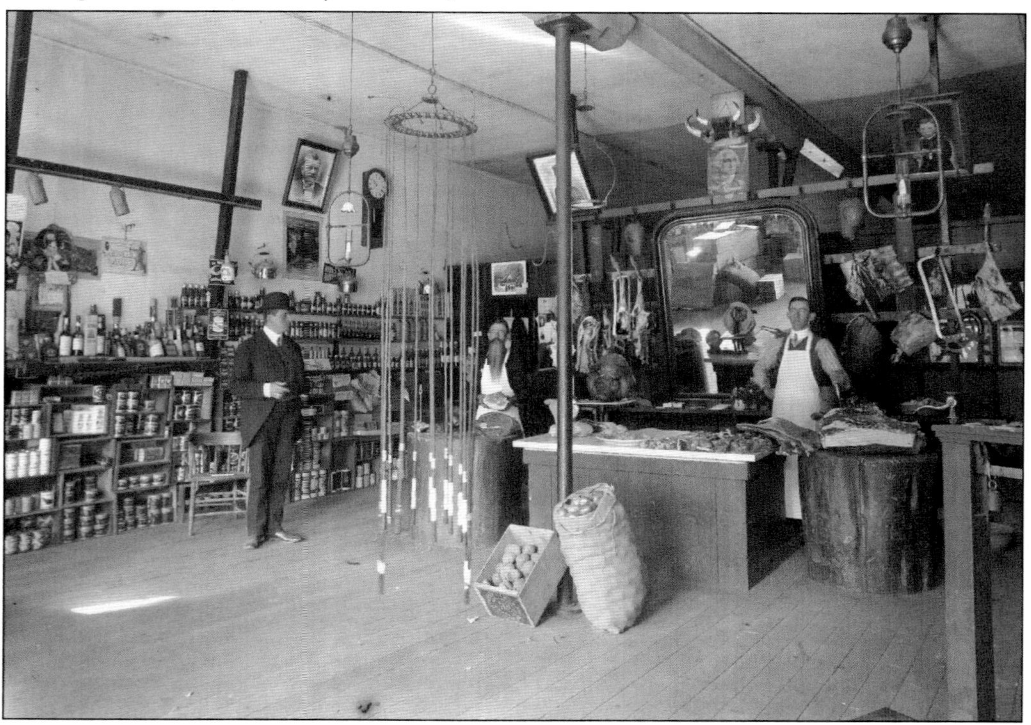

Here is the interior of the C.A. Richards Store on November 8, 1901. Note the buggy whips display hanging from the ceiling. (Courtesy of NVHS.)

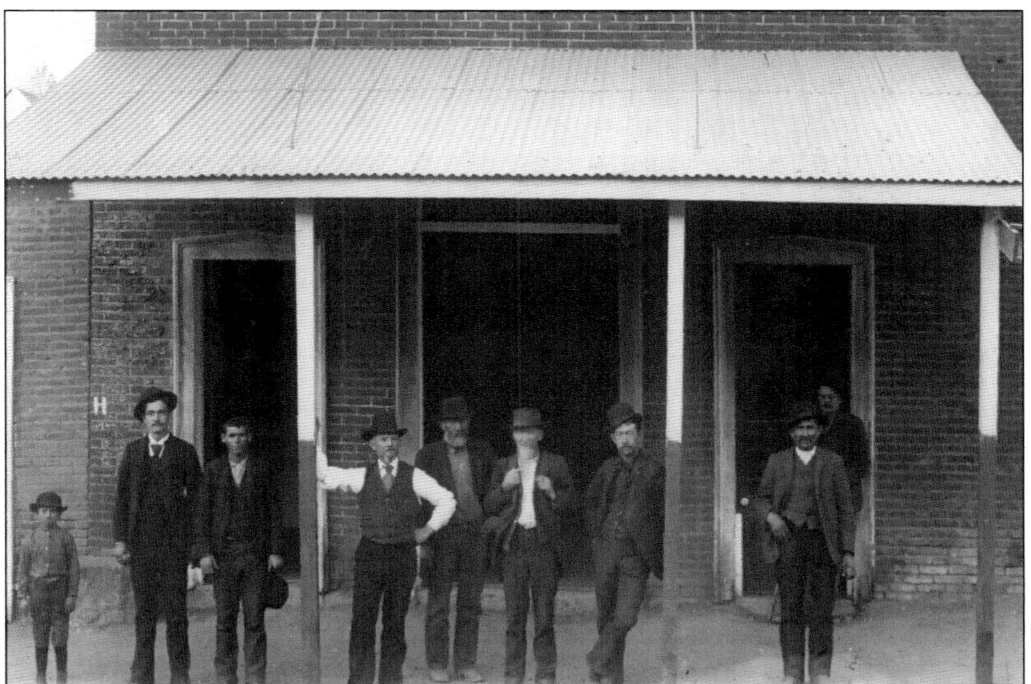

Austin is seen here around 1900. This building is gone but was located on the south side of Main Street. At the time of this photograph, it was most likely used as a warehouse for transshipping freight. (SC.)

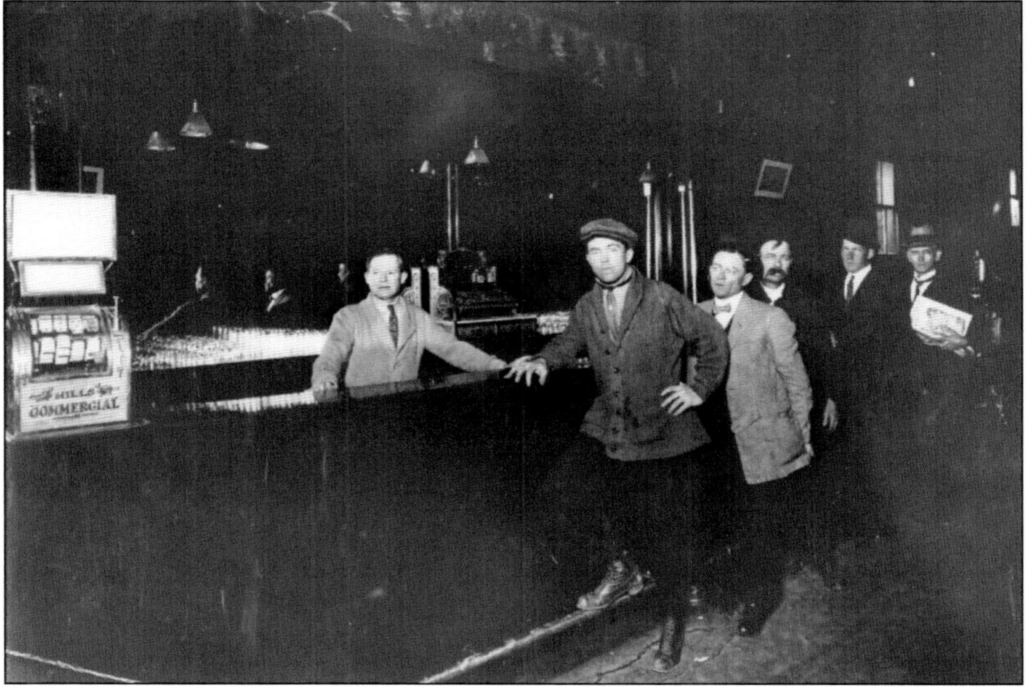

Tommie Eagan's Sam's Saloon was on Austin's Main Street in 1909. Notice the slot machine on the bar to the left. This early model rolled on a nickel and used actual playing cards attached to the reel. Payouts were usually made in beer, whiskey, or cigars from the bar. (Courtesy of NVHS.)

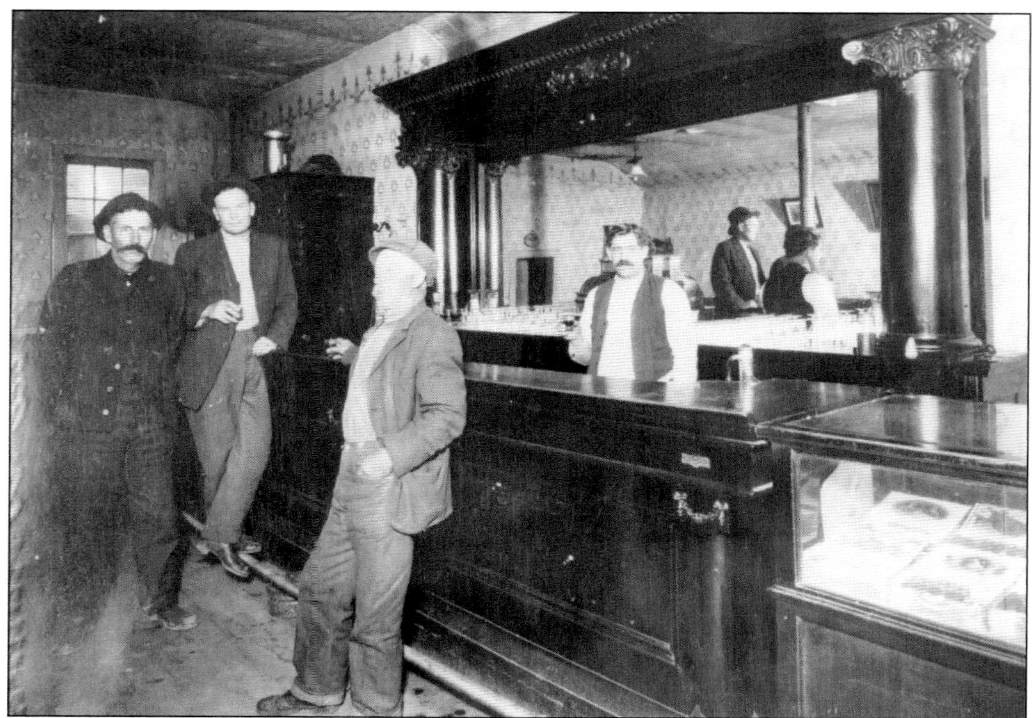

This is the Silver State bar around 1910. Emanuel Aberasturi is the barkeeper, and the two men leaning on the bar are identified as Charley Bray and George Givins (foreground). (Courtesy of NVHS.)

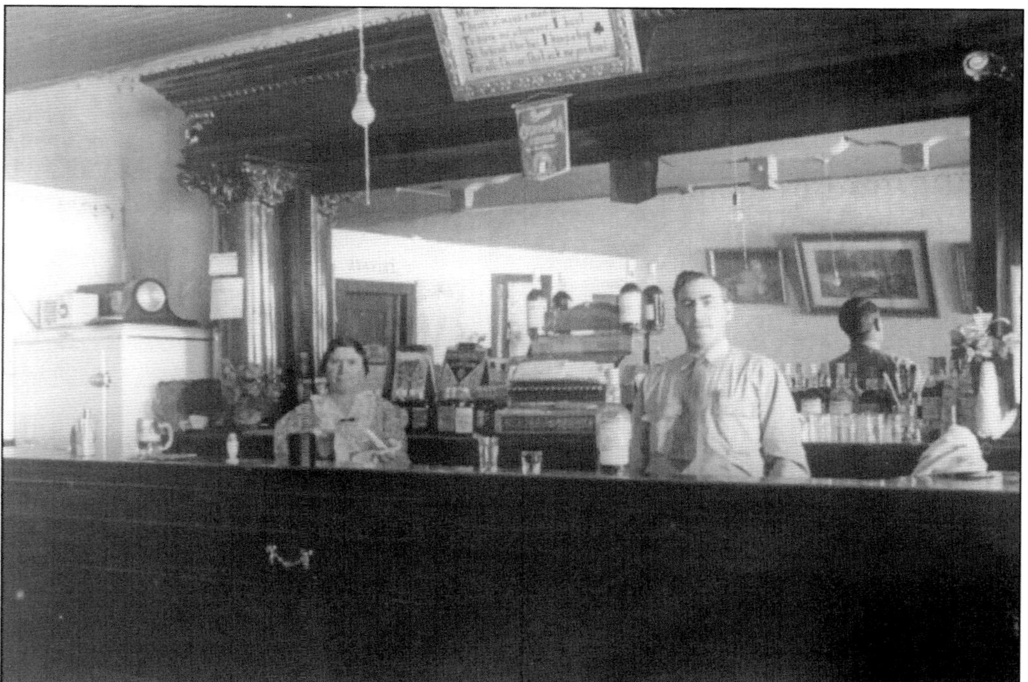

Here is the Silver State in the 1940s. Frank El Dophy and his wife are behind the bar. They are remembered, even today, as always serving a full shot of whiskey. (Courtesy of JBC.)

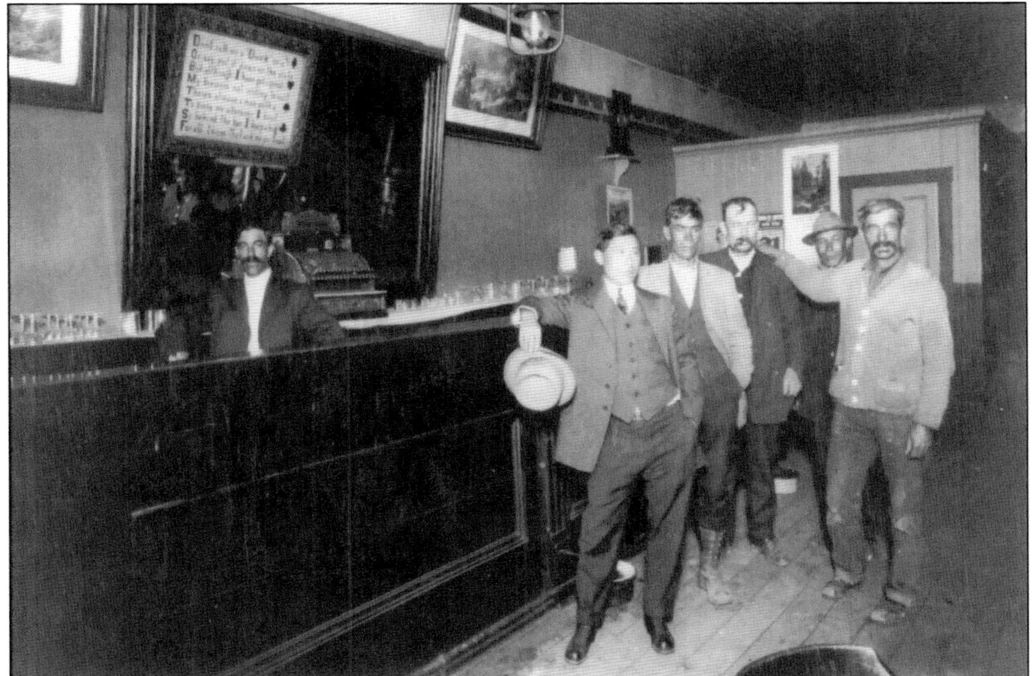

This is a bar scene inside the Hogan Hotel on Main Street, photographed shortly before Prohibition. The barkeeper might be Domingo Aeorda. Hogan became part of the Austin Hotel, which burned down in 1970. (Courtesy of JBC.)

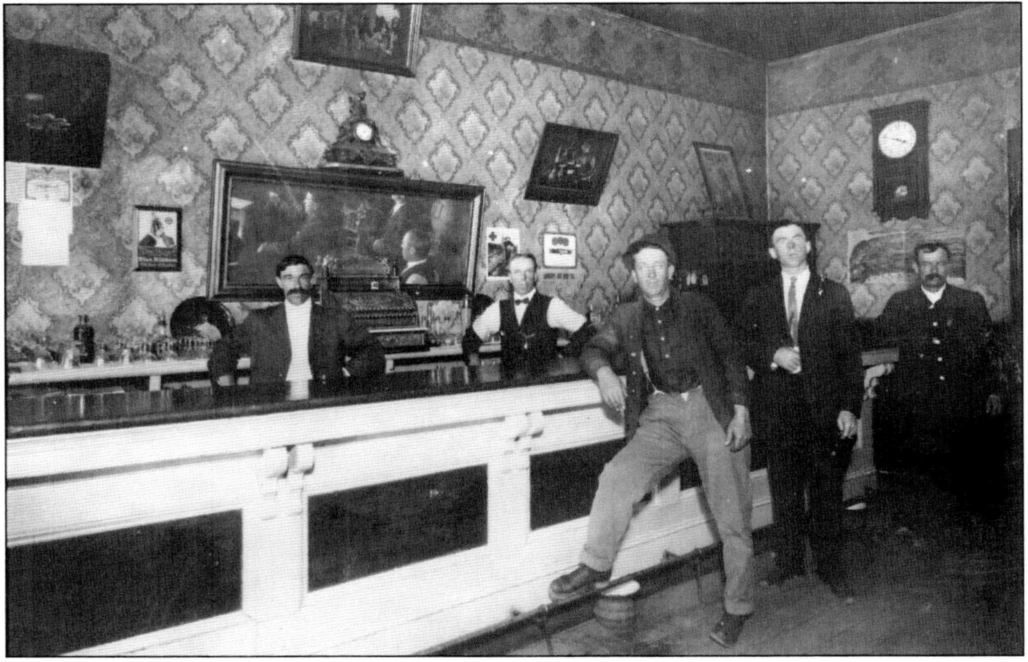

This is Jack Dunston's Saloon in 1909. It was formally known as the King and Easton Saloon. Those behind the bar are, from left to right, Domingo Aeorda and Jack Dunston. Those at the bar are, from left to right, Fred Litchen, Mr. Murray, and Jack Buirier. Unfortunately, the building collapsed in 1947 and is no more. (Courtesy of NVHS.)

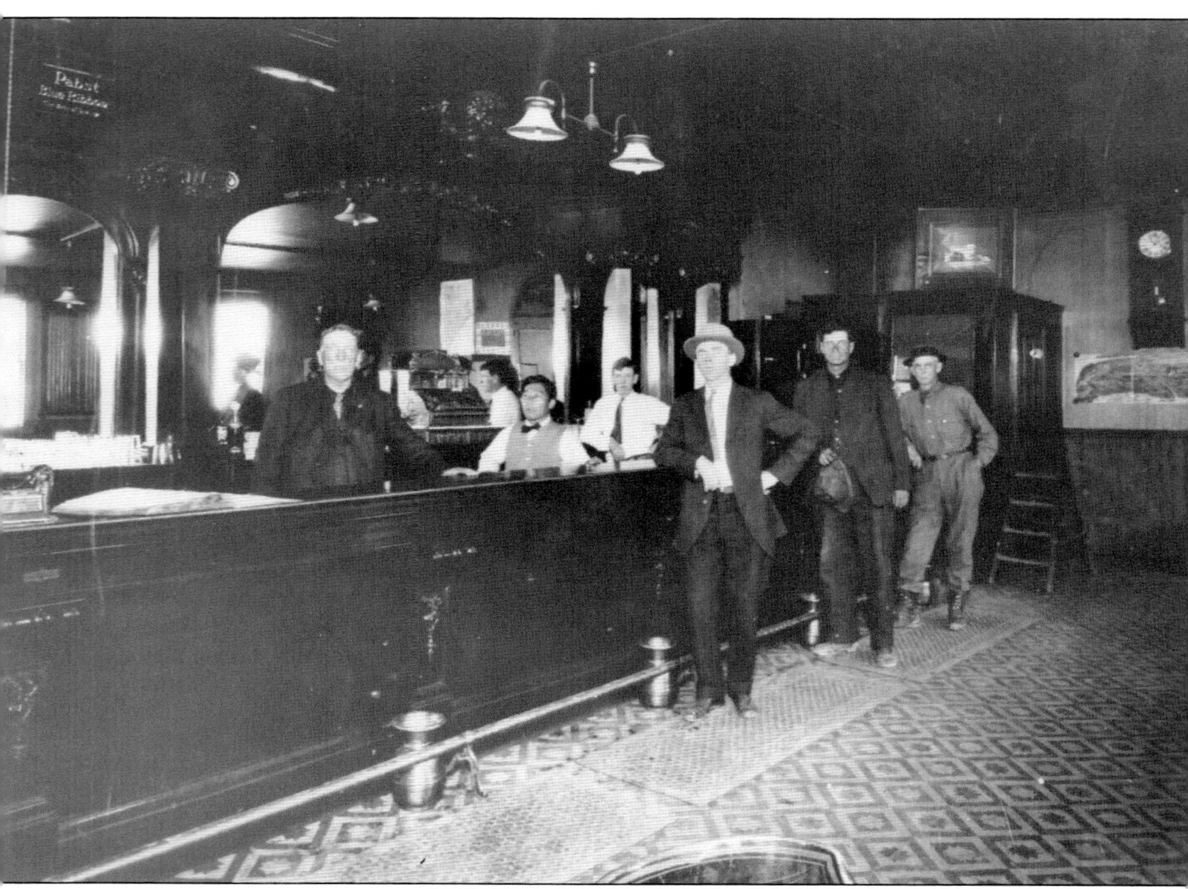

An Austin institution even today, this interior photograph shows the International Hotel in 1909. The International has the distinction of being one of the oldest saloons in the state of Nevada. Moved to Austin from Virginia City in 1863, it has been quenching man's thirst ever since. The back bar is original, made by Brunswick back East and shipped around Cape Horn, then dragged by wagon over the Sierra Nevada Mountains, and finally across 180 miles of dessert to its home in Austin. The spittoons are gone, and the bar itself has moved to the front of the room, this area, now the back, hosts a billiards table and small dance floor. Fortunately, some things never change, and a drink can be had at the saloon's opening at 6:00 a.m. Still a hot spot on Austin's social scene, many a party starts or ends here at the International. See photographs on pages 12, 23, and 34. (Courtesy of NVHS.)

Four

Family and Friends

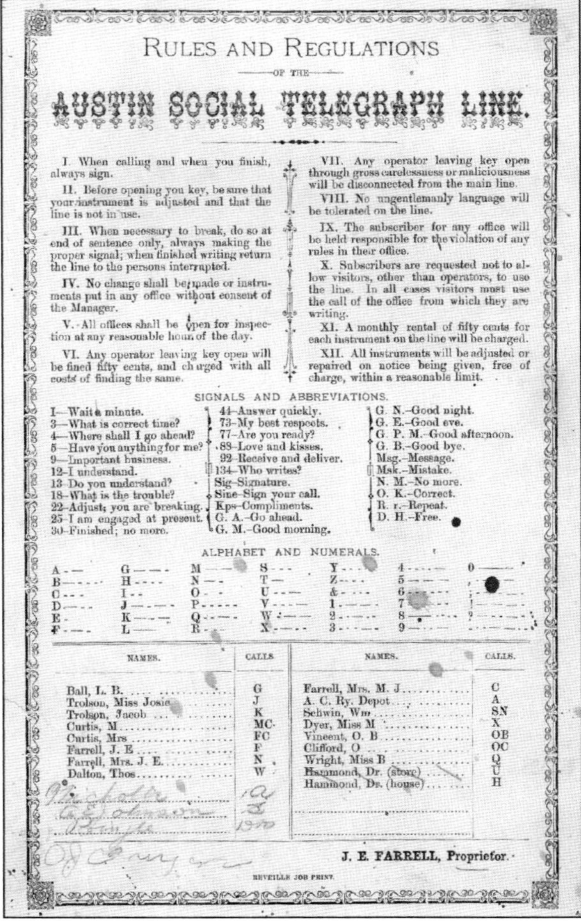

RULES AND REGULATIONS

—OF THE—

AUSTIN SOCIAL TELEGRAPH LINE.

I. When calling and when you finish, always sign.

II. Before opening you key, be sure that your instrument is adjusted and that the line is not in use.

III. When necessary to break, do so at end of sentence only, always making the proper signal; when finished writing return the line to the persons interrupted.

IV. No change shall be made or instruments put in any office without consent of the Manager.

V. All offices shall be open for inspection at any reasonable hour of the day.

VI. Any operator leaving key open will be fined fifty cents, and charged with all costs of finding the same.

VII. Any operator leaving key open through gross carelessness or maliciousness will be disconnected from the main line.

VIII. No ungentlemanly language will be tolerated on the line.

IX. The subscriber for any office will be held responsible for the violation of any rules in their office.

X. Subscribers are requested not to allow visitors, other than operators, to use the line. In all cases visitors must use the call of the office from which they are writing.

XI. A monthly rental of fifty cents for each instrument on the line will be charged.

XII. All instruments will be adjusted or repaired on notice being given, free of charge, within a reasonable limit.

SIGNALS AND ABBREVIATIONS.

1—Wait a minute.
3—What is correct time?
4—Where shall I go ahead?
5—Have you anything for me?
9—Important business.
12–I understand.
13–Do you understand?
18–What is the trouble?
22–Adjust; you are breaking.
25–I am engaged at present.
30–Finished; no more.
44–Answer quickly.
73–My best respects.
77–Are you ready?
88–Love and kisses.
92–Receive and deliver.
134–Who writes?
Sig–Signature.
Sine–Sign your call.
Kps–Compliments.
G. A.–Go ahead.
G. M.–Good morning.
G. N.–Good night.
G. E.–Good eve.
G. P. M.–Good afternoon.
G. B.–Good bye.
Msg.–Message.
Msk.–Mistake.
N. M.–No more.
O. K.–Correct.
R. r.–Repeat.
D. H.–Free.

ALPHABET AND NUMERALS.

A .—	G ——.	M ——	S ...	Y	4 ....—	0 ——
B —...	H	N —.	T —	Z	5 ———	, .—.—
C .. .	I ..	O . .	U ..—	&	6	; ..—..
D —..	J —.—.	P	V ...—	1 .——.	7 ——..	! ———.
E .	K —.—	Q ..—.	W .——	2 ..—..	8 —....	? —..—.
F .—.	L ——	R . ..	X .—..	3 ...—.	9 —..—	..——..

NAMES.	CALLS	NAMES.	CALLS.
Ball, L. B.	G	Farrell, Mrs. M. J	C
Trolson, Miss Josie	J	A. C. Ry. Depot	A
Trolson, Jacob	K	Schwin, Wm	SN
Curtis, M	MC	Dyer, Miss M	X
Curtis, Mrs	FC	Vincent, O. B	OB
Farrell, J. E	F	Clifford, O	OC
Farrell, Mrs. J. E.	N	Wright, Miss B	Q
Dalton, Thos	W	Hammond, Dr. (store)	U
		Hammond, Dr. (house)	H

J. E. FARRELL, Proprietor.

REVEILLE JOB PRINT.

Before e-mail, and before the telephone, there was the telegraph. It was the Internet of the Victorian Age. This call card was for the Austin Social Telegraph, a private subscription messaging system wired for the town of Austin only. Like today's texting, there were abbreviations to reduce time wasted pounding out dots and dits. Each user had a unique designator. "MC" was for Mr. Allen Curtis, manager of the Manhattan Silver Mine and partner in the Bank of Austin. "F" was for Mr. Farrell, who was also connected with the Manhattan Silver Mine and later senator to the state legislature. Crude by today's standards of communication, it was effective nonetheless. (Courtesy of NVHS.)

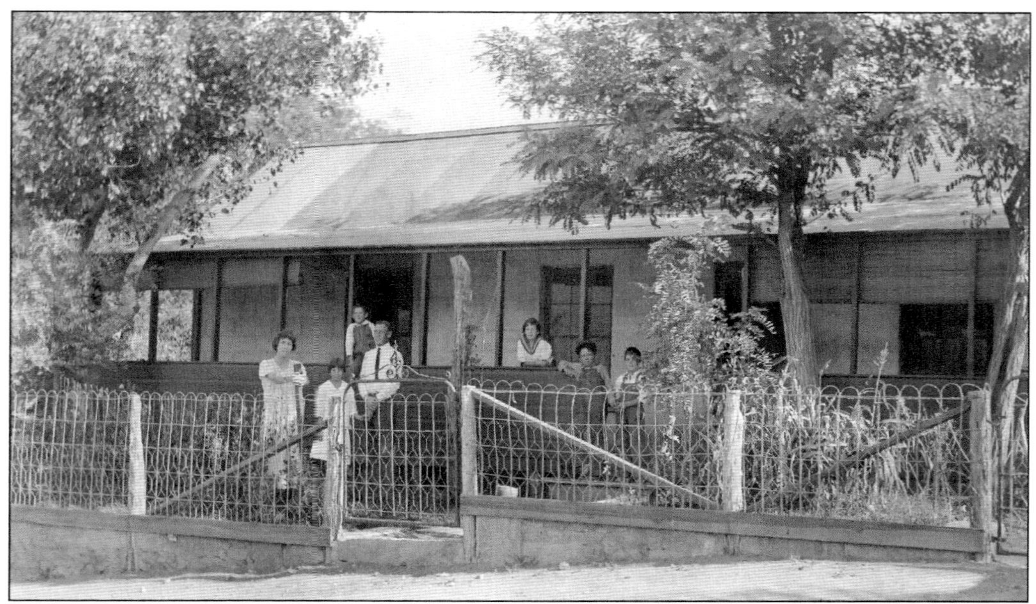

The Acree family lived on Court Street when this photograph was taken. Bert Acree was married to Millie Byer, and they had four children; Bert was also county recorder for many years (see page 42). Those pictured are, from left to right, Millie, Adele, Dale, Bert, Rene, Clayton Byer, and Tom. (Courtesy of CC.)

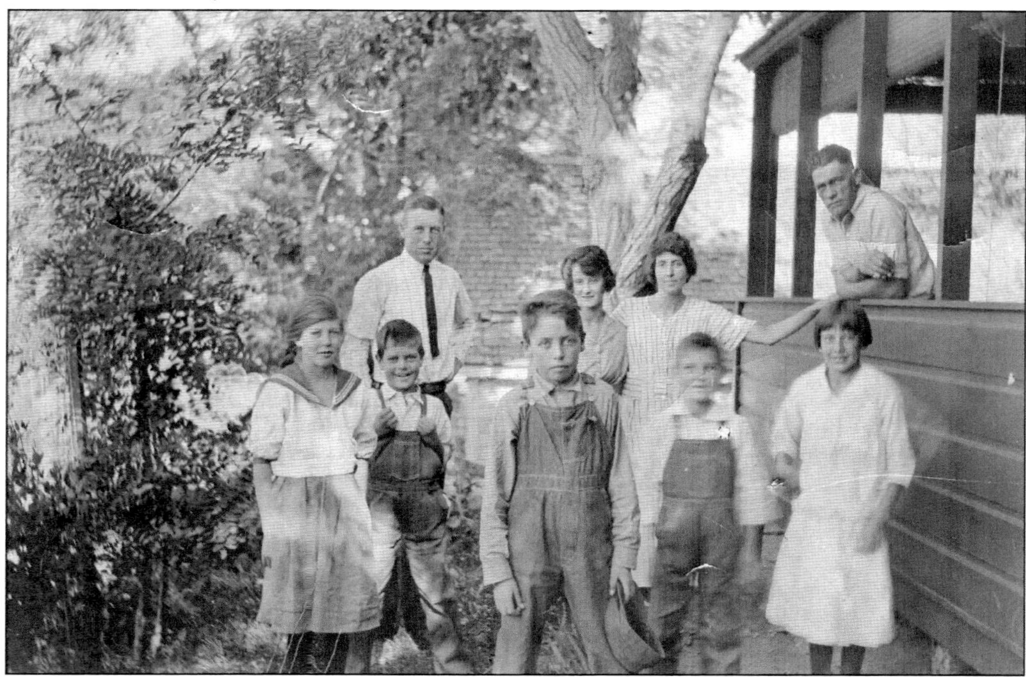

Millie Acree's mother Elizabeth Jones was credited with bringing the "yellow rose of Austin" to the area. It proved very hardy, flourished, and spread. It can be seen to the left in this photograph, and today it is found all over town. Those pictured are, from left to right, (second row) Bert, Thelma Godfrey, Millie, and Clayton Byer; (first row) Rene, Jack Collins, Tom, Dale, and Adele. (Courtesy of CC.)

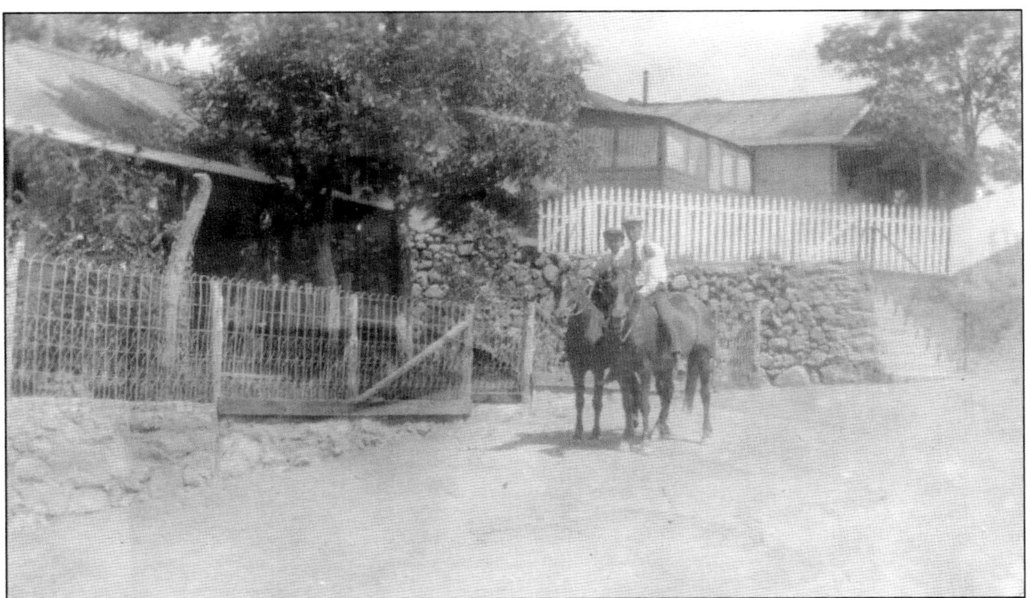

Here is the Acree house on Court Street. Unfortunately, the house is no more; however, the rock retaining wall still stands. The Acrees moved to Sixth Street at Overland in 1926, giving this house to their daughter Rene in that same year. She married Stan Maestretti. (Courtesy of CC.)

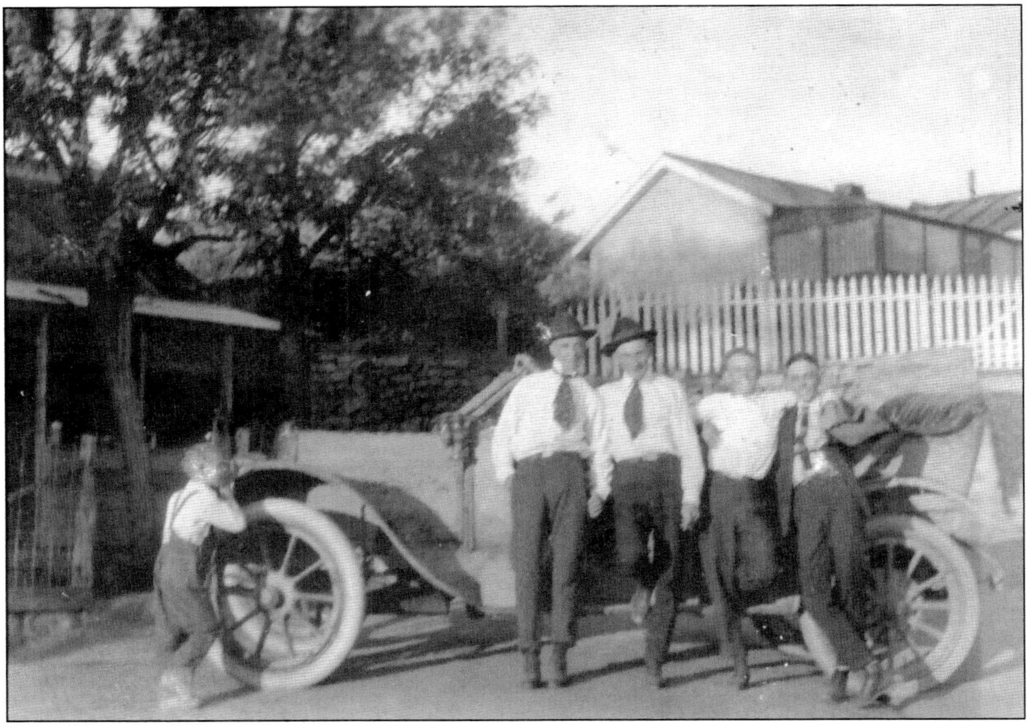

This photograph was taken in front of the Acree house on Court Street. The styling of the car is around 1914, and the two boys standing together are Dale and Tom Acree. (Courtesy of CC.)

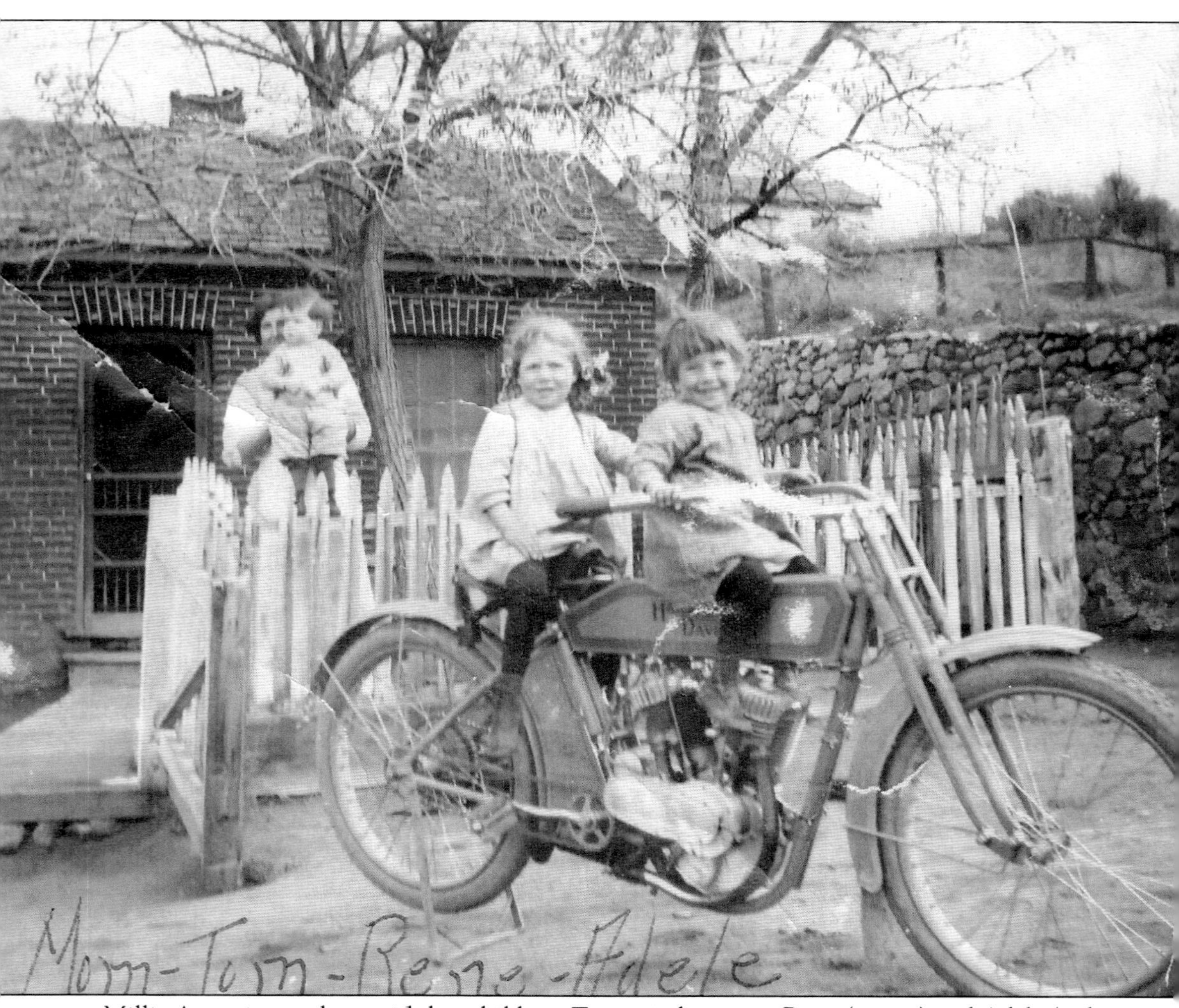

Millie Acree is seen here with her children. Tom is in her arms; Rene (center) and Adele (right, holding the handlebars) are sitting on the motorcycle. This is a very early Harley Davidson. In 1910, the company started building its bikes with the signature twin cylinder V that the company is known for today. Originally one cylinder, the company effectively doubled the horsepower with this new engine. This model is no later than 1916 and was reported to go as fast as 60 miles per hour! (Courtesy of CC.)

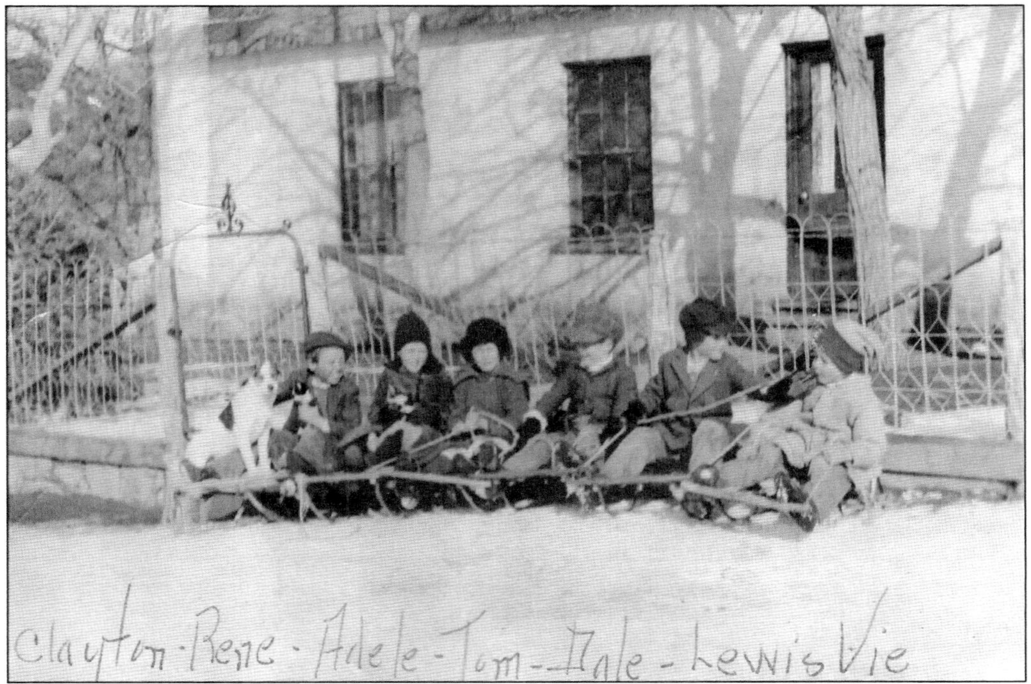

Austin kids are shown on sleds. Those pictured are, from left to right, Clayton Byer, Rene, Adele, Tom, Dale Acree, and Lewis Vie. They are sitting in front of the Easton house on North Street. The house still stands today (see page 84). (Courtesy of CC.)

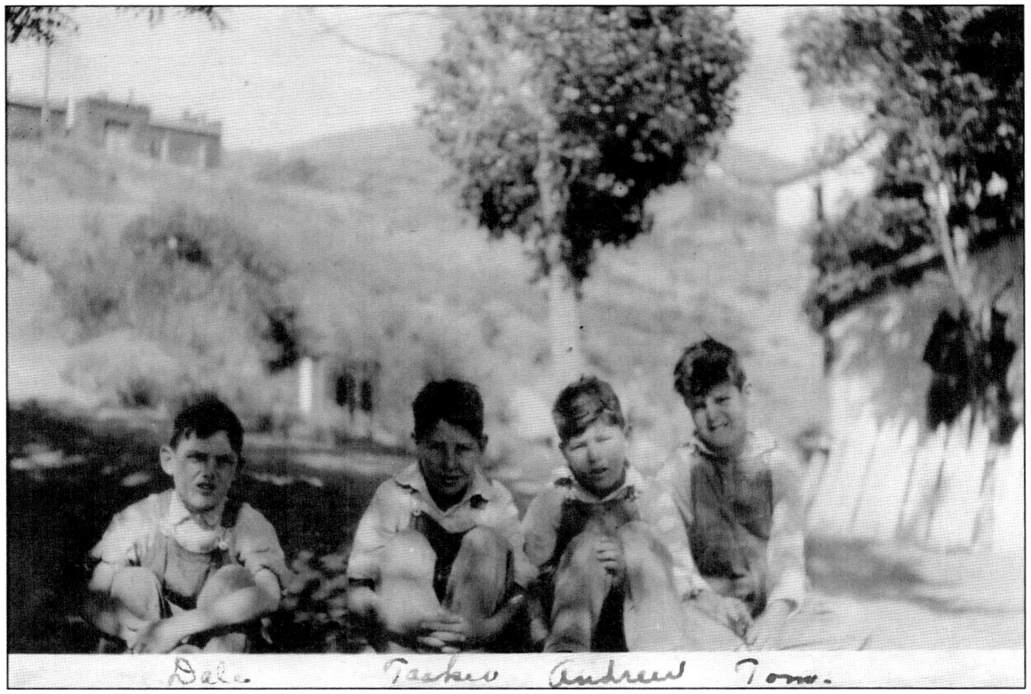

Dale and Tom Acree are on either end of this photograph; the middle two boys are Tasker and Andrew, last names unidentified. The old 1880s Austin School is located up the hill and to the left (see page 59). (Courtesy of CC.)

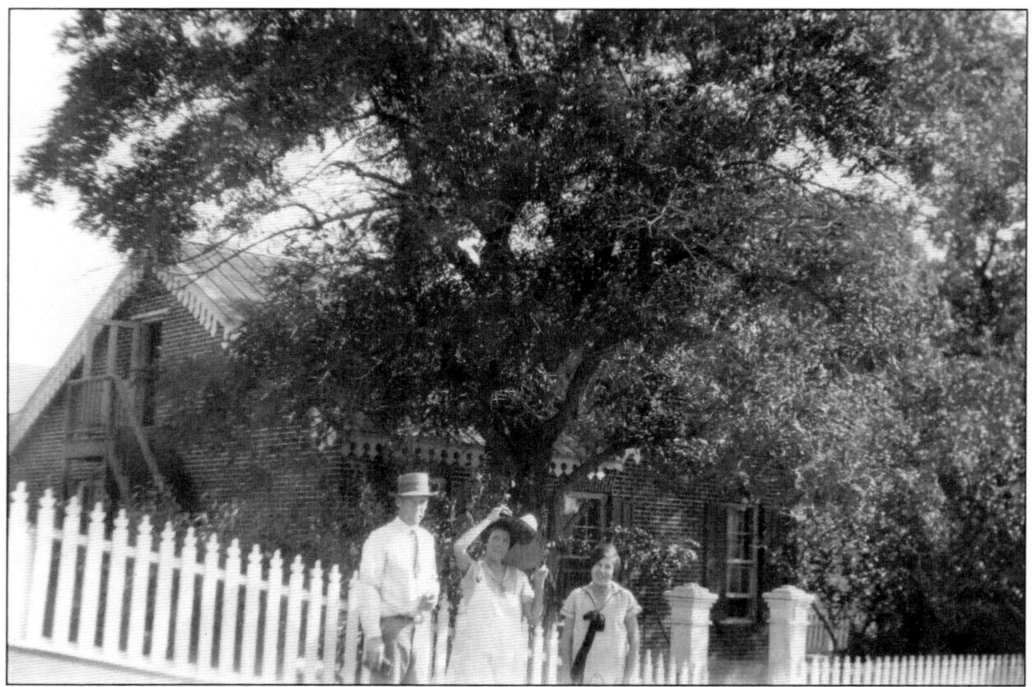

Bert, Millie, and their daughter Rene are in front of their house at the corner of Sixth and Overland Streets. This was an early Austin house with extensive Gothic Revival trim. The house, still know today as the "Acree" house, stands looking much as it did over 140 years ago. (Courtesy of CC.)

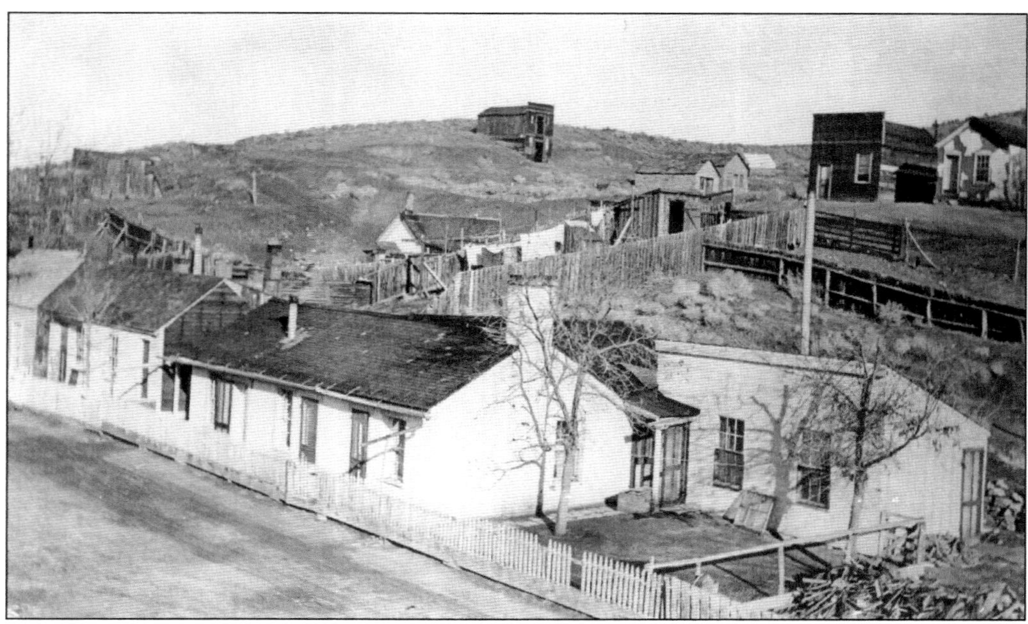

This old house on North Street still stands; at one time, Neil and Elsie Easton lived here. Its thick walls are indicative of the adobe construction. The Eastons owned the International Hotel for many years. China Ridge is located behind the house. (Courtesy of NVHS.)

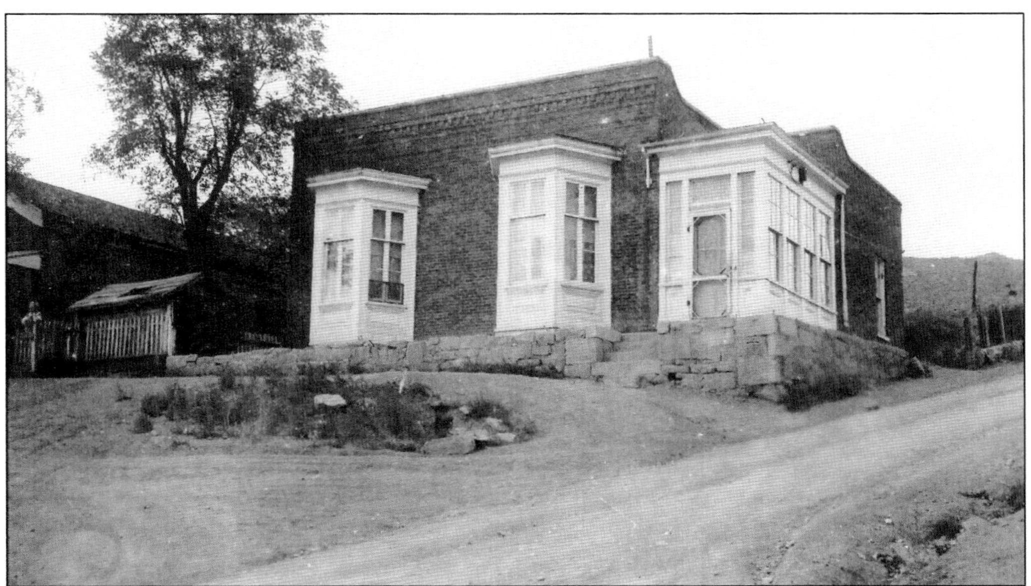

Today, this house, a private residence on Union at Virginia Streets, stands above St. Augustine on Virginia Hill. In the past, it was used to board teachers and miners in the 1950s. (Courtesy of SC.)

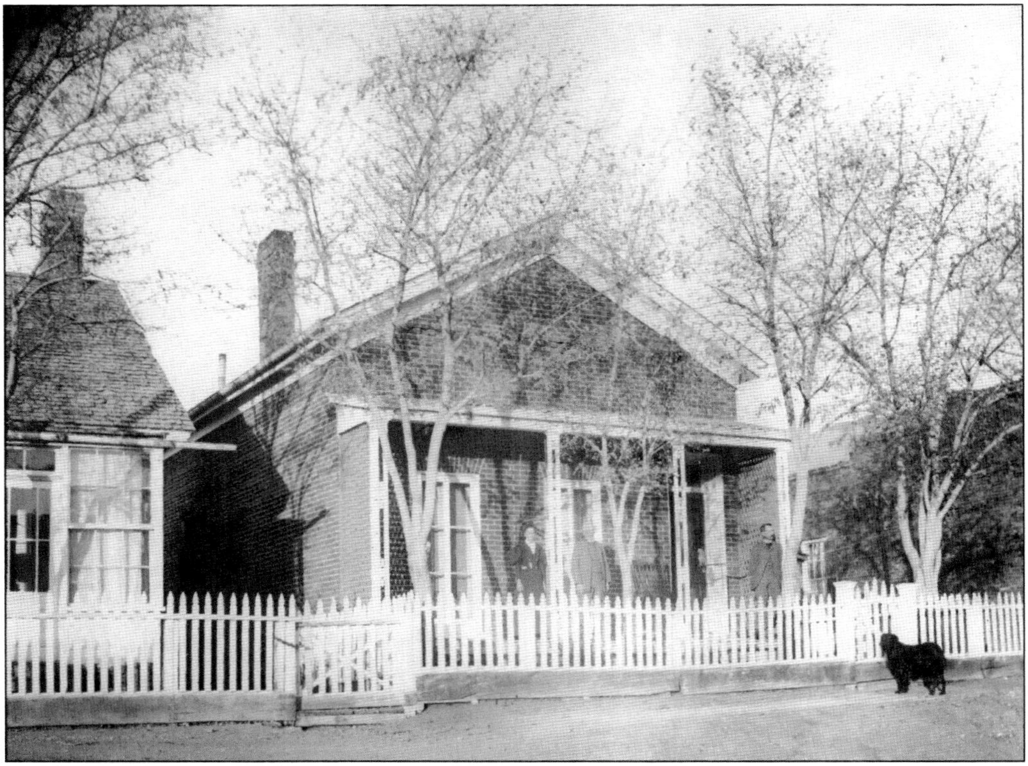

This fine old Austin house belonged to Allen Curtis. It is still in use with many of the original features, including sliding doors and decorative stencils on the walls. Curtis was the superintendent and manager of the Manhattan Silver Mine and had banking and other interests in town. The brick outhouse in back is still functional. (Courtesy of AHS.)

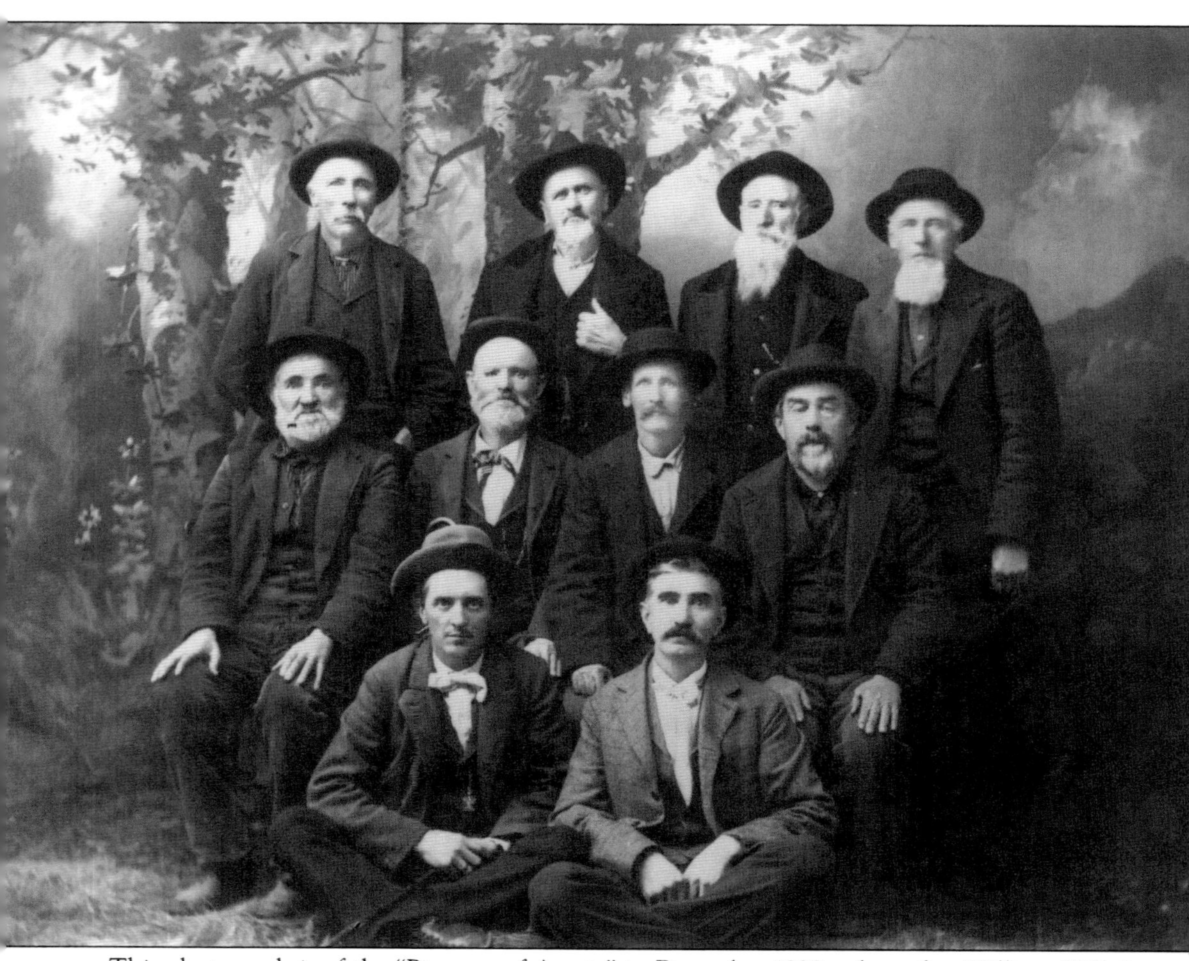

This photograph is of the "Pioneers of Austin" in December 1898, taken after William "Billy" Joans was elected attorney general. Those shown are, from left to right, (third row) Ed Rocht, George W. Dale, John Bicknell, and Hank Ensign; (second row) Edwin Crane, Jim Moss, Jason N. Baker, and William "Billy" Joans; (first row) Johnny Thompson and Davy Todd. Many of these old names lay cold in the graveyard below Austin. (Courtesy of NVHS.)

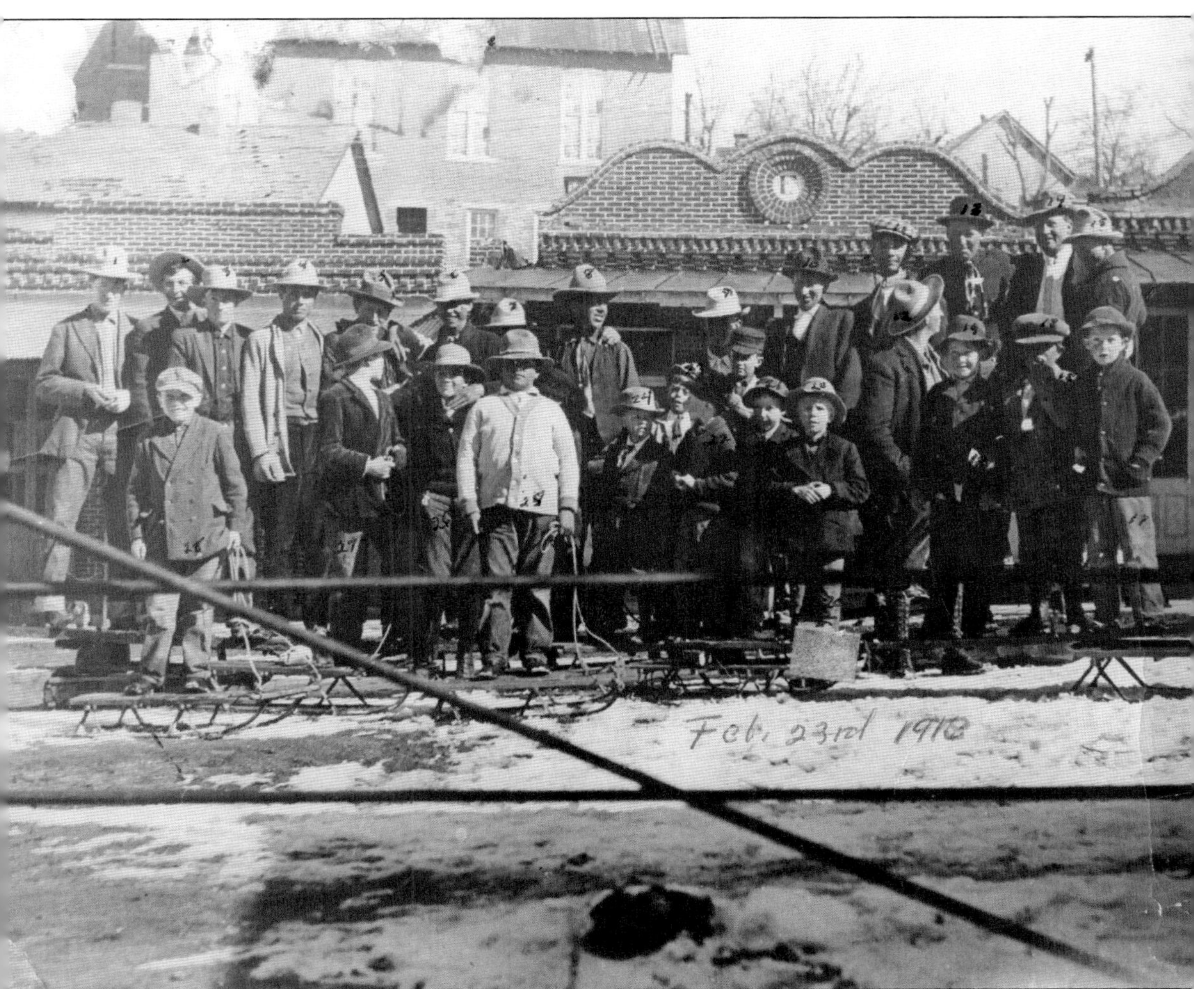

On February 23, 1913, members of the Austin Sled team gathered for this portrait along Main Street. The owners of an 18-man bobsled used to come down Austin Summit, and isurprisingly, the bobsled could hold more than half the team. Those pictured are (1) Joe Dory, (2) F. Bernd, (3) Hanson Streshley, (4) Walter Schmidtlien, (5) August Streshley, (6) L. Schmidtlien, (7) Ed Vigus, (8) Jo Borrego, (9) P. Dory, (10) unidentified, (11) W. Stiener, (12) Abe Sower, (13) Doc Callahan, (14) W.W. Streshley, (15) Frank Schmidtlien, (16) J. Rast, (17) W. Rast, (18) C. Byer, (19) C. Easton, (20) George Cooke, (21) W. Laird, (22) J. Miller, (23) unidentified, (24) W. Pieffer, (25) B. Spencer, (26) G. Laurent, (27) Chester Eason, and (28) Jiggs Malloy. (Courtesy of JBC.)

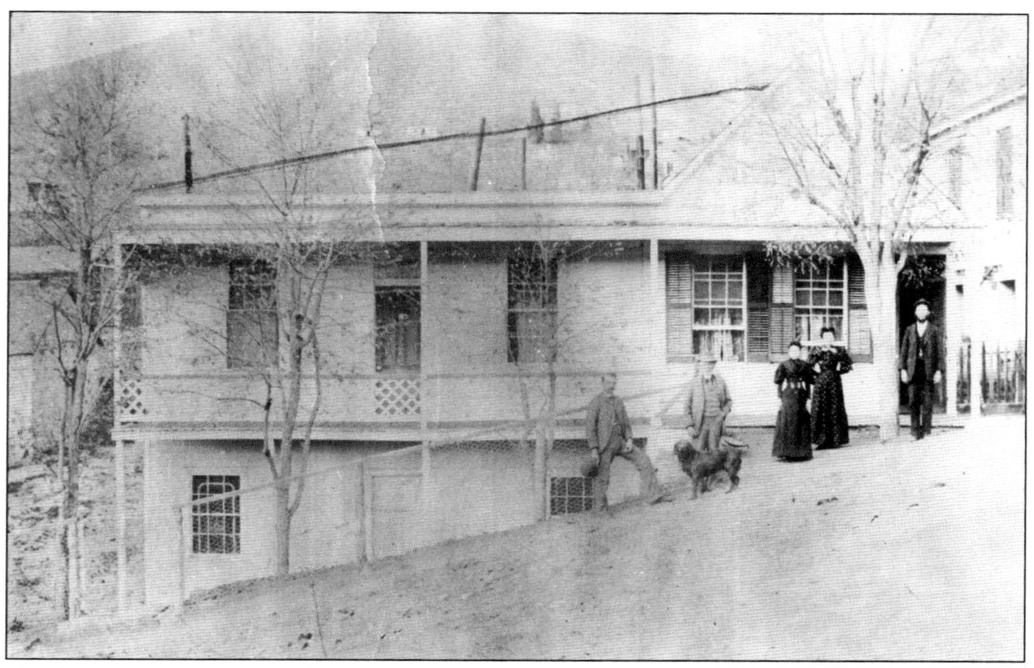

This house at the corner of Cedar and Union Streets is a private residence and serves as bed and breakfast today. Those pictured in this1880s are, from left to right, Oscar Clifford, Sam Cresenzo, Lucy Cresenzo, and two unidentified people. (Courtesy of NVHS.)

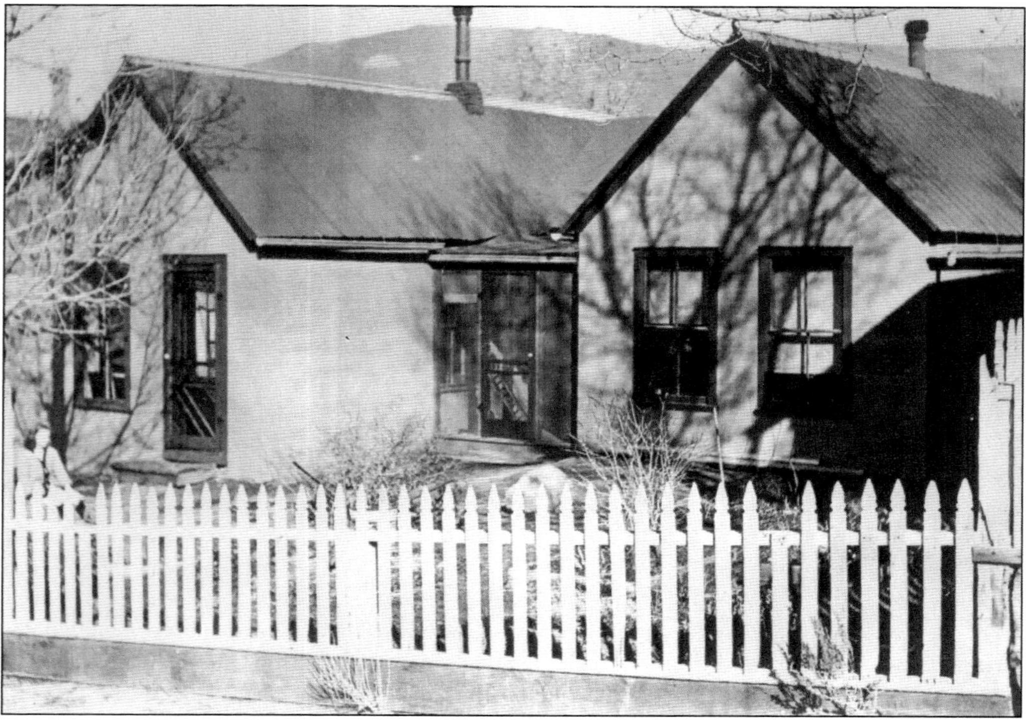

This Water Street residence was known in the 1890s as the McIntire house. It stands today as a private home. Delia was a local artist. Several of her paintings grace Austin's residences today. Sam worked the mines (see page 50). (Courtesy of NVHS.)

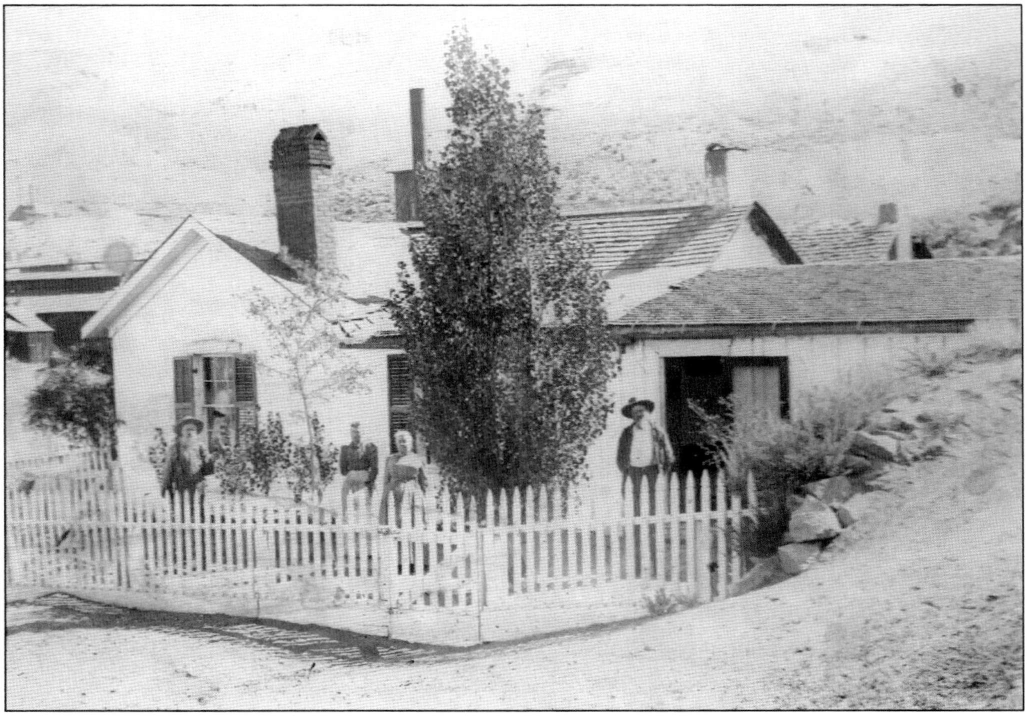

The Nevada National Bank owned this house on Court Street for years, and the local bank president lived here. Today, it is a private residence. (Courtesy of JBC.)

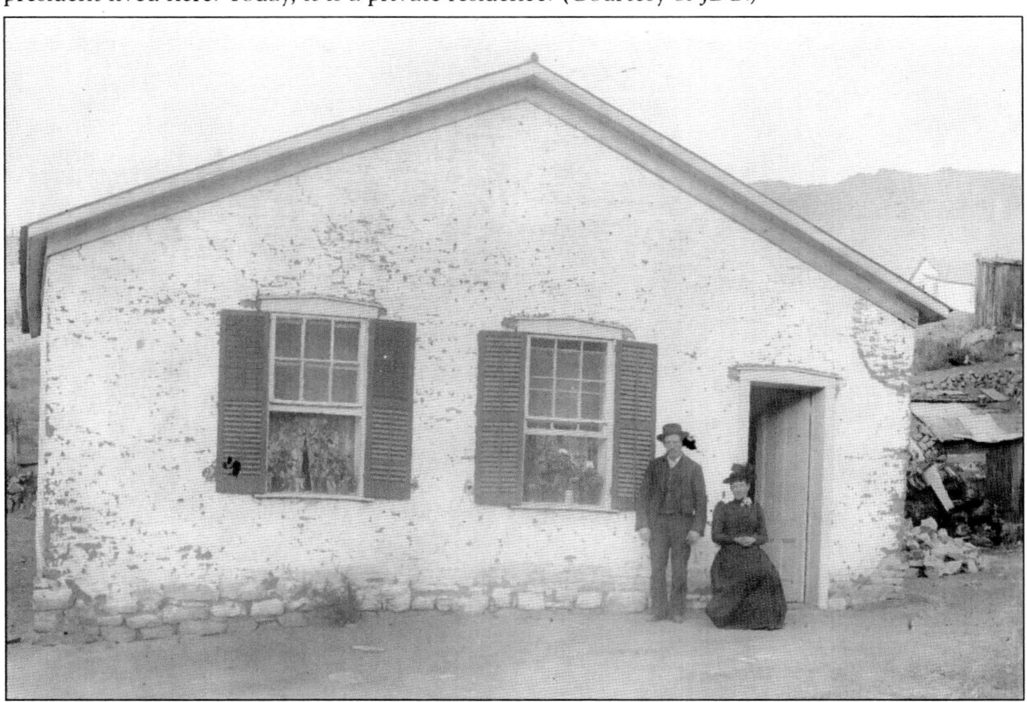

Located on Main Street, this very old house was constructed with adobe brick. In this photograph from 1896, Jim and Bell Roberts stand in front of it, which was their home for many years. Today, the house is used as a bed and breakfast. (Courtesy of SC.)

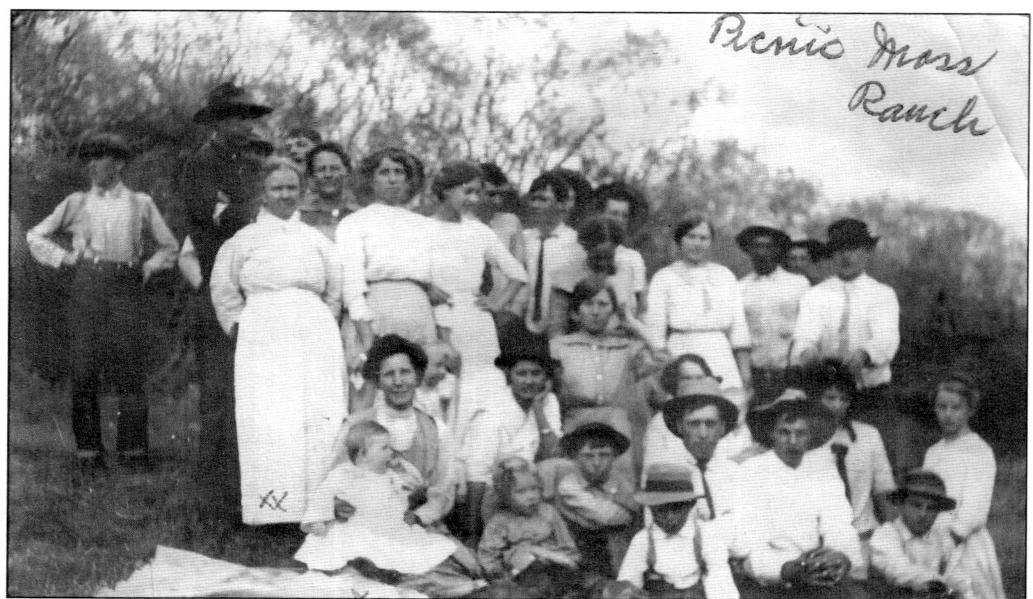

The Moss family homesteaded a ranch just to the east, over Austin Summit. This photograph was taken at a Moss and Roberts's family picnic around 1905. (Courtesy of SC.)

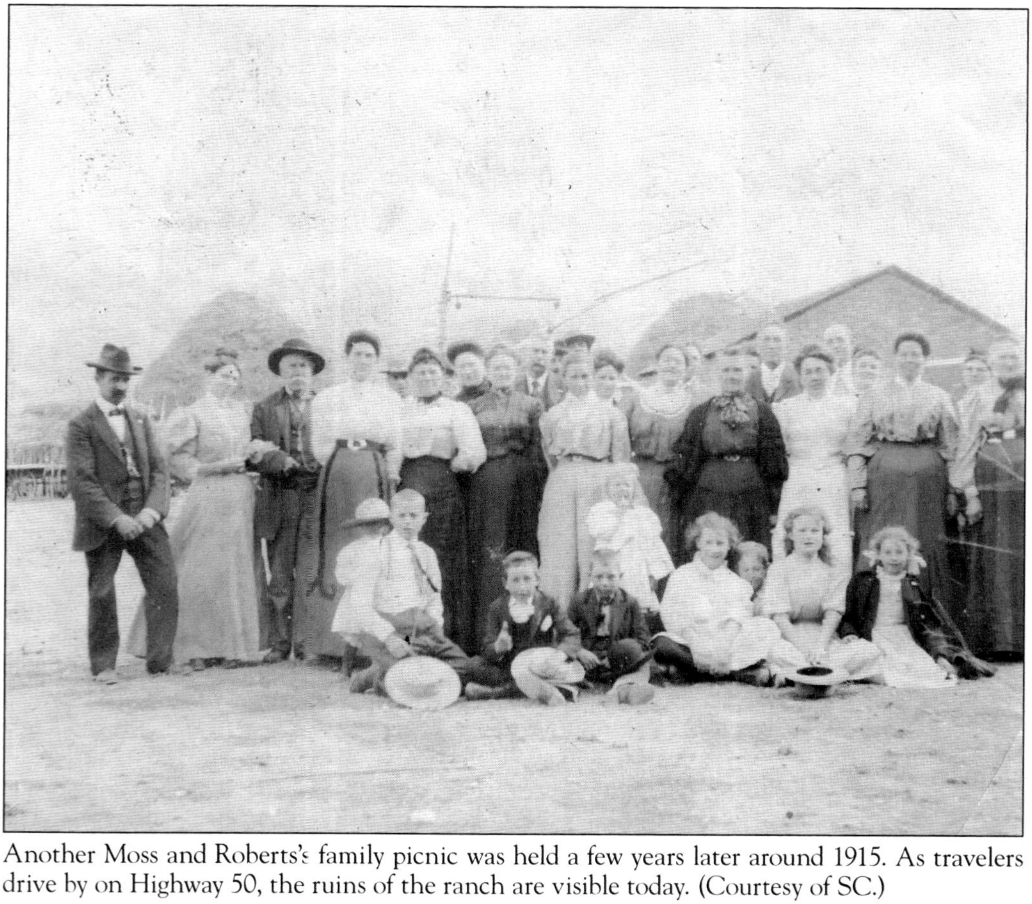

Another Moss and Roberts's family picnic was held a few years later around 1915. As travelers drive by on Highway 50, the ruins of the ranch are visible today. (Courtesy of SC.)

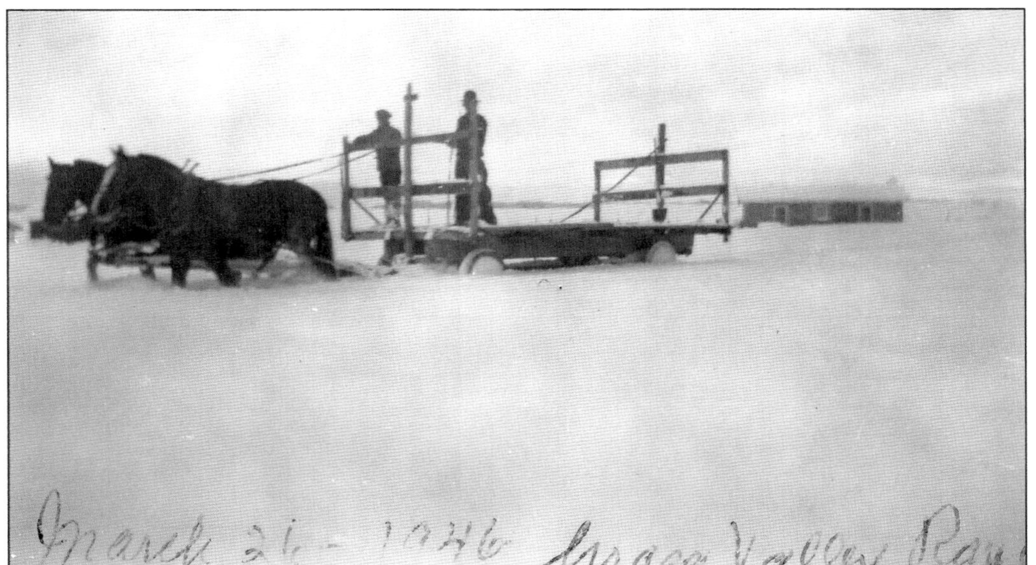

On March 26, 1946, Will Roberts is at the reins of this hay wagon at the Grass Valley Ranch, a few miles north east of Austin. At the time of this image, the owner was Dick Magee, then Knudtsen, then Inchauspe, then Lancaster. These were all family operations, and the ranch is still in business today. (Courtesy of SC.)

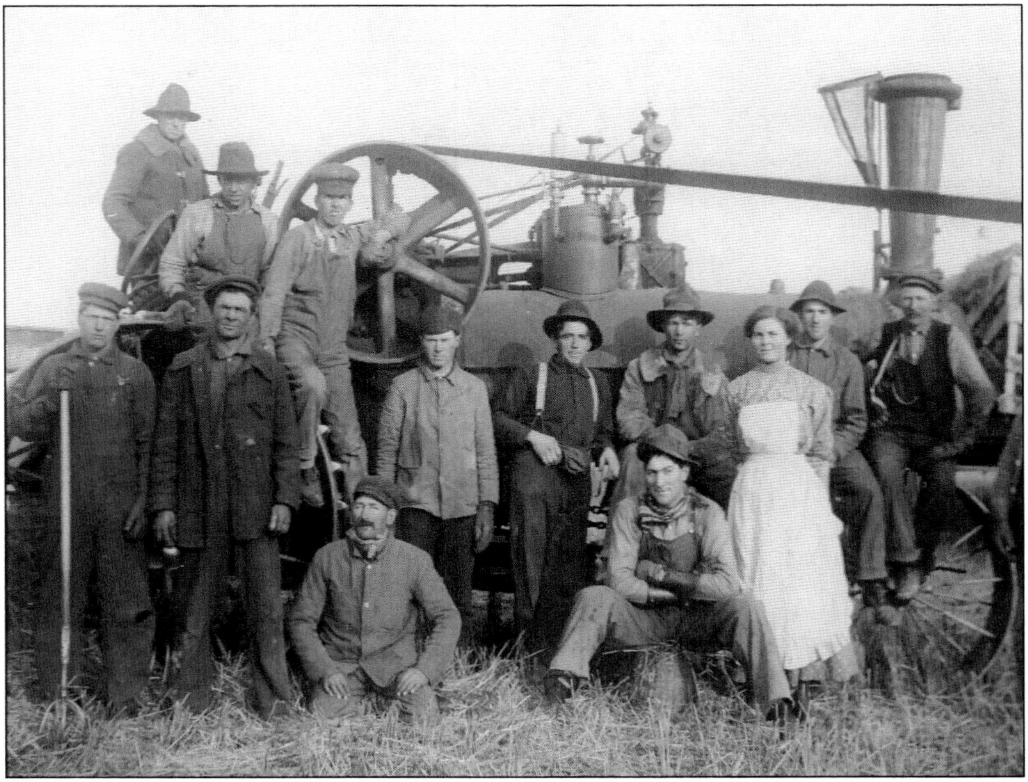

The Hess ranch was located in the Reese River Valley to the west of Austin. This steam thresher dates from around the turn of the century. Dry farming for grain was tried, in addition to raising livestock, but was never very successful. (Courtesy of JBC.)

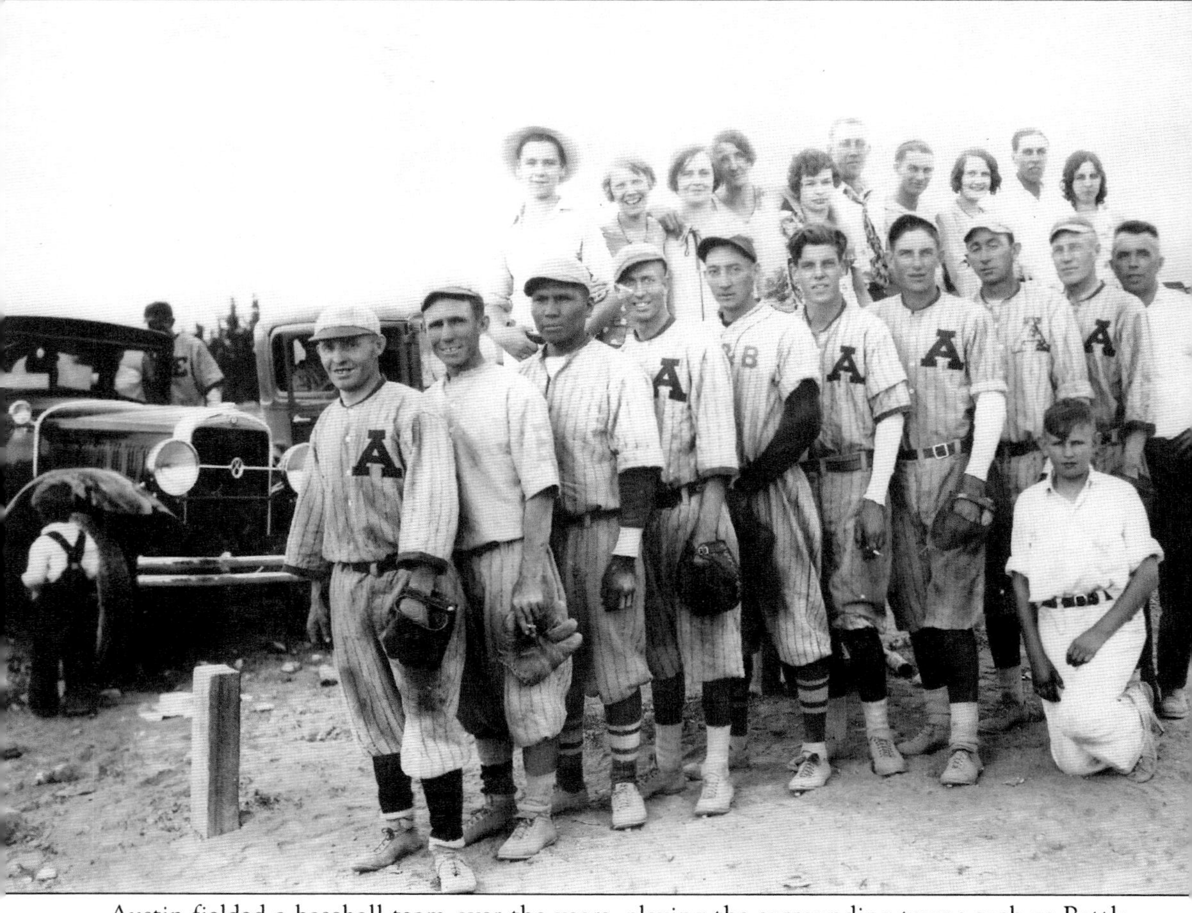

Austin fielded a baseball team over the years, playing the surrounding towns such as Battle Mountain, Eureka, Manhattan, and Tonopah. This team photograph is from 1930. Austin also occasionally had a women's ball club; some of the woman in back were part of that team. Those pictured are, from left to right, (second row) A. Berasture, unidentified, Orel Gurr, unidentified, Powning, Ellen Powell, Millie Acree, Lousia Dron, Loreana Dron, and Billie Ring. Only the first seven people from the right are identified as follows: Bob Hogan, Bert Acree, Dale Acree, Tom Acree, Julian Glock, Howard Brown, and Kenneth Easton. The car to the left is a new 1930 La Salle. (Courtesy of SC.)

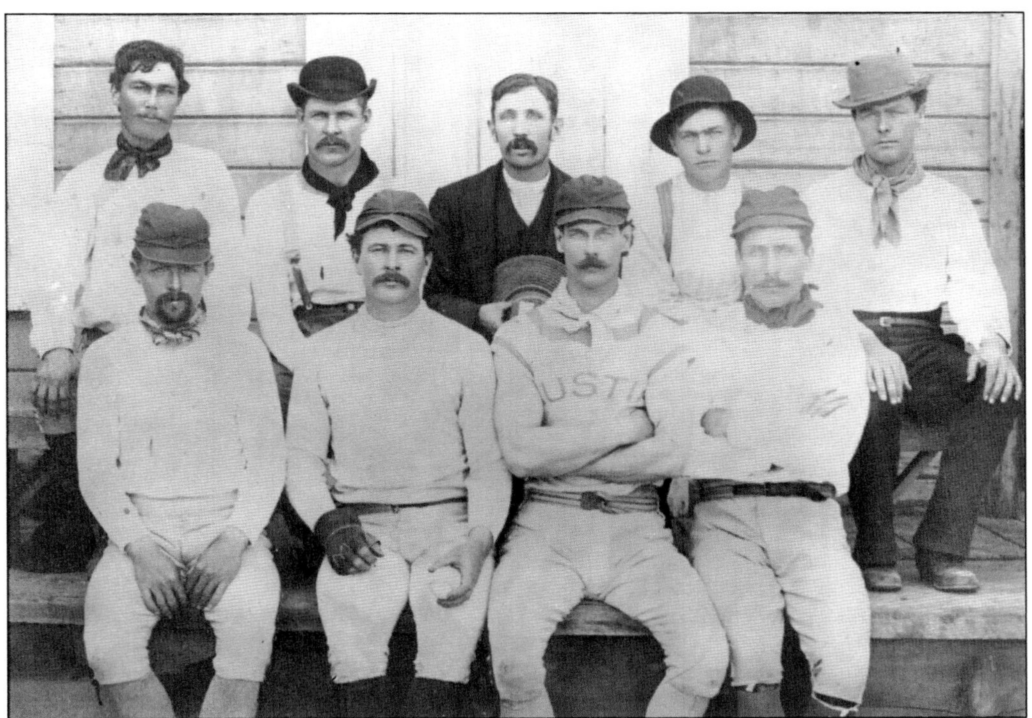

William Easton in the dark suit is the team captain in this 1890s photograph of Austin's ball club. William Easton's father owned the International Hotel. (Courtesy of NVHS.)

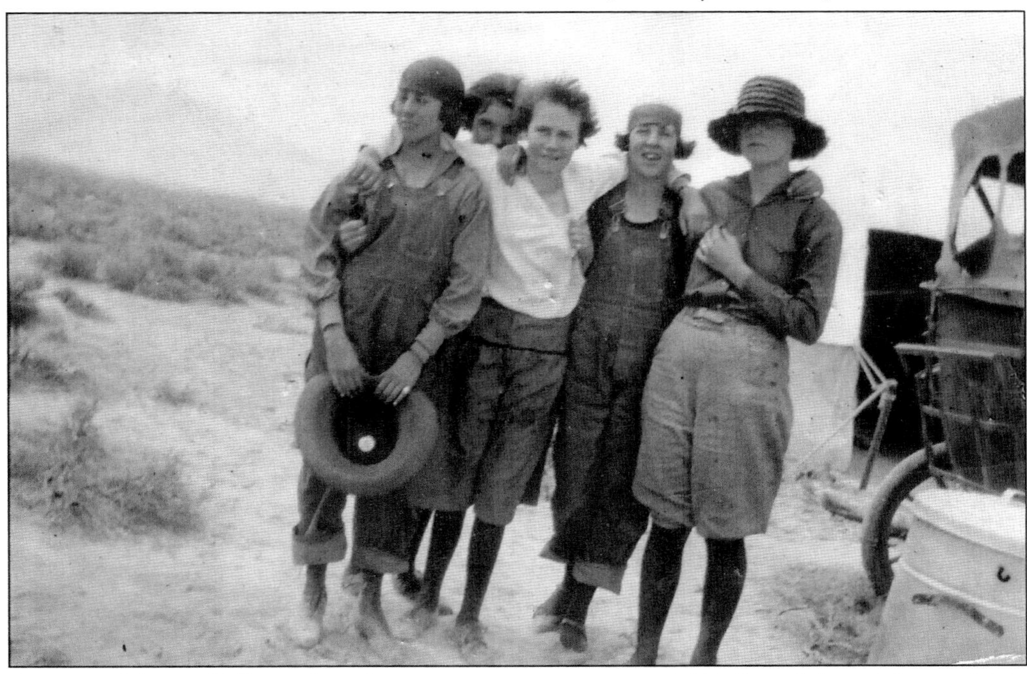

A group of Austin Belles gathers for an impromptu portrait in 1924. From left to right are Adele Acree, Rene Acree, Mary Malloy, Orel Gurr, Dolly Crowell, and Ruth Crowell. Ruth Crowell's mother, Clara, was from Lander County and Nevada's first woman sheriff, being appointed in 1919. (Courtesy of CC.)

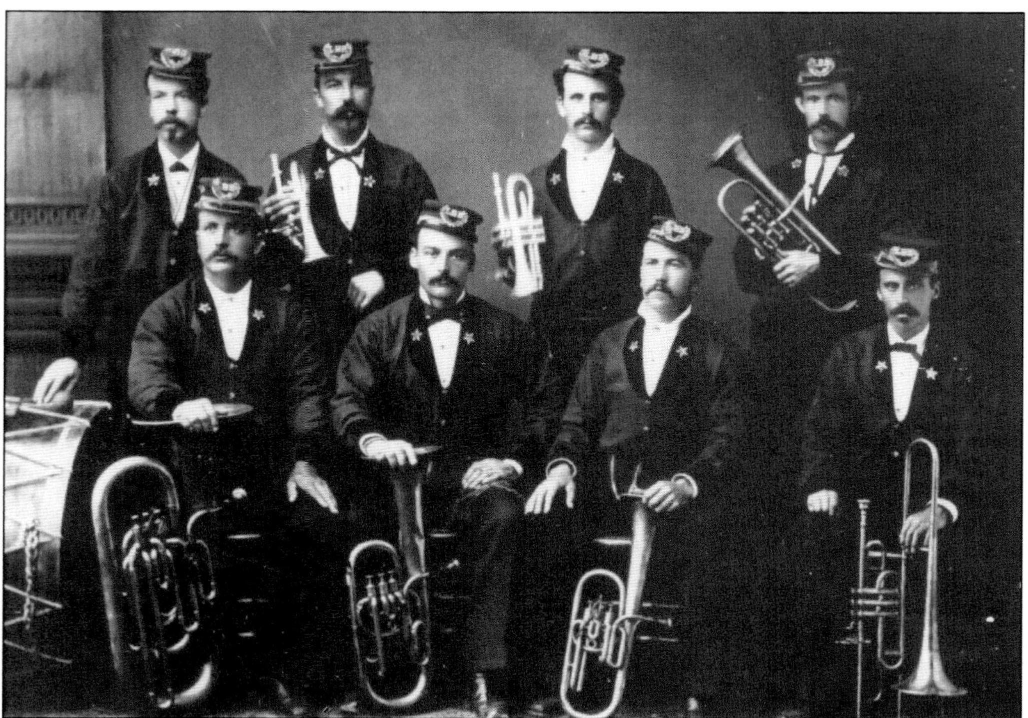

Here is Austin's brass band from the 1890s; they played at local picnics, parades, and other civic functions. (Courtesy of NVHS.)

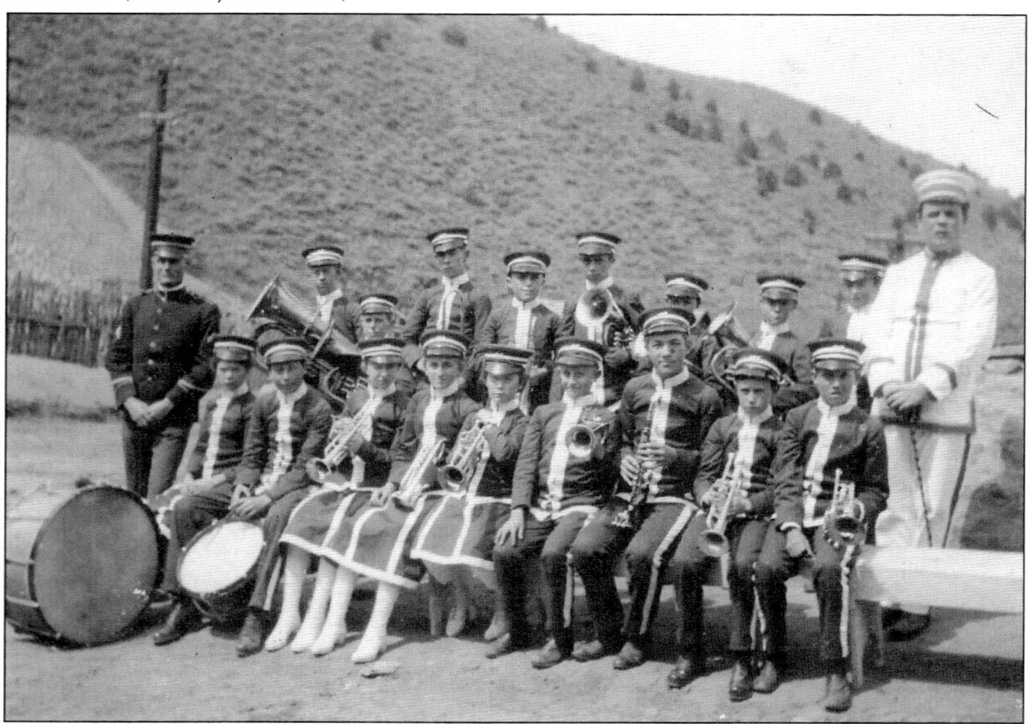

Austin's high school band is playing at the ball field, located below the town in Clifton, in the 1930s. Today, it is the sight of the rodeo grounds. (Courtesy of JBC.)

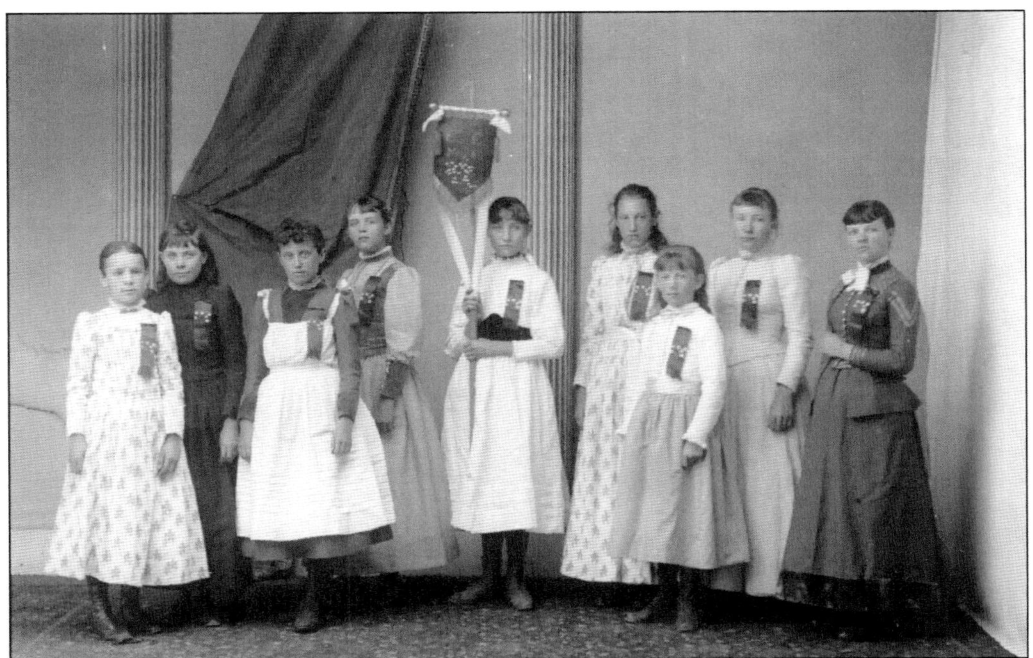

The Charity Club was a young women's organization of the Daughters of Rebekah, the women's auxiliary of the Independent Order of Odd fellows. From left to right are Lousie Pohl, Marjorie Williamson, Luella White, Clara Weller, Bessie Reed, Emma Pohl, Mary Falvey, and Emma Wallace. (Courtesy of SC.)

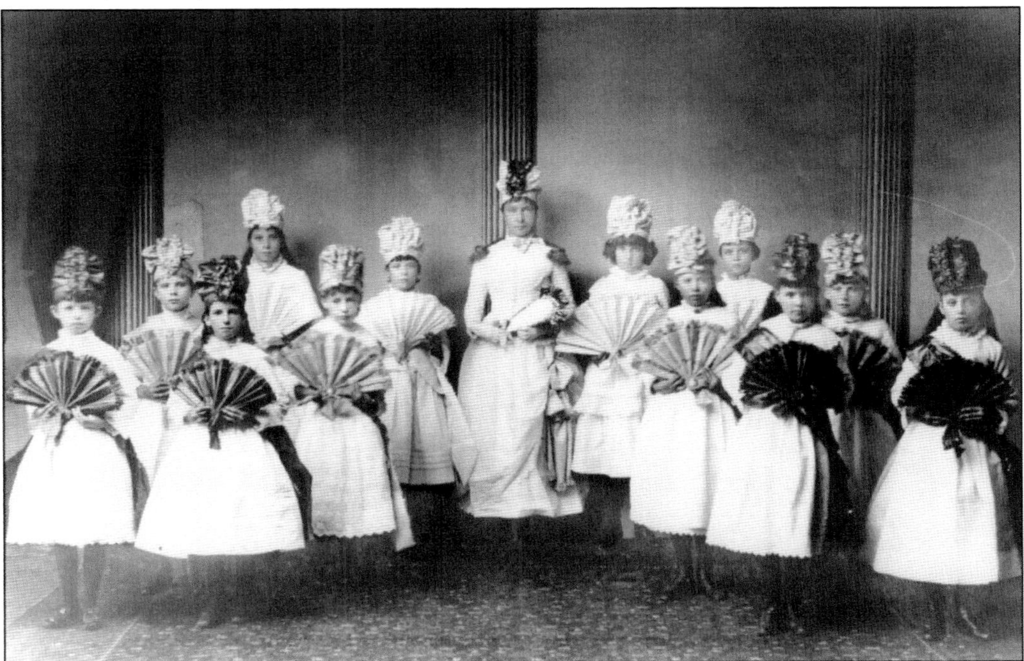

These girls are dressed for a pageant. These two photographs appear to have been taken in the Masonic hall around 1890. From left to right are Tesse Huber, Maude Wallace, Vi Roberts, Lottie Shively, Marry McIntire, Addie Jones, Virginia Smith, Constance Trollson, Anne Pearce, Clara Weller, Mattie Morris, Flora Trevthan, and Luella White. (Courtesy of NVHS.)

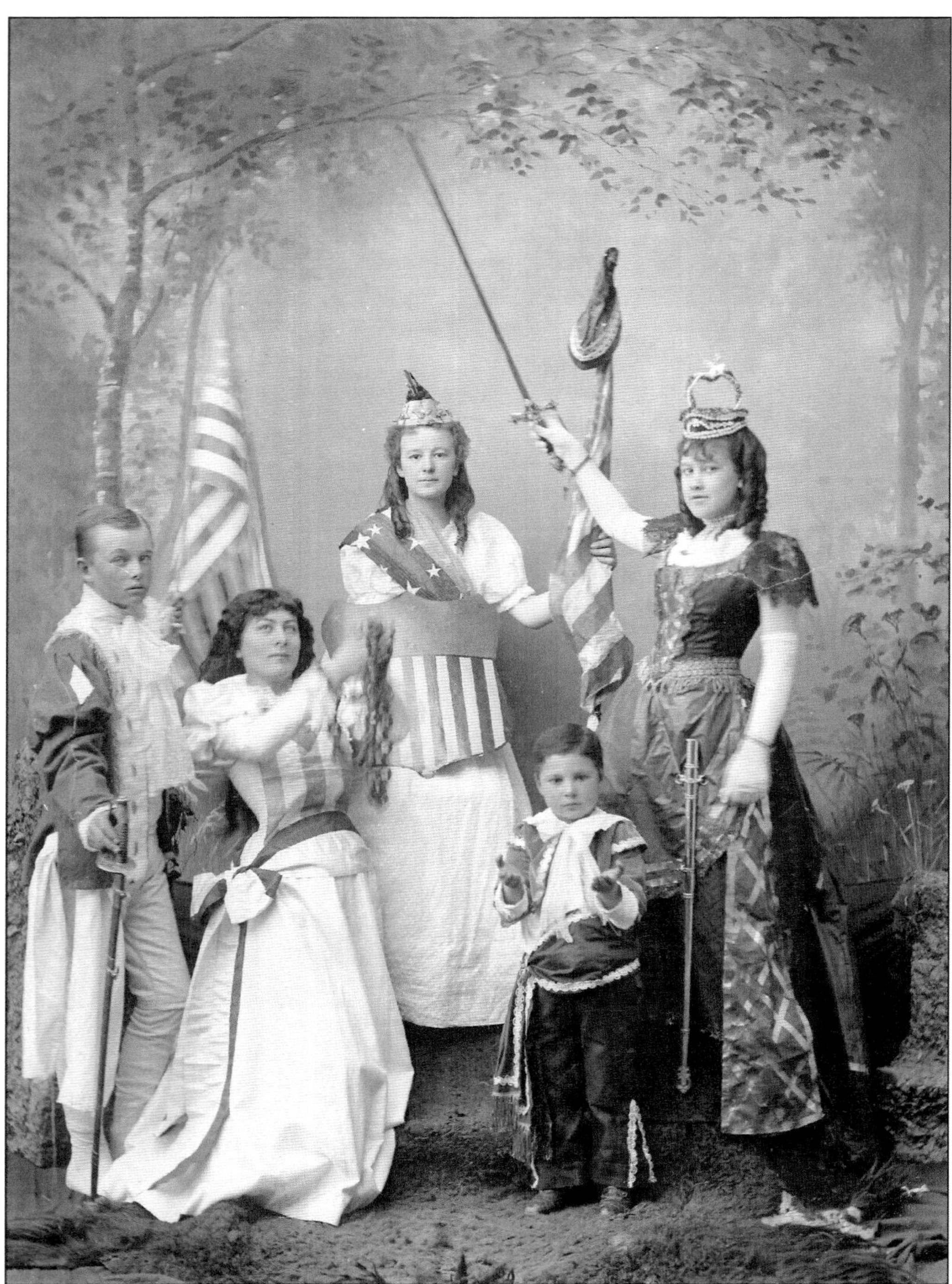

This unusual 1890s portrait of the Meyer family appears to have some connection to America's victory in the Spanish-American War. The chains the women are lifting up represent freedom for Cuba and the Philippines. The Meyers owned the Black Bird Ranch, 11 miles east of Austin. Henry Meyers was a teamster, often hauling the large freight wagons out of Austin and Fallon. A few old buildings of the ranch can be seen when driving by on Highway 50 today. (Courtesy of JBC.)

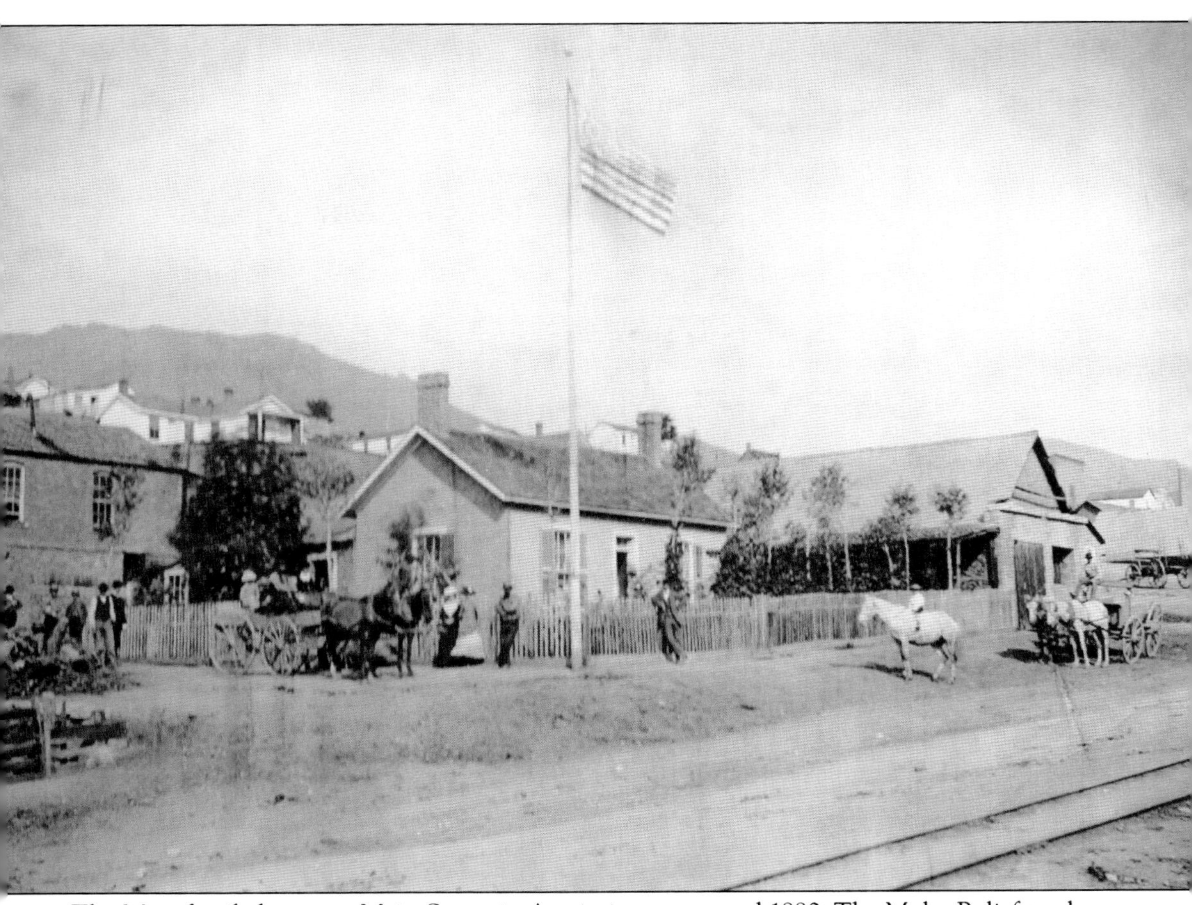

The Moss family home on Main Street in Austin is seen around 1880. The Mules Relief tracks are to the lower right. The Moss family was one of the first to settle in Austin, arriving in 1863 from Salt Lake. As the family grew, the older children lived in the house shown to the left in this photograph. To the right of the house was a blacksmith shop with stables. Joe Trevorthal and Lizzie Moss are seen standing in the door and are looking onto Eddie (driver), Louisa, and Belle Moss sitting in the wagon on the left. Ed, Emma, and Harriet Moss are standing along the fence on the left-hand side of the flagpole; Joe Moss II is standing by the fence to the right of the flagpole. John Moss III is seen second to the right, sitting on a horse, and Ralph Moss is riding in other wagon to the far right. Today, the Moss house still stands, and the blacksmith shop has been converted into a small house owned by Moss descendants. (Courtesy of SC.)

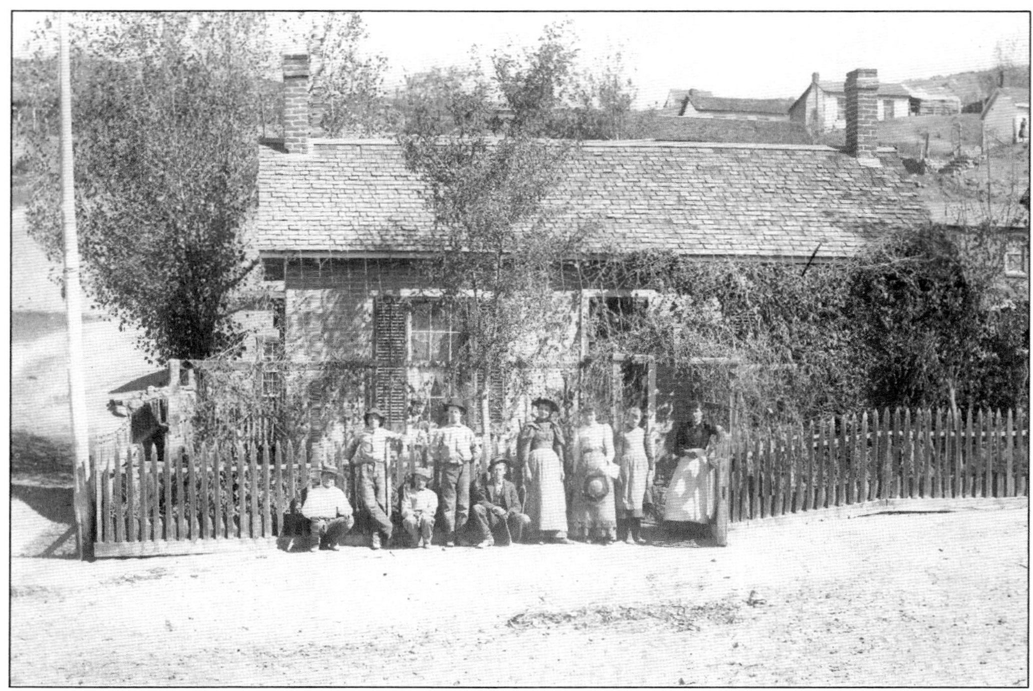

As seen in the page before, the Moss family home has the same flagpole at the corner. A log love seat lies just to the left of the building and was used by courting couples. At least 11 marriage proposals are accredited to its fame. The house and log still line Main Street today. (Courtesy of JBC.)

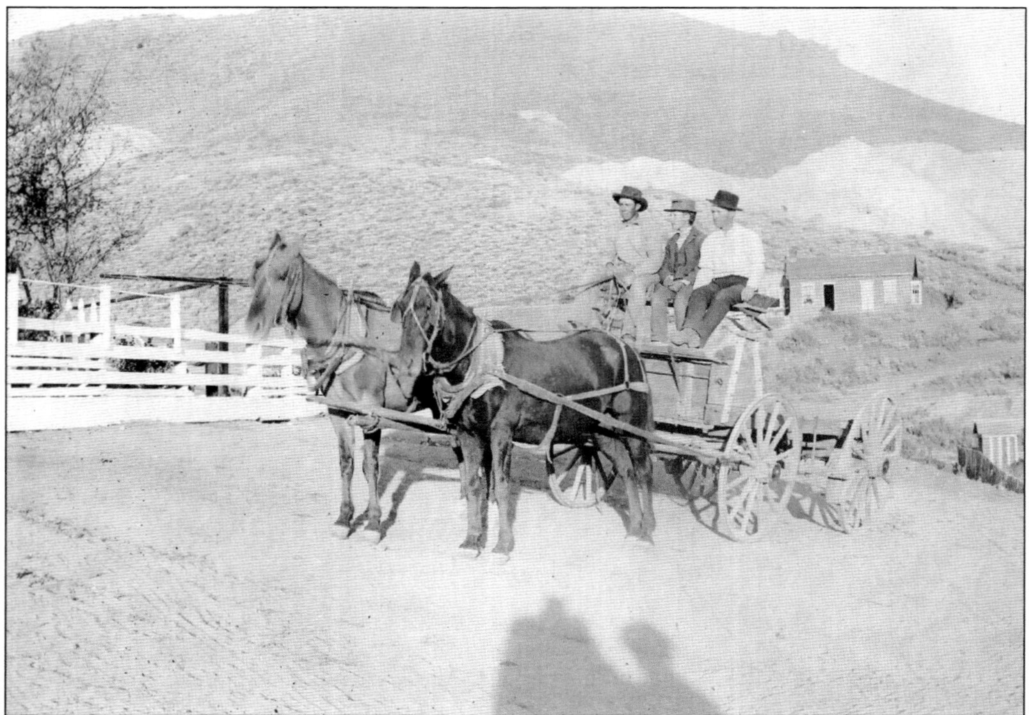

Ralph Moss is driving, and Harry Moss is sitting in the center. Austin mine tailings are seen in the background, and the photographer's shadow is in the foreground. (Courtesy of SC.)

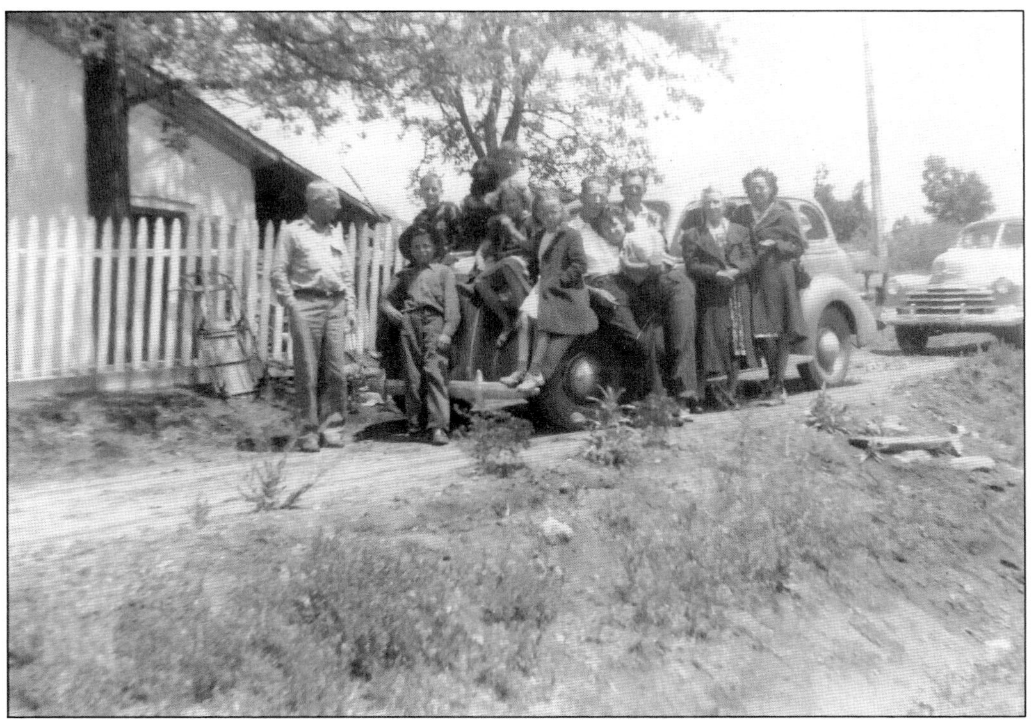

Belle Moss married Jim Roberts. The family has gathered for a quick portrait. A 1946 Chevrolet is in the background. (For a clearer view of the house, see page 89.) (Courtesy of SC.)

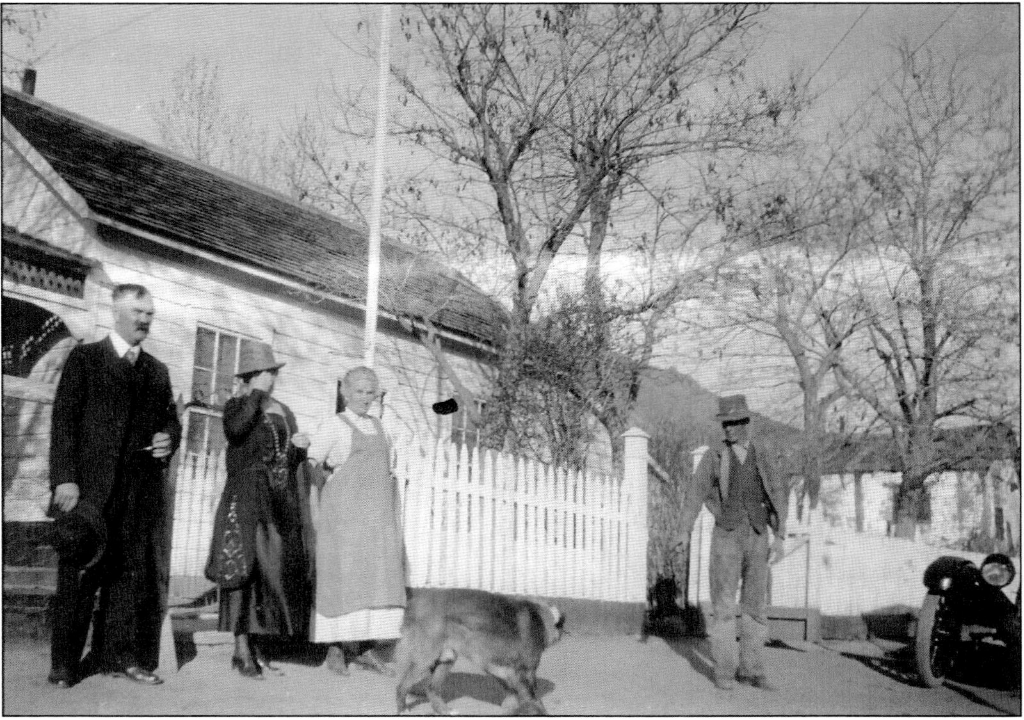

The man in the black suit is George Thorpe, standing in front of his house. For many years, he was the town's undertaker. The car is a 1920 Overland. (Courtesy of SC.)

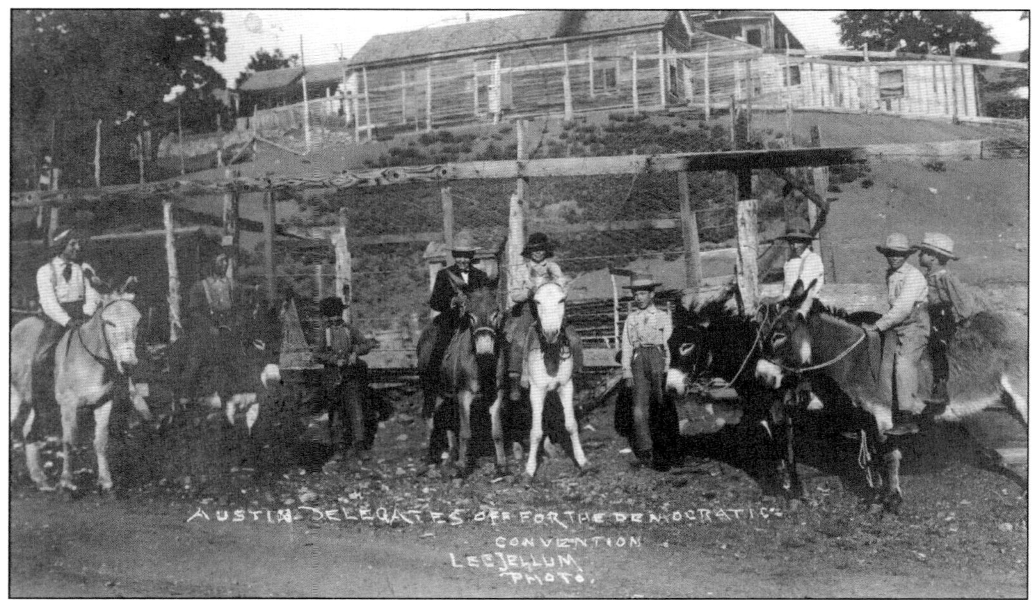

One wonders about this old c. 1910 photograph, titled "Austin Delegates off for the Democratic Convention." The children sitting on these donkeys could hardly be old enough to vote! (Courtesy of Bremmer Collection/ NVHS.)

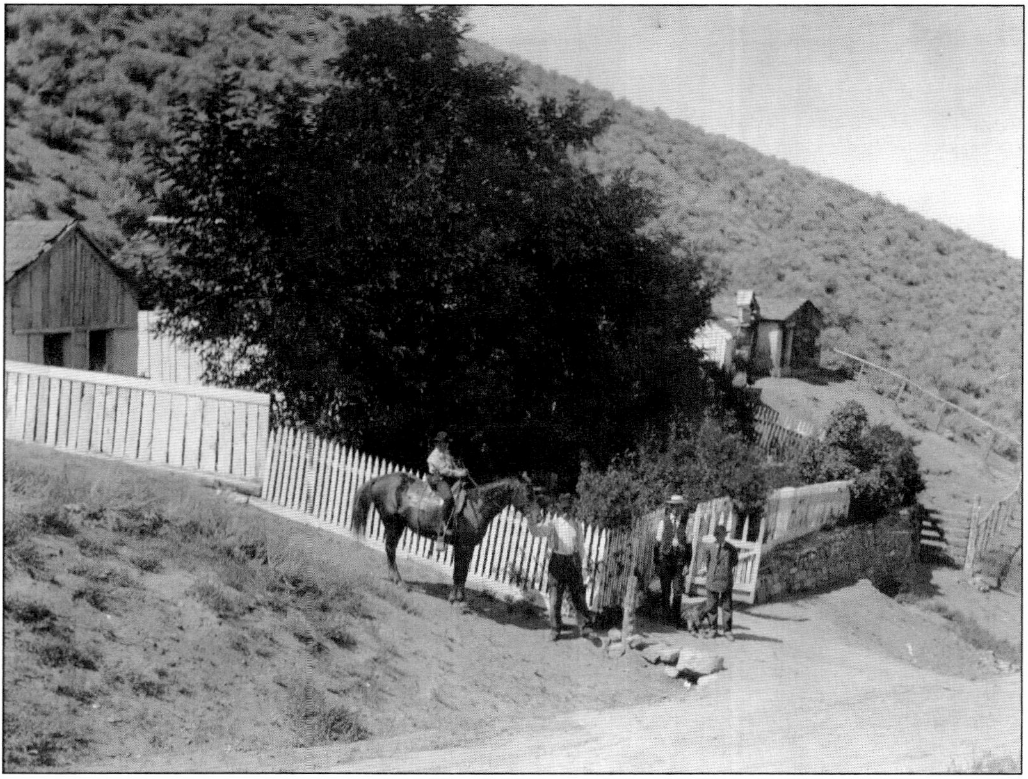

This old house, mostly unseen, is the Sophie Thorpe house, standing to the south side of Main Street toward upper Austin. The Thorpe family consisted mostly of ranchers. Ruins of their old homestead can be found a short ways north of Austin Summit. (Courtesy of SC.)

Five

People and Portraits

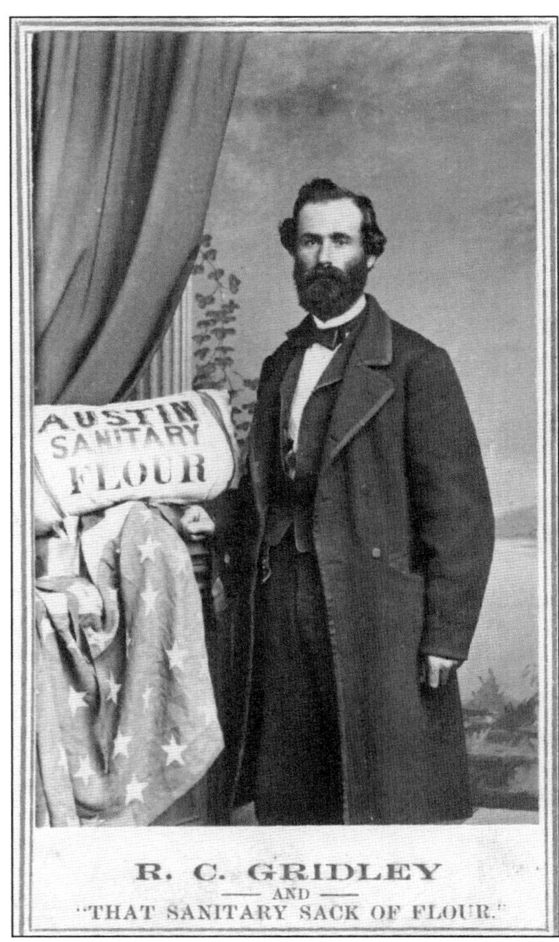

On April 19, 1864, with the Civil War still raging, Ruell Gridley lost a bet in a local election and had to carry a 50-pound sack of flour from Gridley's Store, through the town, and down to Clifton. Ruell made it as far as the Bank Exchange saloon down Main Street. After several rounds of whiskey, the bet was considered paid. Speeches broke out, and then there was an auction for the sack of flour. About $350 in gold coins was the winning bid, and the money was donated to the Sanitary Fund. The flour sack was returned to Gridley and then auctioned off again and again. By the end of the day, over $4,000 was raised for the Sanitary Fund, the precursor of the Red Cross. Ruell took his sack of flower on the road to mining camps through out the west, auctioning it off again and again and raising over $175,000 to help the wounded soldiers of the Civil War. (Courtesy of NVHS.)

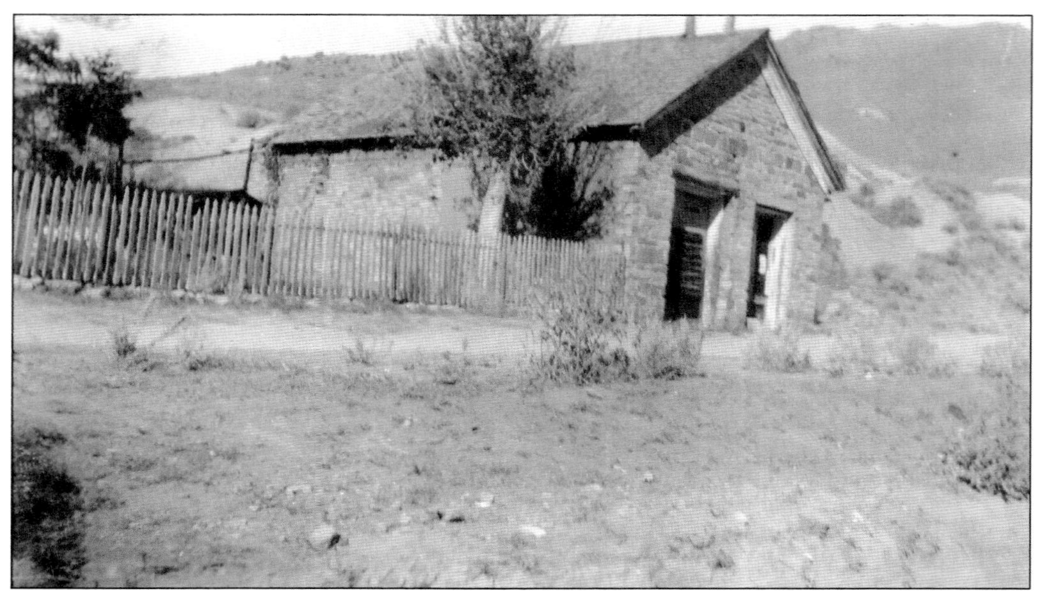

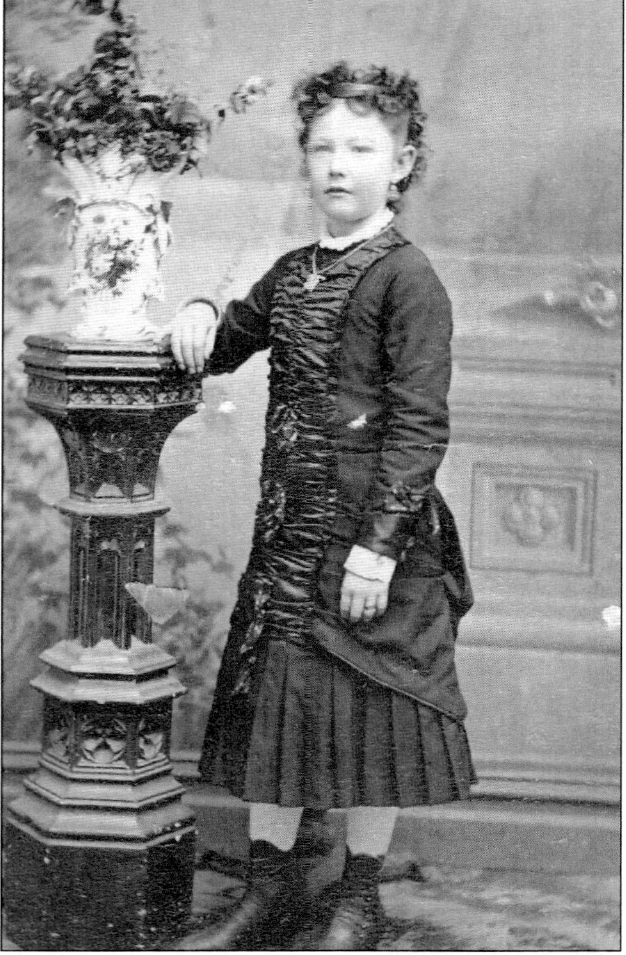

Gridley's Store still stands in upper Austin on Main Street. It has been restored and, for several years, was the Austin Historical Society's museum. Today, the museum has moved to larger quarters a short ways down Main Street, and the old building is used for storage. (Courtesy of JBC.)

Dr. Wixom, his wife Maria, and daughter Emma moved to Austin from Grass Valley, California, in the early 1860s. He established a practice, and his office still stands just behind St. Augustine. Instead of following her father's footsteps, Emma took up singing. (Courtesy of SC.)

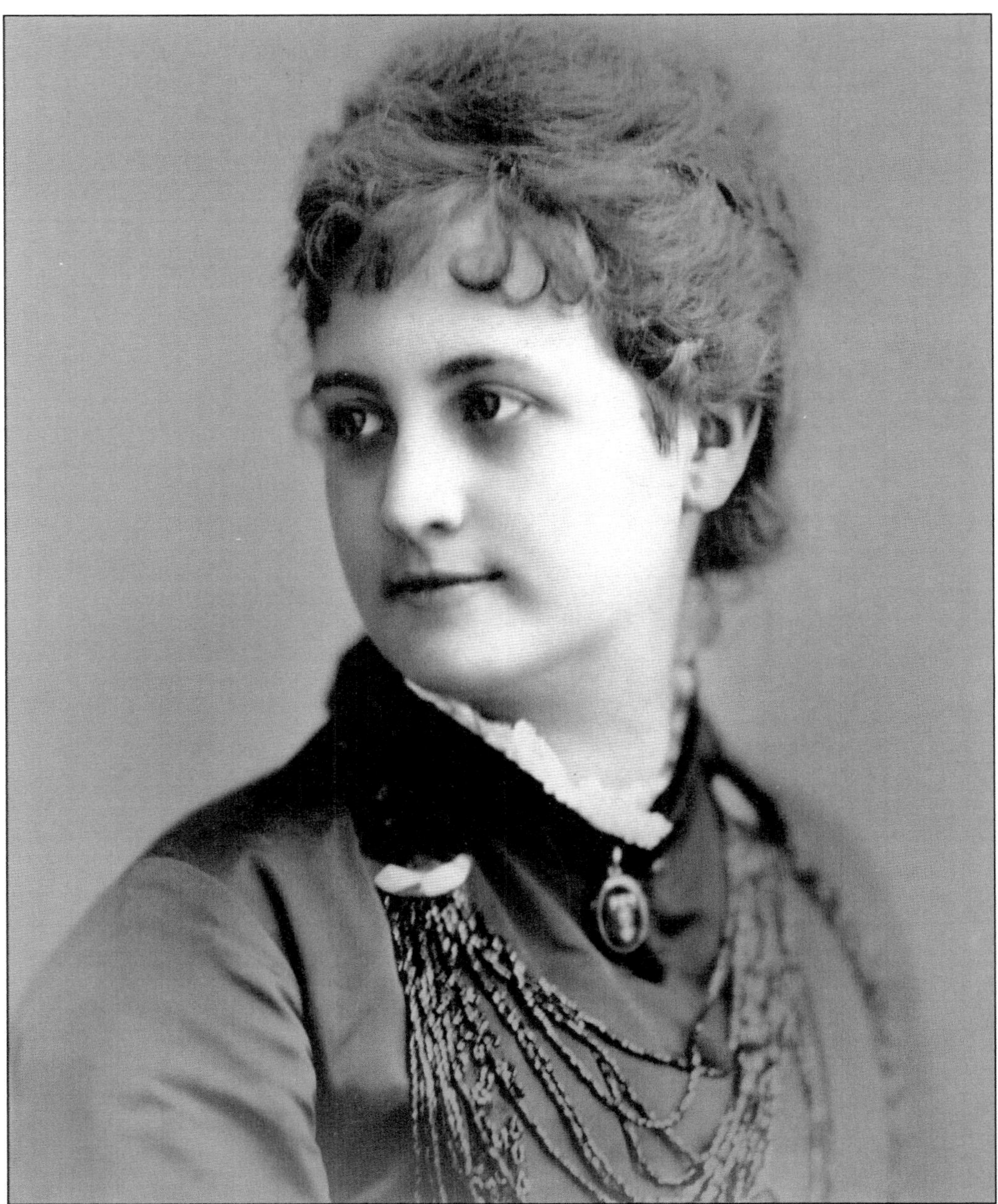

Emma Nevada, as she became known, excelled in languages and music. She readily learned the local Native American languages of the Paiute, Washoe, and Shoshone tribes. Attending Mills College, a women's school in Oakland, California, she became proficient in Spanish, Italian, French, and German. She sang as a coloratura soprano all over the West. Known as the "Comstock nightingale," she eventually sailed for Europe and had a successful career overseas. Her career spanned from 1880 to 1910, singing on both continents. On one occasion, she returned to Austin. Meeting her at the Clifton station, a wagon was summoned, and the townsmen harnessed themselves in. She was pulled up the canyon to the Methodist church. To standing room only, she performed a free concert in benefit of the Methodists. In fact, she sang twice in order to let everyone have a chance to hear her sing. She always remembered her youth in Austin fondly. (Courtesy of NVHS.)

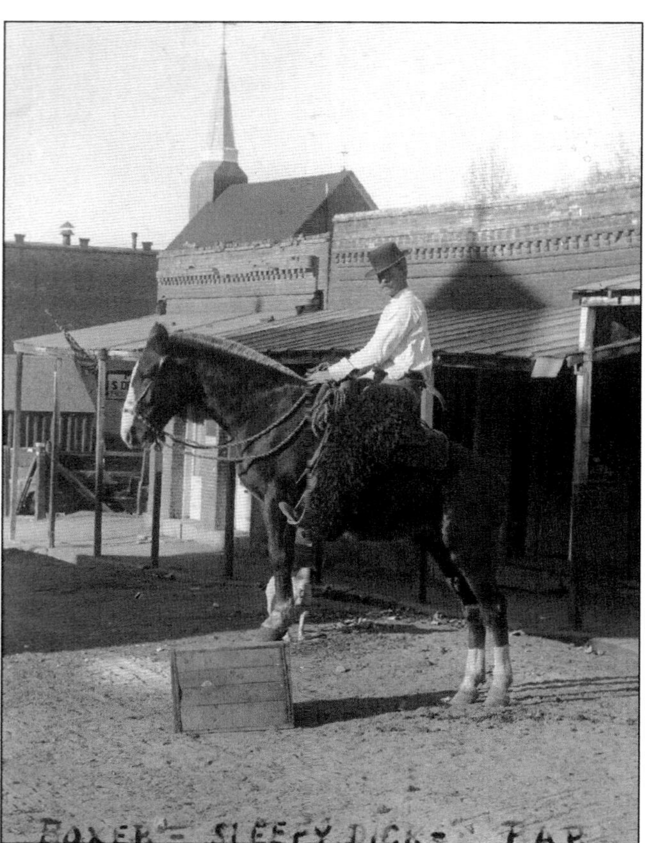

Cowboy Sleepy Dick and his horse Boxer are doing a few tricks on Main Street. The church spire belongs to St. Augustine (see page 72). (Courtesy of NVHS.)

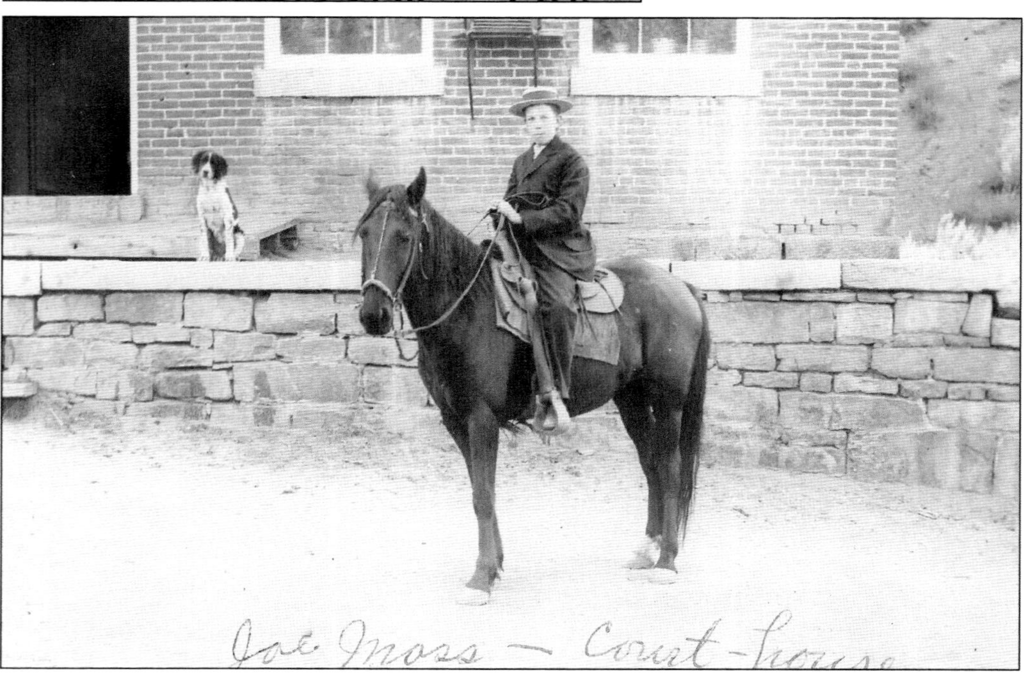

Joe Moss sits astride a horse n front of the Lander County Courthouse. Cars have replaced the horse, but the old courthouse looks the same today (see pages 28 and 42). (Courtesy of SC.)

Having come from Switzerland, A.P. Maestretti was an early Austin-area settler. He owned Smith Creek Ranch, a station on the Pony Express. He was a friend of Shoshone Chief Toi Toi and Dr Wixom, Emma Nevada's father. Smith Creek Ranch continues in operation today, and many of his descendents still populate Austin. (Courtesy of AHS.)

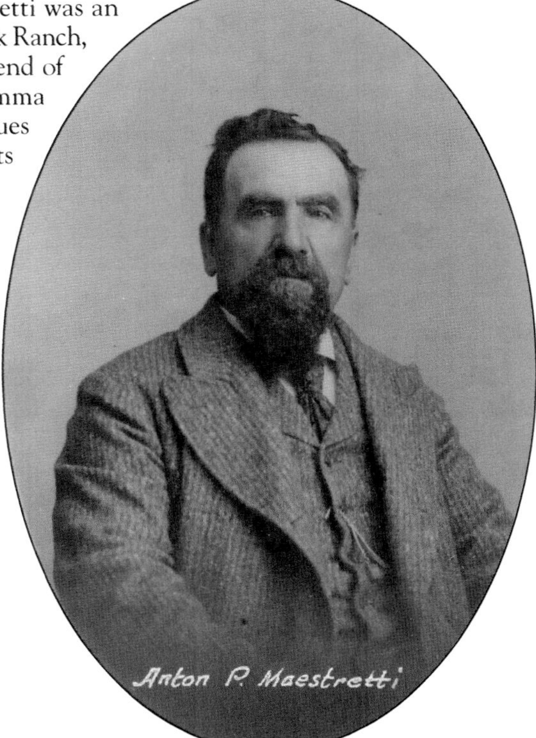

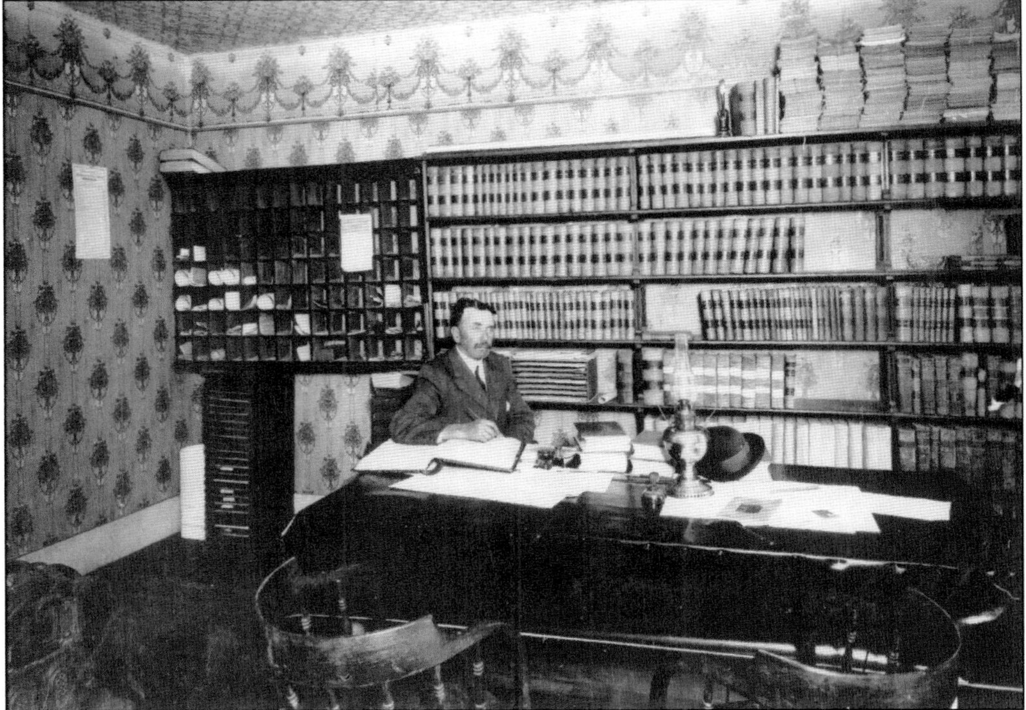

Judge Malloy is seen working in the County Clerks Office at the Lander County Courthouse in 1909. (Courtesy of NVHS.)

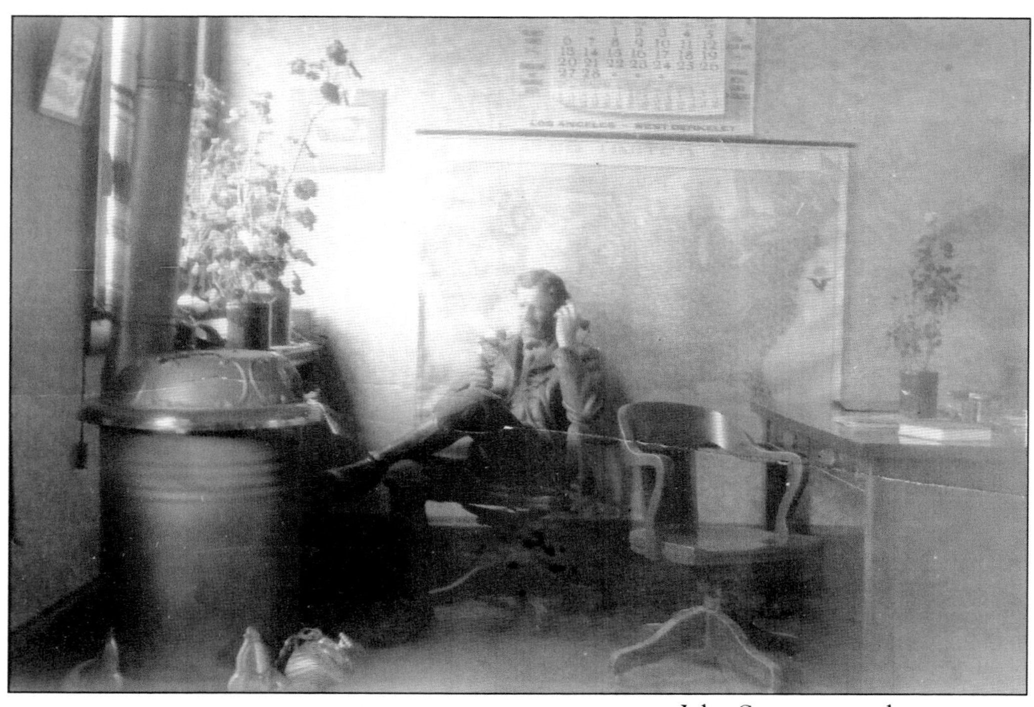

John Spencer was the county treasurer and is seen in his office at the Lander County Courthouse around 1910. (Courtesy of JBC.)

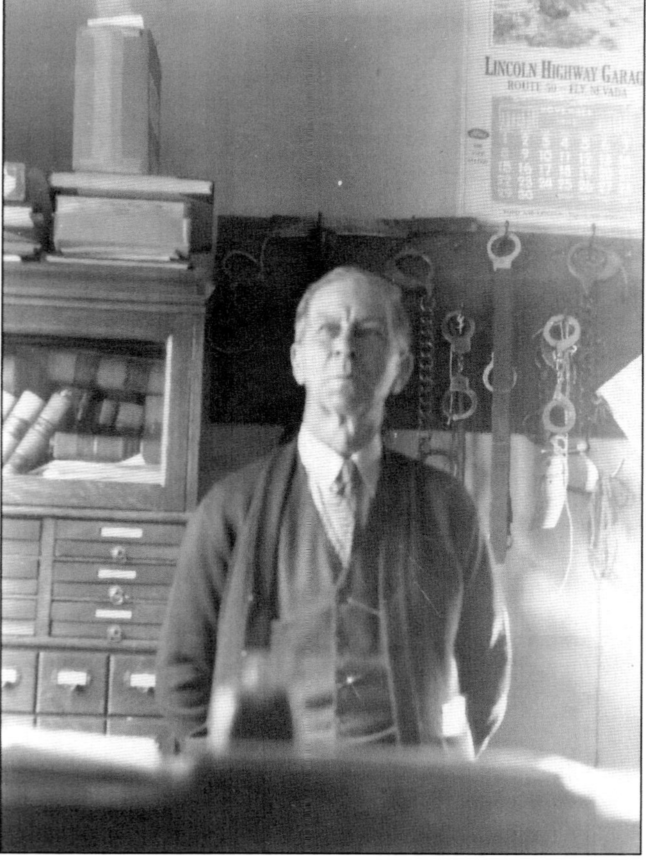

Jim Moore was the sheriff of Lander County around 1910. Note the accoutrements hanging on the wall behind him. (Courtesy of JBC.)

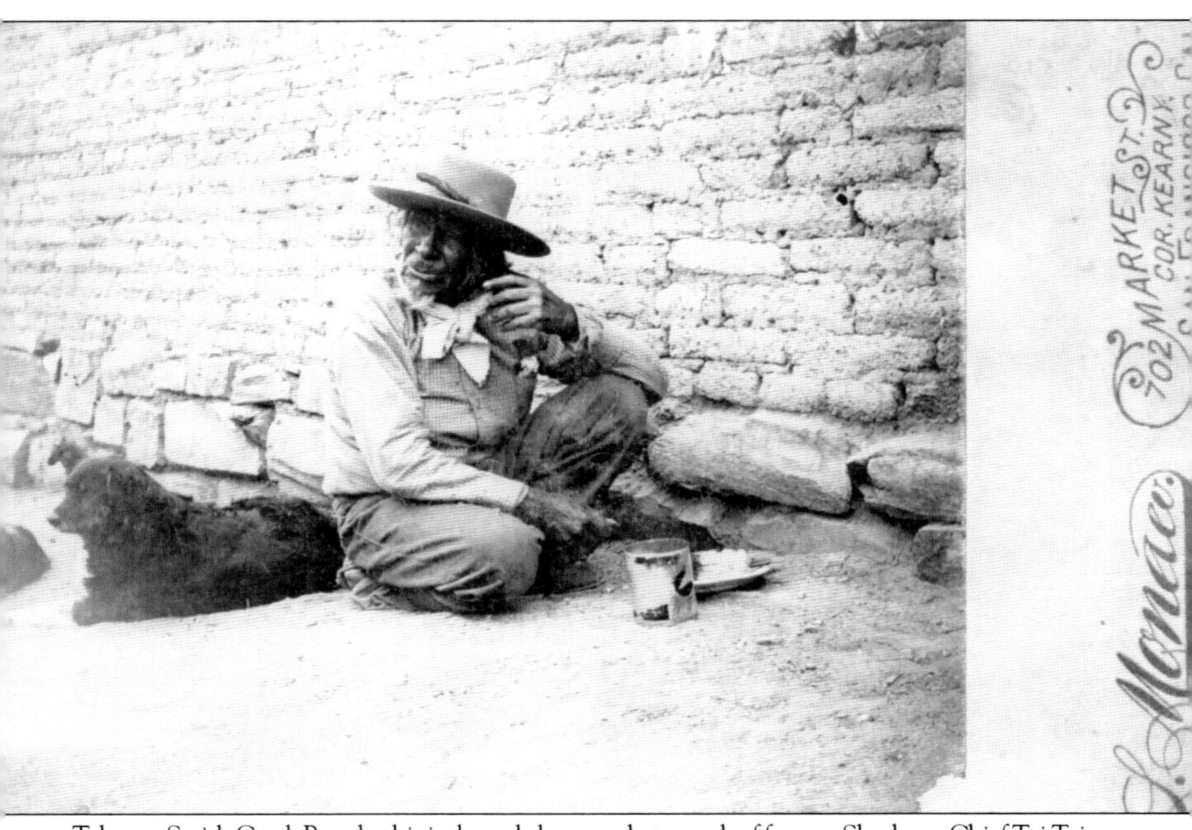

Taken at Smith Creek Ranch, this is the only known photograph of famous Shoshone Chief Toi Toi. He kept his people out of the Indian Wars of the 1860s, was a lifelong friend of A.P. Maestretti and Dr Wixom, and called Emma Nevada "Heap Big Song Bird." The Smith Creek Ranch was originally a station for the Pony Express. Part of the original station still stands and is used as a ranch building today. (Courtesy of NVHS.)

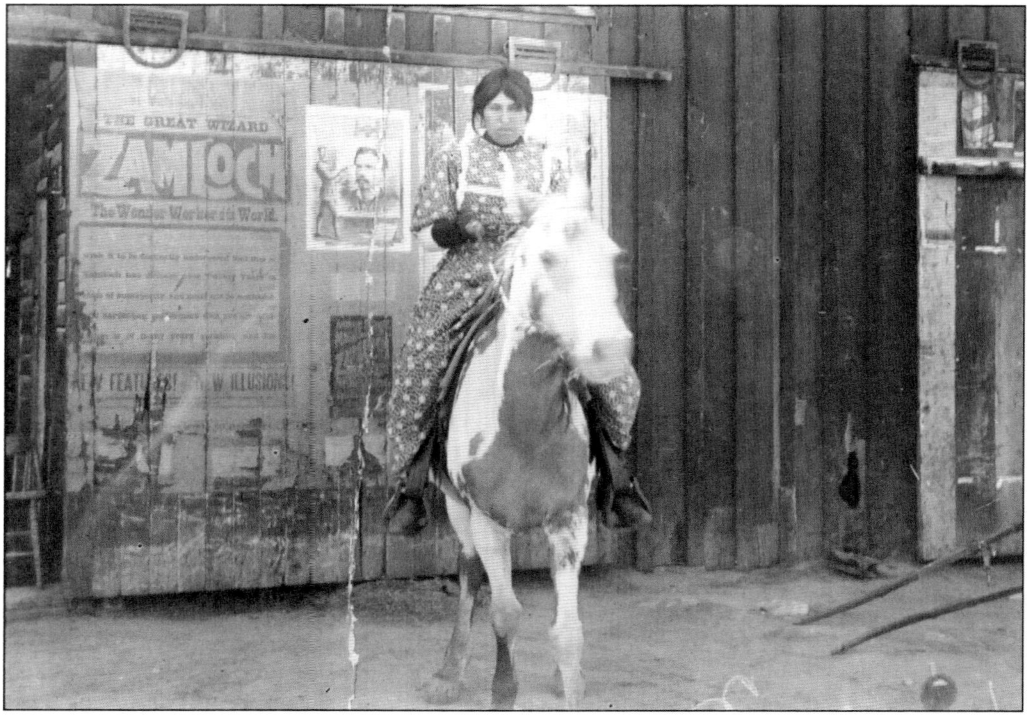

This Shoshone woman, known as Mary Ann, is pictured a on horse around 1910 in front of the Steiner Livery on Main Street (see page 21). (Courtesy of NVHS.)

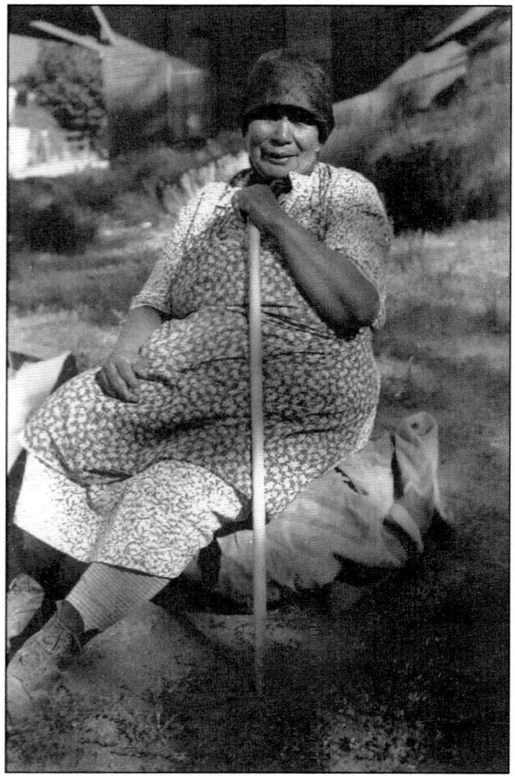

Annie Piffero did laundry around town. The area behind the courthouse was originally known as Mormon Gulch. In later years, many of Austin's Native Americans lived there. (Courtesy of SC.)

Austin resident Katie Johnson is seen with her children. The baby is in a papoose—a Native American backpack for infants. (Courtesy of SC.)

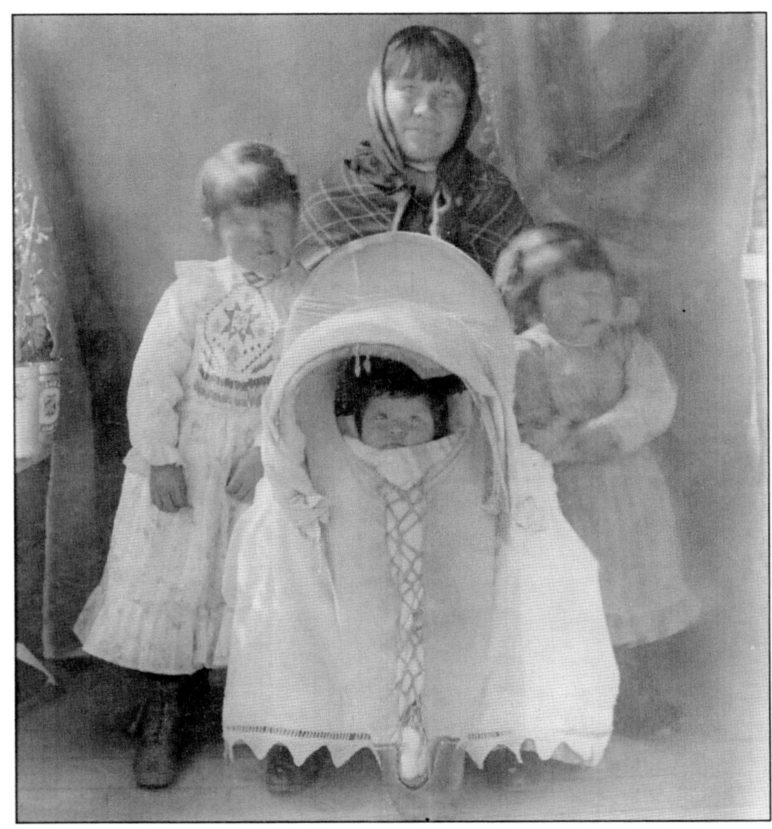

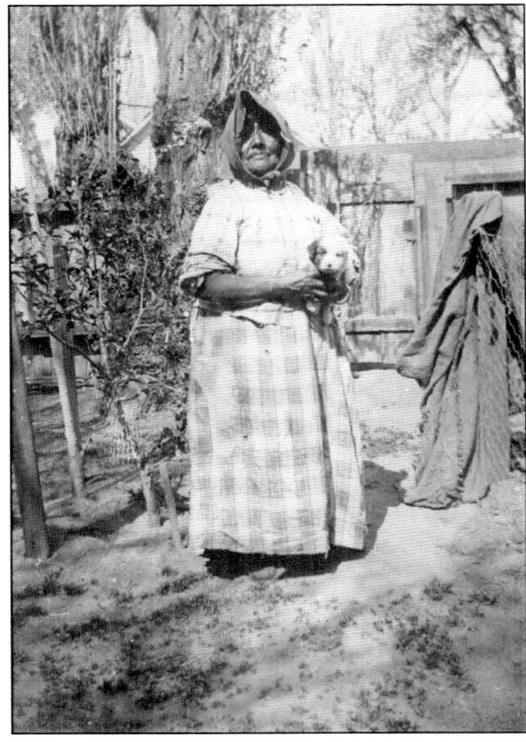

Although Emma Potts lived in Austin, she identified herself as a Washoe. Shoshone Native Americans originally inhabited the area around Austin. (Courtesy of SC.)

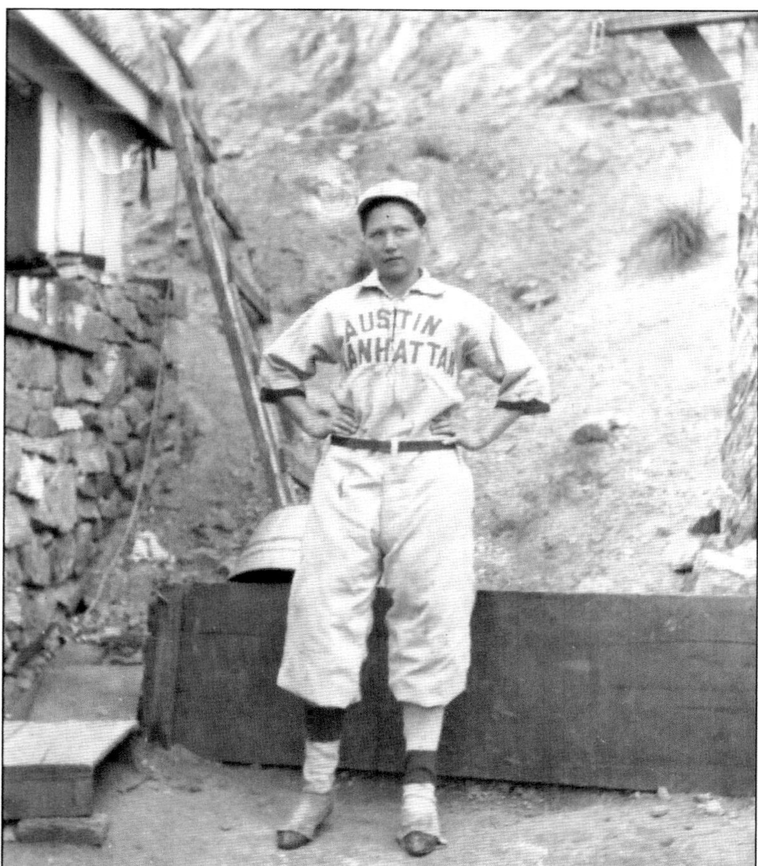

Baseball was a part of the Austin social scene since the 1870s. The woman is in a team uniform for the Manhattan Mines. She is Geraldine Streshley. (Courtesy of JBC.)

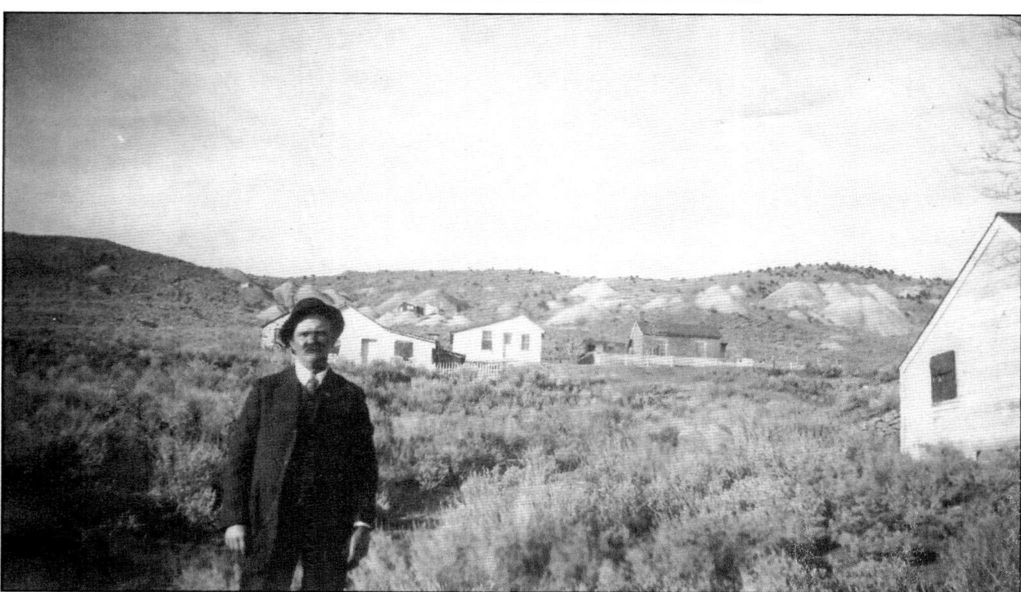

Jim Thorpe, the local undertaker, stands to the left of the old county hospital and morgue. The small white house behind him still stands; however, some additions have been made to the house. Old mine tailing can be seen on the hill. (Courtesy of SC.)

Clara Triplett Byer was the mother of Millie Byer. Clara passed away in 1892 from "black typhoid." She and three others from Austin contracted the fever from bad water at the Byer's homestead, 30 miles east of Austin. (Courtesy of CC.)

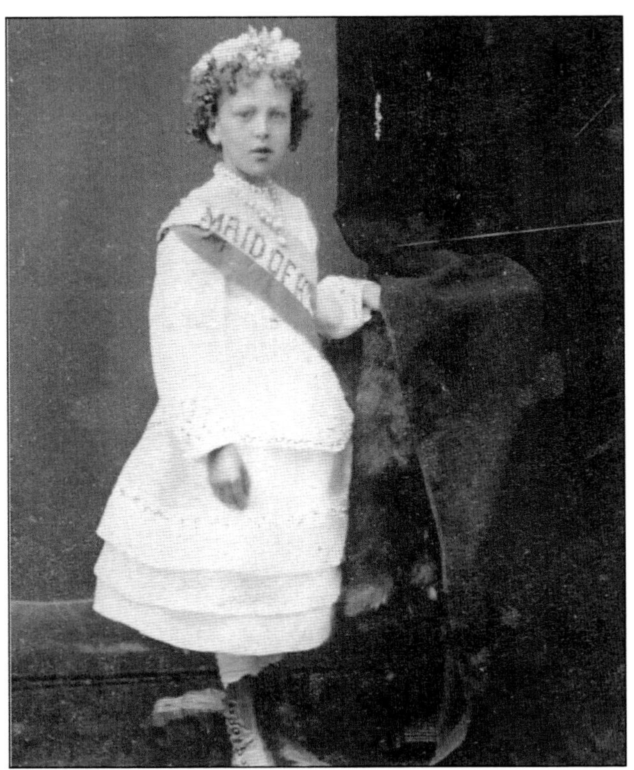

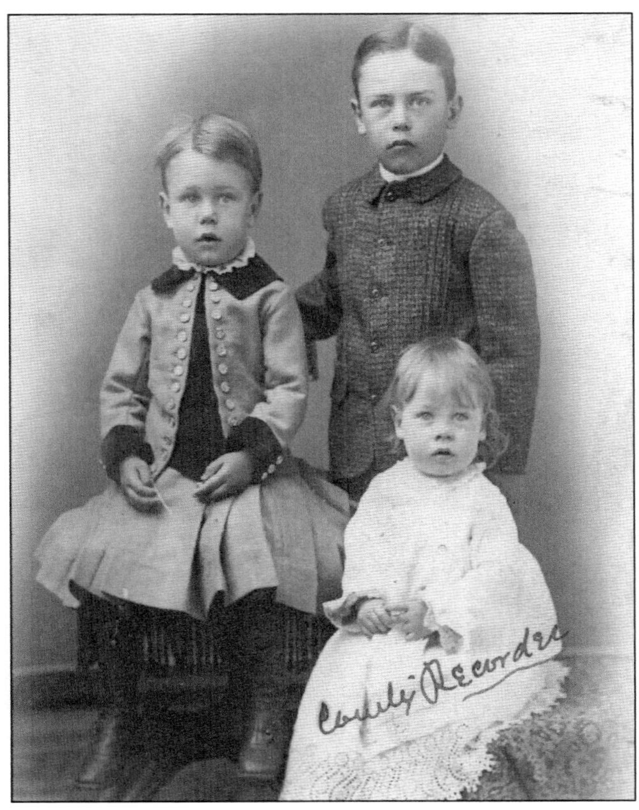

Millie Byer married Bert Acree. Bert, the youngest in this photograph, is seen wearing a dress. It was not uncommon for male children to wear a dress until about age six in Victorian times. The photograph dates from around 1890. Bert later became Lander County recorder. (Courtesy of CC.)

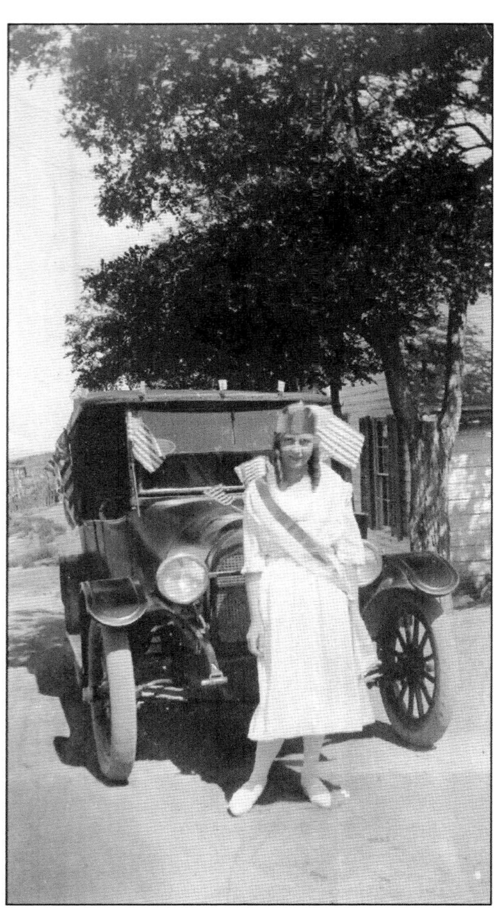

Bert and Millie had four children. One of their daughters, Rene, is pictured here, obviously part of some parade on Main Street. The car dates to the early 1920s. (Courtesy of CC.)

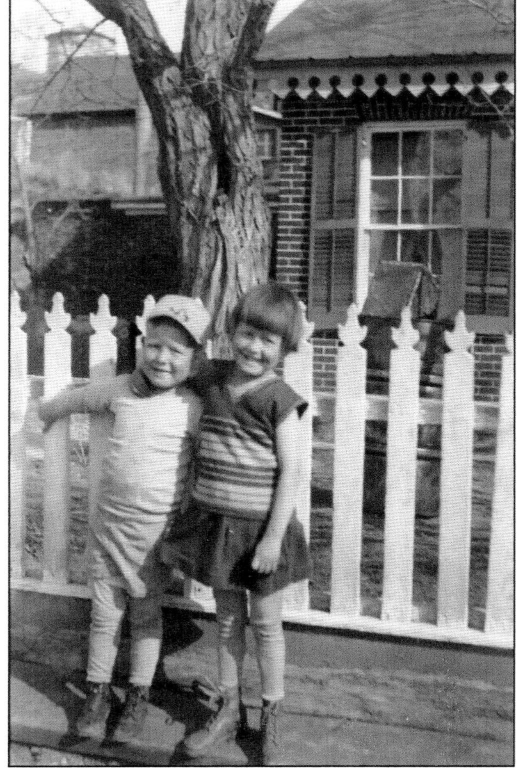

Rene Acree married Lee Maestretti, and they had two children, Stan and Shirley, who are standing in front of Bert and Millie Acree's house. (Courtesy of CC.)

Maestretti family members include, from left to right, (standing) Maggie, Will, and Don; (sitting) Lee and William Maestretti. (Courtesy of CC.)

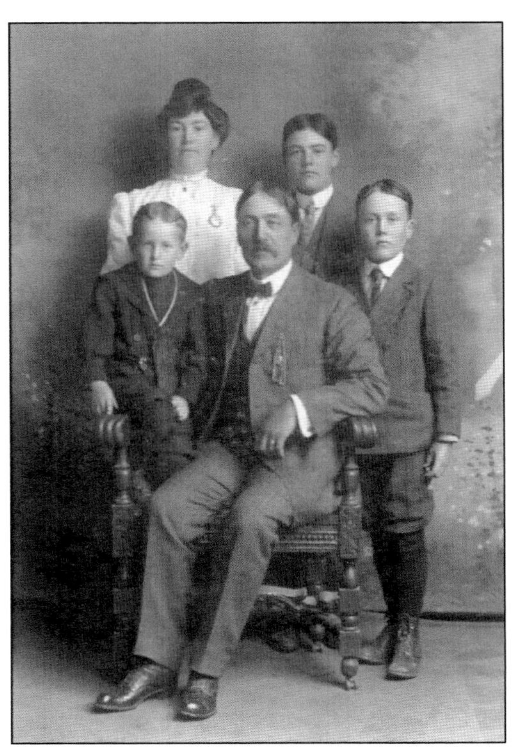

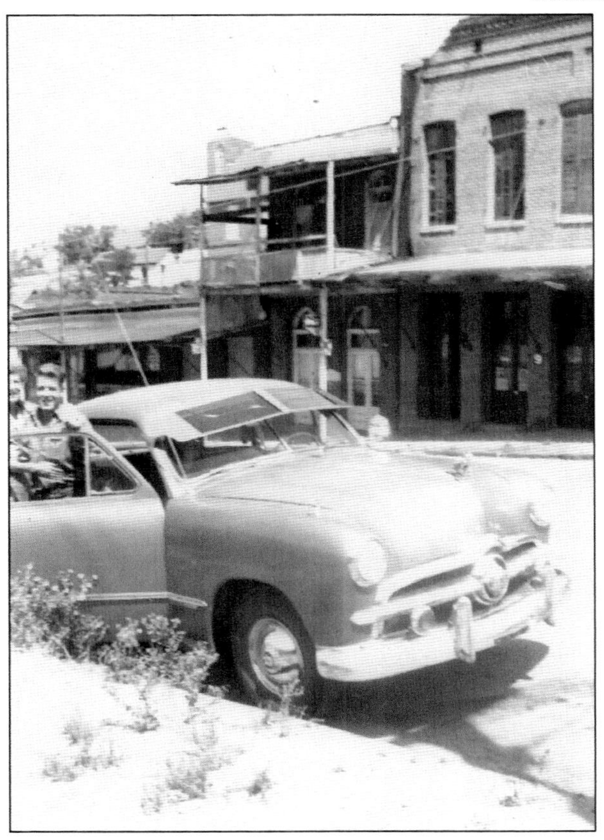

Stan Maestretti is parked on Main Street with his new 1950 Oldsmobile. The Masonic hall is the building to the right. (Courtesy of CC.)

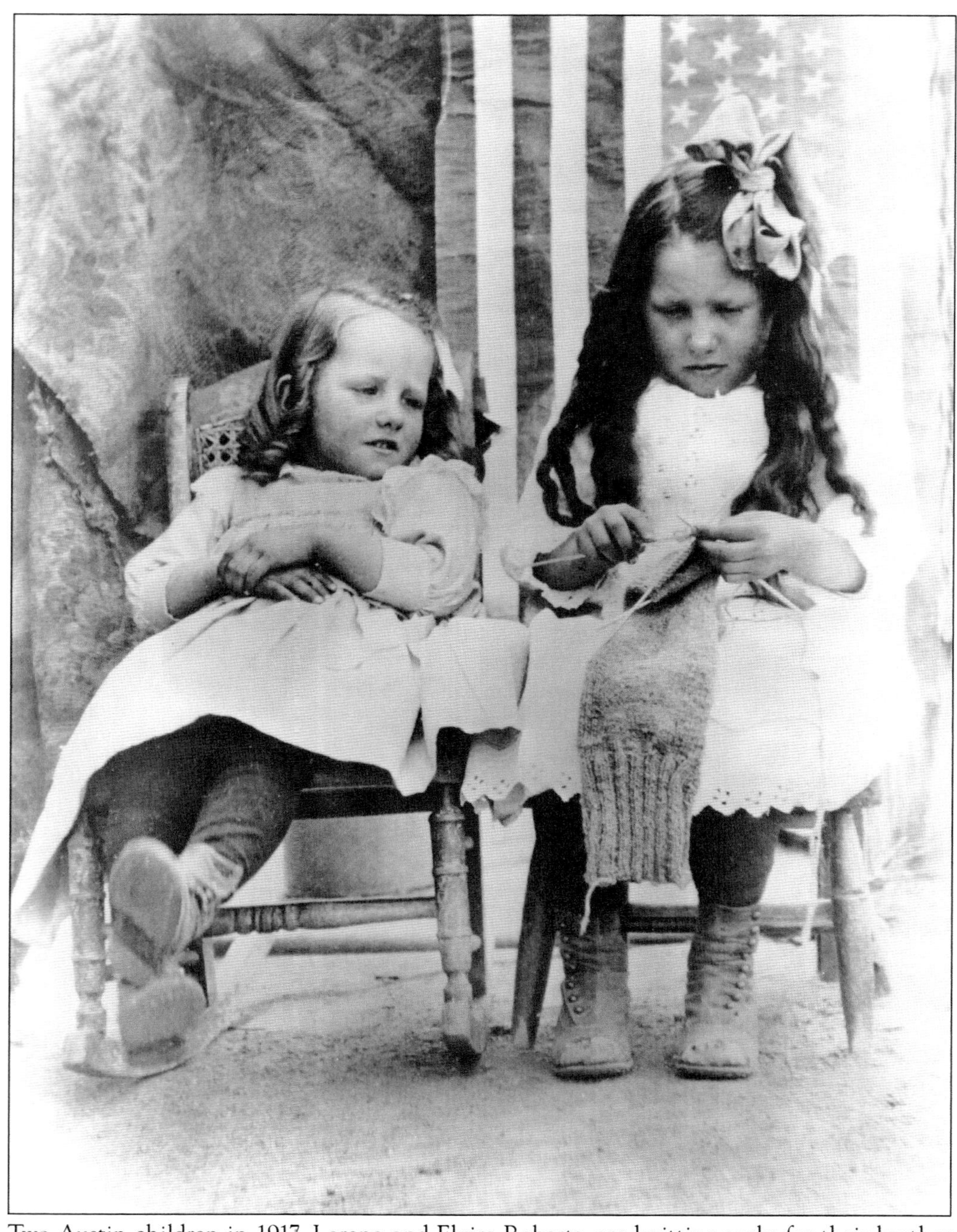

Two Austin children in 1917, Lorena and Elvira Roberts, are knitting socks for their brother stationed in France during World War I. "I was just learning to knit by Jennie Johnson," is found on the back of the image. (Courtesy of SC.)

Very young Sam (left) and George Crescenzo are seen in dresses, as was the custom in the Victorian era. After one of Austin's early fires, George went on to construct the Crescenzo Building, located a few doors below the Masonic hall. (Courtesy of SC.)

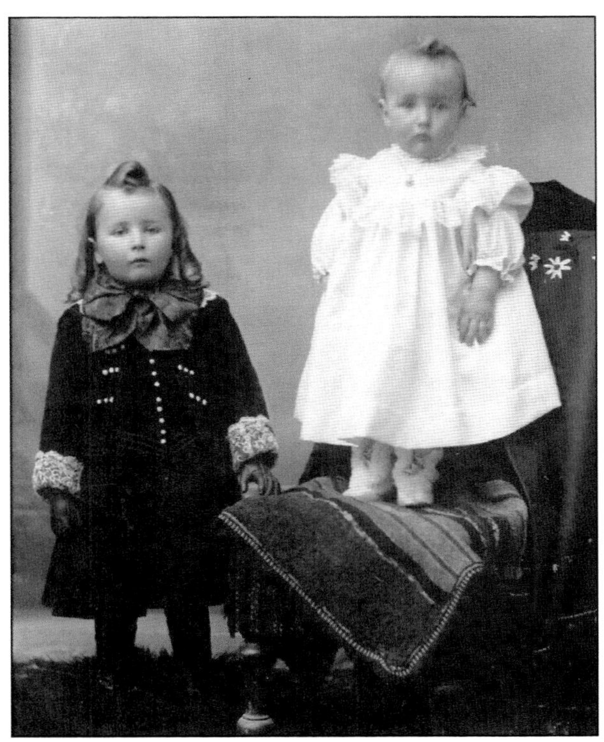

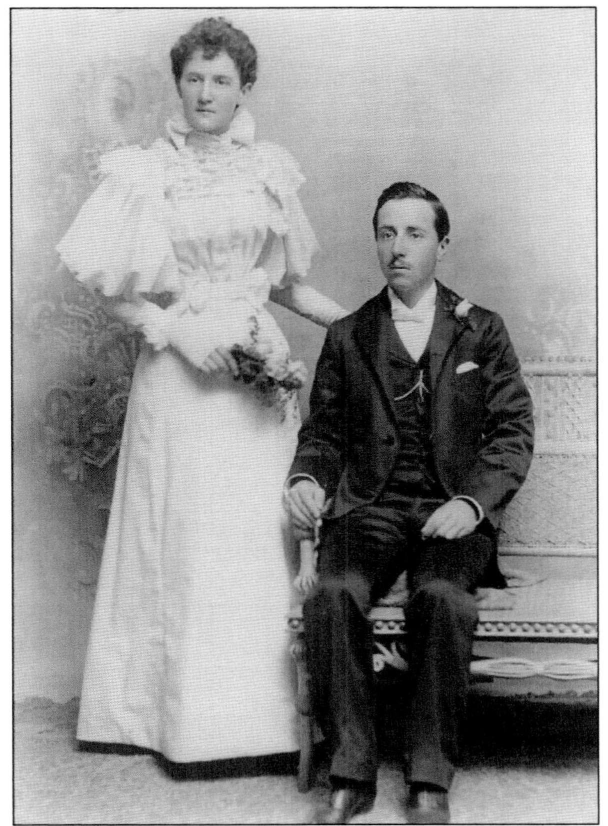

It is the wedding day of Belle and Johnny Crescenzo. They ran the Crescenzo Store for over 30 years. At one time, it was the largest dry goods emporium between Virginia City and Salt Lake. Today, the building still stands and is still a store selling old treasurers, books, and postcards for travelers along Highway 50. (Courtesy of SC.)

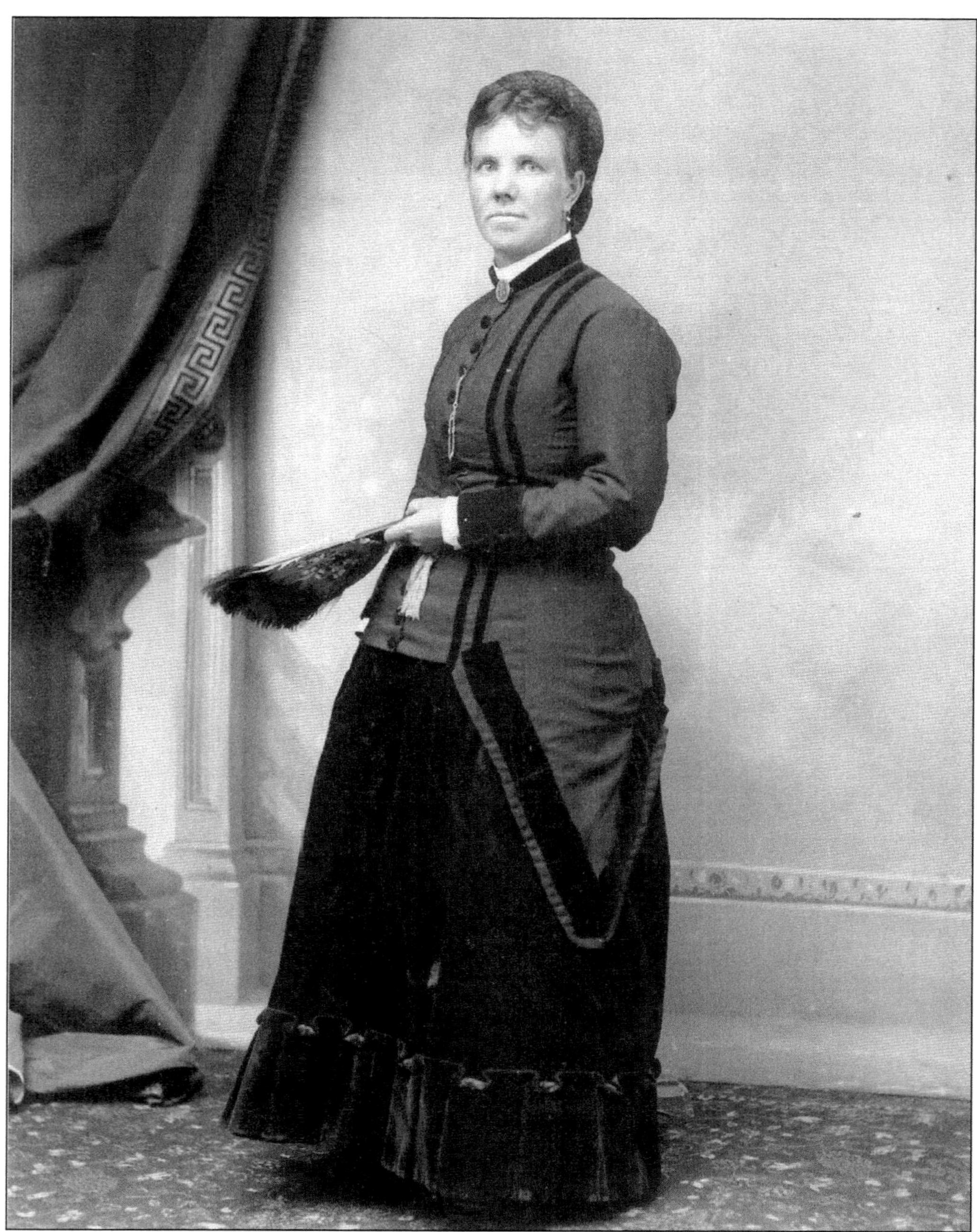

Louisa Wardle Moss was born in England; she became a Mormon and immigrated to the Utah Territory. She crossed the plains with a handcart brigade, only to get caught in an early winter storm. She survived, while many perished. Married to Joe Moss in Salt Lake, her husband was part of the Morrisite Apostasy (followers of Joseph Morris, who disagreed with Brigham Young about polygamy). In 1863, with little more than a wagon and fearing for their lives, they fled Salt Lake bound for the Nevada Territory. While passing through Jacobsville, along the Overland Stage Road, they heard about the rich silver strike a few miles away in Pony Canyon. Louisa and Joe Moss settled in Austin and prospered. She was Austin's first white woman. Their house is still standing (see pages 97 and 98). (Courtesy of SC.)

Lousia and Joe Moss's daughter Belle married James Roberts in 1895 in the Methodist church. The Roberts came West from with the Crescenzos from Nova Scotia. James and Louisa did a little of everything. He was a miner and town constable for many years. She was the matron of the county hospital and a member of the Daughters of Rebekah for over 50 years. Together, they ran Austin's soda works. (Courtesy of SC.)

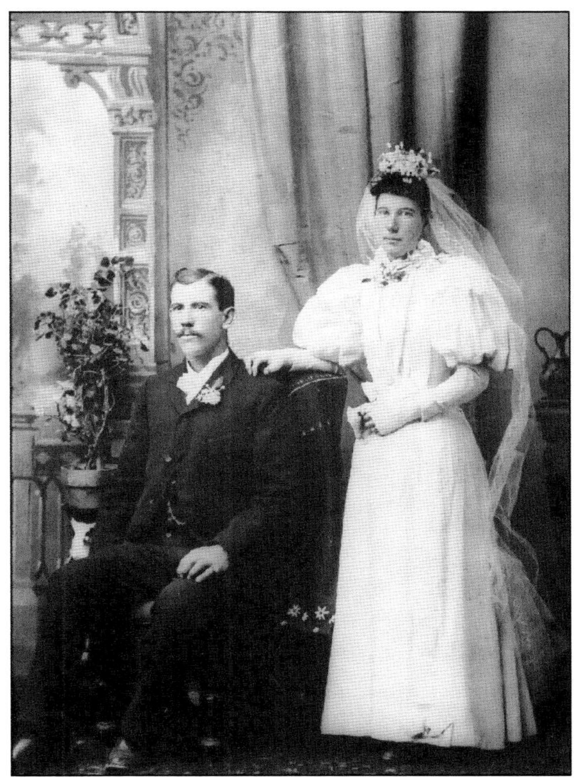

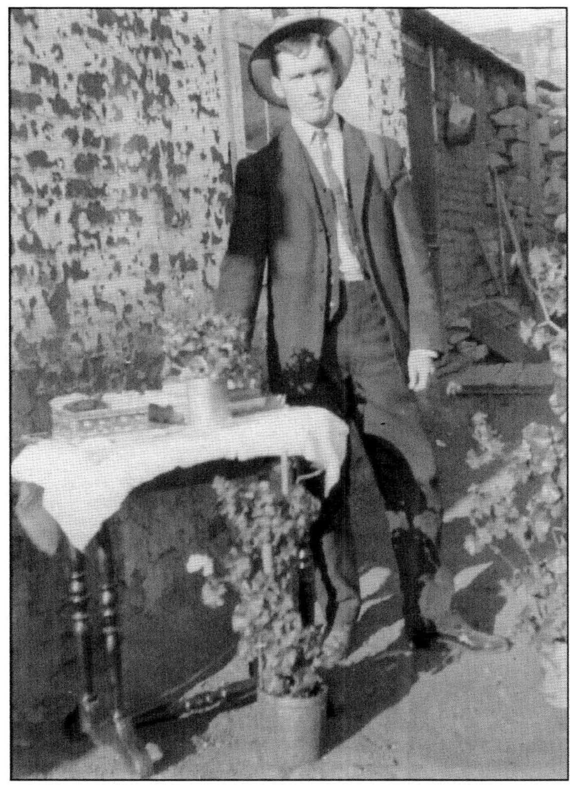

Will Moss was Belle's brother. He worked in the mines and ranches around Austin. The potted flowers are hollyhocks, and today they grow wild around the old Moss home. (Courtesy of SC.)

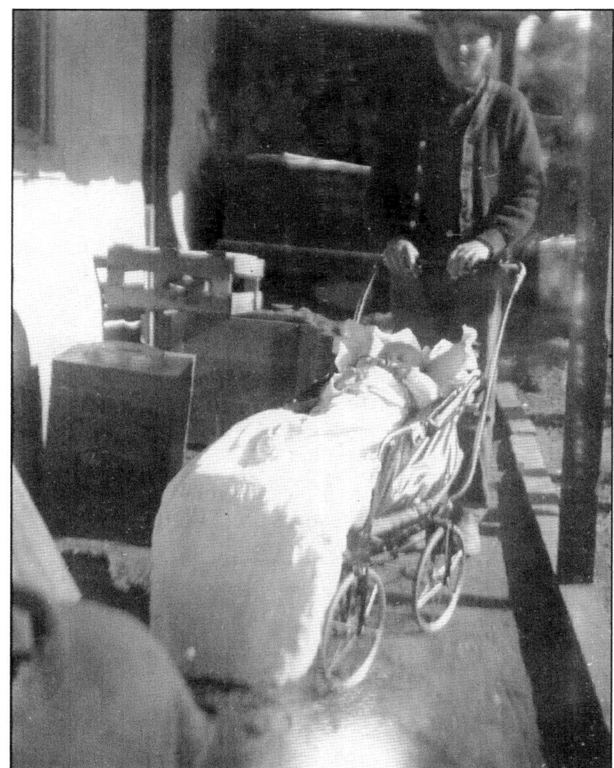

Will Roberts stands over his younger brother Austin. Will served in World War I and was badly wounded. Returning from France a year after the war ended, he worked the Grass Valley Ranch a few miles northeast of Austin. His brother Austin served in World War II and settled in Reno. (Courtesy of SC.)

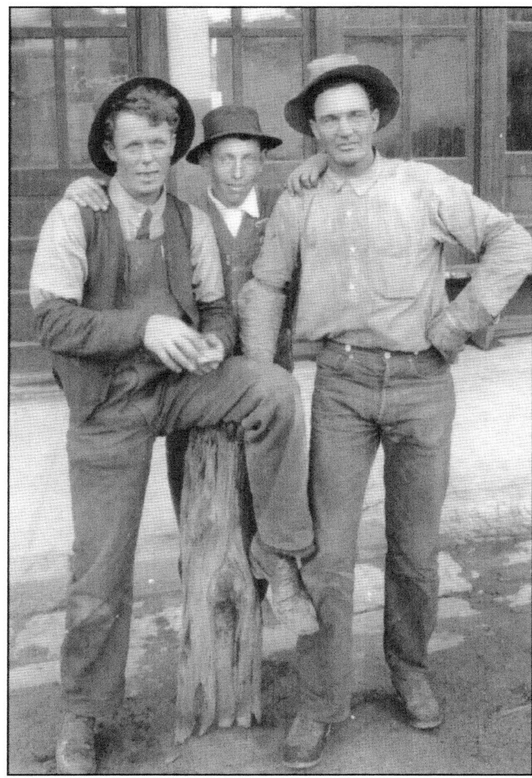

Tucker Streshley (on the right) and friends are standing by an old hitching post. Behind them is the old entrance to the International Hotel. (Courtesy of AHS.)

Six

Fini

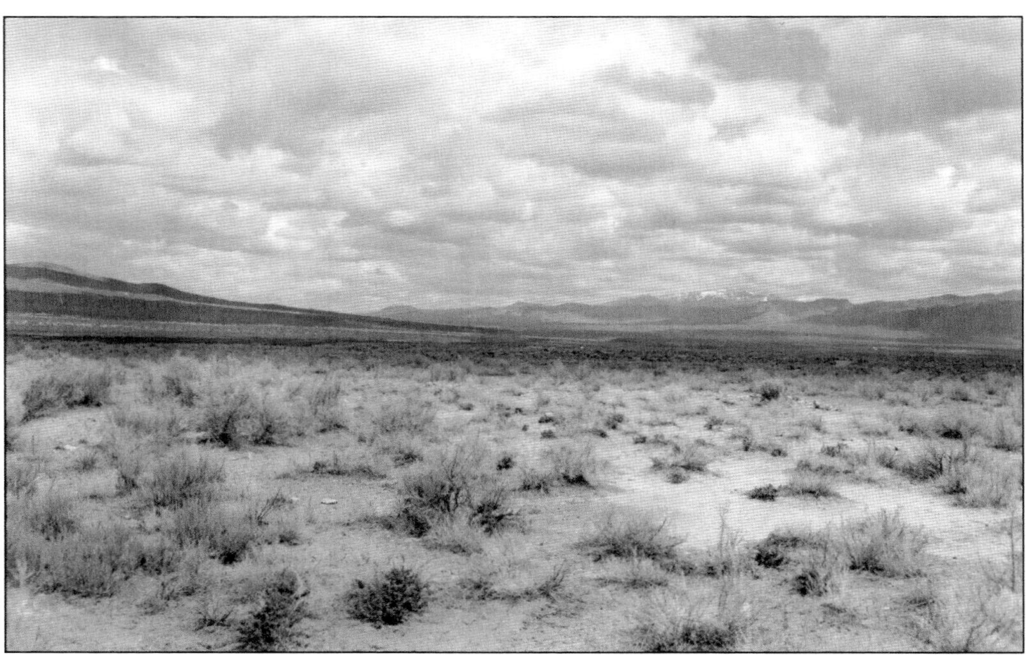

Like so many towns and mining camps in Nevada's outback, not much survives to tell their story—just memories and the wind. This is the sight of Jacobsville in 1957. Only a couple piles of rocks mark the foundations of a busy little settlement. The Pony Express, the Overland Stage, and Lander County's first center of government all called this little patch of desert home. Like the surrounding hamlets of Amador, Yankee Blade, Clifton, Canyon City, Ravenswood, Skookum, Ledie, Clinton, and Birch Creek, only a few rocks and broken bottles mark their graves. Jacobsville is no more. Yet, Austin survives. Fires, floods, mining booms and busts, and the loss of the county seat have not broken this old camp. The town still gathers for weddings, school graduations, Fourth of July celebrations, and funerals. In 1955, Oscar Lewis wrote a book about Austin's history, aptly, titled *The Town That Died Laughing.* For those of us living here, we are still waiting . . . and laughing.